Those Were the Days

Those Were the Days

Why *All in the Family* Still Matters

JIM CULLEN

Rutgers University Press

New Brunswick, Camden, and Newark, New Jersey, and London

Library of Congress Cataloging-in-Publication Data

Names: Cullen, Jim, 1962– author.
Title: Those were the days : why All in the family still matters /
  Jim Cullen.
Description: New Brunswick : Rutgers University Press, 2020. | Includes
  bibliographical references and index. | Summary: "All in the Family;
  history of the show—why it matters now. How it was progressive for its
  time"—Provided by publisher.
Identifiers: LCCN 2019012948| ISBN 9781978805781 (cloth) |
  ISBN 9781978805774 (paperback)
Subjects: LCSH: All in the family (Television program)
Classification: LCC PN1992.77.A483 C85 2020 | DDC 791.45/72—dc23
LC record available at https://lccn.loc.gov/2019012948

A British Cataloging-in-Publication record for this book is available from the British Library.

♾ The paper used in this publication meets the requirements of the American National
Standard for Information Sciences—Permanence of Paper for Printed Library Materials,
ANSI Z39.48-1992.

www.rutgersuniversitypress.org

Manufactured in the United States of America

For Wally Levis
Left, Right, and Centered

Contents

Those Were the Days

Introduction

Broad(cast) Humor

Popular culture—art for the masses—is a mysterious thing.

There's all manner of ways in which it isn't mysterious at all. For centuries, popular culture has been embedded in a tightly organized capitalist system. That system consists of artists, audiences, and a set of commercial subsystems—distribution, marketing, publicity, among others—designed to bring them (profitably) together. Formulas, also known as genres, have evolved to reach audiences with a demonstrated interest in paying for certain kinds of stories. The variables may change, but the iron hand of commerce will always guide, if not rigidly determine, outcomes.

In other ways, though, popular culture can be unpredictable. For one thing, commerce isn't static. Businesses are subject not only to changing market conditions but also to technological innovation, which often determines what gets produced—and how. For another, it's never possible to entirely predict how successful a given work is going to be. The history of entertainment is replete with surprise hits, unexpected flops, and sleepers that emerge later, or more durably, than foreseen at the time. Finally, the fingerprints of humanity are too variegated and quirky to be easily managed. People buy a work of art—literally and figuratively—to see things, hear things, and learn things that they didn't expect, count on, or pay for.

Conversely, artists need money to survive, but money isn't the only or even primary reason why they make art, and they will often pour all kinds of surplus value, economic and otherwise, into producing something without expecting or getting a return on their investment. Here, too, outcomes are uncertain: you make hits the same way you make flops; collaborations click or they grind; talents crest or recede in ways you can't always foresee. Works of art are labors of love, and love is a mysterious thing.

One other point about popular culture is worth mentioning at the outset: it's inextricably bound up in history. Which is to say that even more than other kinds of art, pop culture is the product of a series of shared, but temporary, circumstances distinct from those that came before and those that come after. Notions of "before" and "after" are variously defined and of varying duration. But when disentangled carefully and rewoven gracefully, versions of the befores, durings, and afters—which is to say histories—help us make sense of our lives in ways we'd have trouble doing otherwise.

Before Norman and After Norman

This book tells the story of a particular television show that spanned the decade of the 1970s. It was unusually successful in its time and has lived on in collective memory as one of the best shows of its kind, specifically that genre known as the situation-comedy, or sitcom. *All in the Family* bears a genealogical resemblance to ancestors such as *The Honeymooners* (1955–1956) and *I Love Lucy* (1951–1957) in its manic energy and engagement with racial and class issues. It also exhibits traits that can be seen in many heirs. *Married . . . with Children* (1987–1997) inherited its penchant for depicting family conflict; *The Simpsons* (1989–) and *South Park* (1997–) carried forward its daring irreverence. *Roseanne* was perhaps its most faithful heir in its consistent focus on class conflict (we'll revisit an attempt to revive that show at the conclusion of this book). One could cite many other examples. But no show has combined these elements quite as effectively as *All in the Family* did.

A great many informed observers consider the creator of *All in the Family*, Norman Lear, as central to the history of the genre. "The way I look at it, television can be broken into two parts: B.N. and A.N.: Before Norman and After Norman," Phil Rosenthal, creator of the highly successful sitcom *Every-*

body Loves Raymond (1996–2005), said in 2016. "He's the most influential producer in the history of television because of this gigantic change that happened when *All in the Family* hit the air."[1]

The "gigantic change" that Rosenthal refers to is the suite of themes, topics, and ideas presented on *All in the Family*, many of which were unprecedented. Before it came along, the sitcom was a highly stylized kind of TV show with clear boundaries of form as well as content. An important early historian of television, Horace Newcomb, described both succinctly. The sitcom, he said, "will fall into four basic parts: the establishment of the 'situation,' the complication, the confusion that ensues, and the alleviation of the complication." (One can still see this pattern in just about any sitcom to this day.) "The essential factor is the remedying of the confusion. It is rather like a mathematical process, the removal of parentheses within parentheses." Newcomb pointed out that this structural logic also has a political logic. "No one intends to cause pain in the shows, no one intends evil. . . . The audience is reassured in its beliefs; it is not challenged by choice, by ambiguity, or by speculation about what might happen under other 'realistic' circumstances. The character is not forced to examine his or her values, nor is the audience."[2]

As Newcomb realized, *All in the Family* revised this formula. To be sure, it maintained many core elements of the sitcom, especially in terms of its structure—which, as we'll see, was surprisingly traditional. But the show pushed boundaries in all kinds of ways, among them its willingness to use profanity, engage taboo topics, and offer ambiguous, even disturbing, endings. Admittedly, it didn't *explode* the conventions of the sitcom—true to form, its protagonist was a bigot, but not a malicious one—and it purveyed ideas that were daring in its time but can seem dated, even lame, today. And yet the show still maintains its power to shock, whether in depicting a frightening rape or a character unselfconsciously uttering hate speech. *All in the Family* has also stood a test of time for its quality: the writing, the acting, production design, and camera work remain impressive a half century later and have engendered durable affection. So it is, for example, that the twenty-first-century comedian Amy Poehler, who called *All in the Family* "the best show ever," has indicated that she named her son Archie in honor of the protagonist.[3]

Waves of Change

But *All in the Family* wasn't created in a (collaborative) vacuum. It was very much a product of its moment. There are two aspects of that moment in particular that are worth considering before we proceed to look at the show in detail.

The first is that *All in the Family* arrived at a time of unusual uncertainty and questioning in American society. It debuted shortly after the social upheaval of the 1960s, a period in which many reforms were made but also a time when many formerly comforting verities—among them the global economic, military, and political pre-eminence of the United States—were in active question. This uncertainty extended to many of the nation's cultural gatekeepers, notably film, television, and music executives, who responded by extending a greater degree of experimentation and autonomy to artists than they were inclined to do before or after this period. This is why, for example, the early 1970s are widely considered a golden age of Hollywood filmmaking in the aftermath of the collapse of the studio system.[4]

Television was always a different proposition, however. In part, that's because larger sums of money were involved over longer periods of time; because advertisers played such a large role in financing its operation; and because of the very large numbers of people involved in watching shows like *All in the Family*—much larger than a typical TV show today. Television was a *broadcast* medium.

Which brings us to the second reason for *All in the Family*'s significance. It's not simply that it was a trailblazing work of popular culture. Such works happen all the time. But few of them happen on a scale that *AITF* did at the very height of the broadcasting era—right before, in fact, it went into decline. We'll look at this history in more detail in chapter 2. But it's worth taking a moment at the outset to position the show as the quintessential product of what might be termed the Age of Broadcasting and how it's different from the one we're living in now.

To at least some extent, we still do live in a broadcast television culture. Then, as now, there were three major networks: ABC, CBS, and NBC; a fourth, FOX, came along in the 1980s. Each of these networks owns a series of local television stations known as affiliates for which they provide programming (they sell it to other entities as well). On any given day, you can turn on a television and watch a continuous stream of shows produced and/ or distributed by the networks, interrupted by advertisements, just as you could back then. You don't have to go to a store to buy such shows, pay a subscription fee to access them, or travel outside your home to see them. We tend to take these facts for granted now, but they're the culmination of a long process, and a long struggle: in a way, you might say, the history of popular culture is a saga in which entertainment started outside the home and ended inside it.[5] This high level of accessibility (assuming you can get decent reception over the airwaves) means that a television show can reach a great many people at once. That's *broad*casting.

However, relatively few people today experience television this way. There have been two key developments in the television industry that have occurred since the 1970s. The first is the rise of cable television. Cable (also delivered by satellite) is a much more variegated proposition than traditional broadcast TV in terms of both the number of shows and the kinds of players, from global networks to hyperlocal stations, that populate its universe. Where once you typically had a handful of choices of what to watch, you now have hundreds. There are channels to sate just about any kind of appetite, from golf fare to cooking shows. Some of this programming is commercial-free; other programming is paid for by advertisers. In any case, in order to watch cable you have to pay for it, typically in the form of monthly subscription fees. Cable emerged as a competitor with broadcast TV in the late 1970s; by the 1990s it dominated the industry in terms of influence, if not always in revenue or the size of its audiences.

But like traditional broadcasting, cable is also now fading as a form of TV content delivery. The advent of the internet in the 1990s, combined with the growing technical capacity to carry content to individuals—first in wired form, then wirelessly—has made it possible to deliver even more television on demand in a greater variety of settings. But the issue here is not simply *how* the shows get to us; it's also the way these new technologies have changed *what* we watch. For much of their early history, TV shows in the United States were financed by advertisers, which paid stations and networks money in exchange for slots of time to ply their wares to potential customers. Obviously, the goal was to make shows that lots of people would watch; less obviously, advertisers had an interest in not presenting content that could negatively affect their businesses, whether as a matter of potentially upsetting viewers or showing them things that would challenge the status quo. It's also worth noting that networks had an interest in producing shows that cost less money rather than more money; profit margins could sometimes be higher on cheap programming (like game shows and talk shows) than on expensive programming (such as scripted dramas shot on location). But when viewers are not a commodity sold to advertisers but rather the actual customers for the content, the rules change in terms of what gets made—and what it's possible to make.

The result, by many reckonings, has been a television renaissance sometimes referred to as "peak TV."[6] While this historical moment doesn't have fixed historical parameters, it's generally regarded as stretching from the last decade of the twentieth century into the second decade of the twenty-first. Observers cite a string of widely celebrated shows—dramas such as *The Wire*, *The Sopranos*, *Mad Men*, *Breaking Bad*, *Game of Thrones*; sitcoms such as *Curb Your Enthusiasm*, *Veep*, *Silicon Valley*, *Girls*—of unusual quality, daring, and appeal. Freed from the strictures of network censors, skittish advertisers, and lowest-common-denominator content, the creators of these shows have been able to develop a sense of depth and complexity previously impossible in the network era.

Like all good things, though, this one has a price. One, of course, is literal. Most people regard a Netflix subscription, hovering at around $15 a month, as trivial. But such shows sprawl across a series of platforms—HBO, Hulu, Amazon Prime, among others—that in effect function as networks like ABC, CBS, and NBC, except that this time you have to pay for them individually. As we're gradually becoming aware, watching such programs has potentially important privacy implications, as data are collected and shared in ways viewers don't know, since these content providers are secretive about their own data (Nielsen ratings in broadcast television are essentially public information, but Netflix doesn't share the numbers on its shows).

Then there are the cultural ramifications of this newer television landscape. The concept of choice is virtually enshrined in American culture: we cherish it and regard more of it as a self-evidently good thing. One of the happier by-products of the new media order is the creation of "the long tail": the new accessibility of niche, obscure, or previously unavailable content that promotes cultural connoisseurship of all kinds.[7] The downside, however, is, in the words of one media scholar, "a more fragmented, individualized media culture."[8] In short, we have less in common than we used to. In the mid-1970s, Archie Bunker was a shared cultural reference point, even if there were disagreements about what he meant. We tend not to have that today.

There are other, more serious, implications in this sense of fragmentation. In the second decade of the twenty-first century, it has become a commonplace to observe that we now tend to be encased in our own cultural and ideological media silos, only seeking and finding content that confirms our pre-existing view of the world. There is also a substantial body of psychological findings that having a plethora of choices is as likely to engender anxiety (in the form of "fear of missing out," or FOMO) as it is satisfaction.[9]

To be clear: the point here is not to argue that one television culture is better than the other. Besides the fact that we don't get to choose the moment we inhabit, there are always trade-offs involved in the choices we make, and variations in the priorities that different people have. But a sense of clarity of where we *do* stand, what we *can* choose, goes to the heart of the historical enterprise. It's in this sense that history is an enormously practical subject. In looking closely at artifacts from the past, we can understand the ways the world we live in has changed, how it has not, what we value, and why. And it also raises the possibility that we may yet resurrect, in our finite, fallible way, the spirit of the artistic enterprise across time and space.

1

Situation Comedy,
Situation Tragedy

The Transitional World
of *All in the Family*

On January 12, 1971, the *New York Times* reported that the U.S. Army had closed all men's clubs in the South Vietnamese city of Tuy Hòa, site of a major Air Force base, after a hand grenade blast hurt twenty-seven soldiers amid a riot at a club there (officials denied there were racial tensions in the incident). President Richard Nixon signed a bill into law that increased access to food stamps for the poor, but restricted the program only to those families whose members were willing to accept work. And George Blanda, the forty-three-year-old backup quarterback and kicker for the Oakland Raiders, was named the male athlete of the year by the Associated Press, beating out much younger players for the honor.[1] January 12, 1971, was also the day *All in the Family* made its debut on national television, halfway through the 1970–1971 television season. Like these and other stories, the show captured a culture that was in transition in the late 1960s and early 1970s.

In a way, to say that the nation was in a state of transition isn't saying much: when *isn't* a culture in a state of transition? But the time of change here, commonly referred to in shorthand as "the sixties," was particularly stark in its pace and intensity, especially compared with the generation that preceded it. As is often the case with historical periodization, the term "sixties" is imprecise, given that in collective memory it's widely regarded as stretching from the mid-1960s to the mid-1970s. *All in the Family* was born halfway through this transformation into a nation of paradoxes. Again, that's not unusual; paradoxes are characteristic of nations in all times and places. But the particular environment in which the show arrived was sharp and distinctive, and one uniquely suited to the emergence of what would become one of the most popular and controversial television shows of all time. (Popular and controversial: that's something of a paradox right there.)

Cultural artifacts reflect their times. On the other hand, it's also possible to imagine at least some of them happening at another time. *The Mary Tyler Moore Show*, which premiered in the same TV season that *All in the Family* did, was a TV program featuring a single woman in the workplace—a scenario that could and did become the basis for sitcoms for the next half century (ranging from *Murphy Brown* in the 1990s to *Homeland* a generation later). Conversely, *Friends*, a show about a group of unattached twentysomethings trying to find their way in New York City, could easily have premiered decades before 1994 (like *That Girl* in the 1960s). The details would vary, but the premise would work. But the idea of a TV show—a *comedic* television show, no less—featuring a bitterly divided family arguing about politics and seriously engaging any manner of taboo subjects for weekly audiences of 50 million viewers for years at a time? There had never been anything like it. And, notwithstanding any number of passing shows with a passing resemblance to it (*Married . . . with Children*, *Roseanne*), there hasn't been since, either. It was, truly and uniquely, a document of its moment.

The Best of Times . . .

And what was that moment? Well, again, it was a curiously divided one. In many respects, the United States circa 1970 was at the peak of its prosperity. The nation as a whole was immensely wealthy—rich in natural resources, rich in social capital, and rich in monetary wealth. It had the highest gross domestic product per person—essentially the world's highest standard of living, financially speaking—and had been in this position for some time.[2]

Not only that, but life in the United States had much improved since the dawn of the 1960s, itself a prosperous time. Over the course of that decade, the nation's per capita gross national product had risen by almost a third; the poverty rate had declined by almost half.[3] But the gains were not merely economic. The passage of the Civil Rights Act of 1964 and the Voting Rights Act of 1965 had demolished the legal foundation of racial segregation in the United States, even if it would persist in other forms. Women were being educated in greater numbers and entering careers that had previously been denied them. Laws protecting the rights of workers, the environment, and consumer safety were on the books. A wave of new technologies—CAT scans, bar codes, microwave ovens—were on their way to becoming facts of everyday life.

The nation was also increasingly taking advantage of another of its assets: immense space. Though the population was growing (the country grew from 151 million in 1950 to over 226 million by 1980), there was still plenty of room. France had four times as many people per square mile as the United States, the United Kingdom nine times, and Japan twelve. Sure, the Soviet Union and China—not especially attractive climates, in any number of ways—were larger, as was Canada. Moreover, the growing U.S. population did significantly reduce the amount of forest on the continent; the replanting of trees to replace cut timber, combined with reforestation of abandoned agricultural land—all this while the United States remained a major food exporter—meant there were about as many trees in the nation as there were during World War II.[4] To be sure, there were colossal waste and destruction in the form of strip mining, oil spills, and other forms of air and water pollution. But awareness of these ills was also beginning to mitigate them, as did the Clean Air Act of 1970, which controlled fuel emissions into the environment.

Though, technically speaking, the nation's frontier had closed in 1890, a collective westward migration continued. A huge swath of territory stretching from Virginia to southern California—known by the new term "Sun Belt"—was growing rapidly. There were a series of reasons for this: an attractive business climate (low taxes and wages); appealing weather (especially when compared with the "Rust Belt" of the Northeast and industrial Midwest); and relatively new infrastructure (good roads, new residential construction, and, not to be underestimated, pervasive air-conditioning). A series of cities—more like metropolitan areas, since there was a strongly suburban character to them—were growing rapidly: Atlanta, Houston, Phoenix, and San Diego, among others. Many of these cities produced or shipped goods for international consumption; all of them benefited from an influx of new arrivals from around the world who contributed their labor to these communities and spiced them with their folkways. In short, the American empire remained a colossus.

. . . The Worst of Times

In retrospect, though, the early 1970s appear to mark something of an American crest, a final moment of confidence and affluence before the start of some marked decline and even despair. A series of alternative realities was already evident to anyone who was even vaguely paying attention. If in some respects it was the best of times, it was also clear that it was the worst of times too.

Perhaps most obviously, it was a time of conflict at home and abroad: the Vietnam War—or, more accurately, as that small story in the *Times* of January 12, 1971, suggests, the Vietnam *Wars*—raged. In 1970 the United States still had almost 300,000 troops in Southeast Asia, down from the approximately half million of 1967, but more than any U.S. deployment since.[5] The presidential administration of Richard Nixon, frustrated by the way the Communist government of North Vietnam was smuggling resources down the Ho Chi Minh trail across its own national boundaries, expanded the conflict by bombing Cambodia in 1970, creating a whole new front in the war as well as precipitating a humanitarian catastrophe in that country when the murderous Khmer Rouge regime seized power and launched a campaign of genocide against its own people. A growing antiwar movement in the United States was incensed by the invasion of Cambodia, triggering a wave of protests that led to the death of four college students at Kent State University in Ohio. It was a time notable for a "generation gap" between older and younger Americans, one vividly captured each week in the arguments between the patriarchal Archie Bunker and his son-in-law, Mike Stivic.

Another realm of social conflict gripping the United States in 1970 was race relations. Though it was a moment of relative quietude—there were neither major African American protests that year, nor were major pieces of legislation signed—the overall mood in the nation was dour. Most civil rights leaders saw the glass as at least half empty. The assassination of Martin Luther King in 1968 still cast a heavy pall, and militant voices, notably those of Stokely Carmichael, George Jackson (charged in the death of a prison guard in 1970), and Angela Davis, dominated headlines.

Meanwhile, other oppressed racial minorities were rising. In 1970, the American Indian Movement (AIM) led a protest by occupying Plymouth Rock, site of the Pilgrim landing in New England in 1620. Asian activists were also raising their voices in the yellow power movement. The Stonewall riot of 1969 kick-started a gay liberation movement that would come into its own in 1970. So would the second wave feminist movement. In 1970, it still seemed possible, even likely, that an Equal Rights Amendment could clear Congress (the proposal was brought to the floor of the House of Representatives by Michigan Democrat Martha Griffiths). But arguments over the role of women in society came fast and furious, and were also reflected in the plots and dialogue of *All in the Family*, where a range of female characters—Archie and Edith's daughter Gloria; their neighbors Louise Jefferson and Irene Lorenzo; Edith's cousin Maude—engaged a series of women's perspectives and experiences.

Though such voices could be loud and angry, they were of course not necessarily signs of national ill health. Indeed, protest often brought about positive change. The antiwar movement, for example, certainly played a role in bringing the Vietnam War to an end, a conflict that most observers came to regard as a mistake (even those, like Archie's friend Pinky Peterson, who lost a son in the war but nevertheless shook hands with a draft dodger at a Christmas dinner at the Bunker home in 1976). The decades that followed the 1970s were marked by significant gains for women and racial minorities, and so the 1970s could be seen as an important turning point for the better. The success of *All in the Family* was a matter of its ability to capture the duality of this moment: the perception of change (which frightened some) and the frustration that it wasn't happening fast enough (which angered others).

In other ways, however, the national tide was going out in ways that have shaped our national life ever since. This is particularly true in the realm of economics. Though the energy crisis that would sap the nation's confidence and vitality was still a few years away, the U.S. economy hadn't been doing all that well even before the eruption of the 1973 war between Israel and Egypt that brought the age of cheap energy in the United States to a close. The U.S. economy grew at an average rate of 5 percent annually between 1947 and 1965, but between 1966 and 1975 that figure dropped to 1.9 percent.[6] President Lyndon Johnson's reluctance to tax Americans to pay for the Vietnam

War, coupled with a sharp rise in defense spending, led to inflation that weakened the U.S. economy and eroded the power of U.S. currency abroad. By 1970 the nation was facing severe pressure from other nations seeking to cash in their dollars for gold, and in 1971 President Nixon would end a long-standing policy of convertibility, allowing the dollar to float relative to other currencies. While this was surely necessary, it also made clear that the international standing of the United States was weakening. First in the world in gross domestic product per person at the start of the decade, the United States slipped to eleventh by 1980, a slide that corresponded with *All in the Family*'s run on prime-time television.[7]

For most Americans, such statistics were remote abstractions. But the growing economic pain was real enough. The cost of living was rising in 1970. Inflation, at an average annual rate of 6.2 percent in 1969, would double to 12.4 percent by 1974, when *All in the Family* ran a four-part episode with the title "The Bunkers and Inflation." Unemployment would reach 7.5 percent in 1975; the fear, and reality, of joblessness factored periodically into the show's plots.[8] With an eye toward his looming re-election, President Nixon imposed ninety-day wage and price controls in late 1971, designed to tamp down rising prices. But when he lifted those controls, the whiplash was all the more painful, particularly for staples like food. The opening credits for the *Mary Tyler Moore Show* were famous at the time for showing its main character looking with disgust at the price of meat in a supermarket as she tosses it into her shopping cart. One hilarious episode of *All in the Family* features Edith's attempts to economize with horsemeat; another involves her getting absurdly good prices on beef from an immigrant butcher who is infatuated with her.

These rising prices defied economic logic. High inflation usually meant low unemployment, as people with jobs tended to buy more stuff, driving prices up. Alternatively, high unemployment meant low inflation, since people without jobs bought less stuff, driving prices down. If one was high, the other was supposed to be low. But by the mid-1970s the nation was experiencing relatively high unemployment *and* high inflation, leading to the creation of a new economic term: "stagflation." Whatever the reasons for the mystery, it was a source of frustration and anxiety.

One result of these developments was that Americans—at this point, mostly white ones—voted with their feet and fled the nation's largest cities in favor of more affordable suburbs or racially segregated districts of the Sunbelt. (In his cheeky but pointed 1975 song "Chocolate City," bandleader

George Clinton of Parliament conferred his blessings on the accomplish-ments of fellow African Americans concentrated in urban areas even as he cast a benevolent eye on those in "vanilla suburbs.") Northeastern cities such as Philadelphia and Washington, DC, shrank; downtown midwestern ones such as Cleveland and Cincinnati became empty, often dangerous husks, surrounded by a belt of wealthier suburbs. Between 1950 and 1980, Chi-cago lost 17 percent of its population, Detroit 35 percent, and St. Louis 47 percent—a process of shrinkage and de-industrialization that was acutely apparent in the 1970s.[9] Archie Bunker, who famously inhabited a neighbor-hood in the New York City borough of Queens, was in this, as in so many other ways, increasingly perceived as yesterday's man.

There was also a growing perception that his native New York was on the verge of collapse—something that Archie Bunker would regularly read about as he sat in his beloved living room chair and read the tabloid New York *Daily News*. Like the populations of other U.S. cities, New York's popula-tion was also shrinking, taking a significant piece of its tax base with it. And like other cities, Gotham was losing its industrial base; the closing in 1966 of the Brooklyn Navy Yard, an economic hub since it first opened in 1806, was only one example of how thousands of jobs were lost (others disappeared when corporations left New York for the Sun Belt). Like other cities, too, New York experienced an influx of poor people, many of them immigrants, who required services the city was relatively generous in providing. New York City also had a large public sector workforce, whose unions negotiated relatively good contracts. To pay those contracts, the municipal government increasingly relied on short-term loans. Add to this a growing crime prob-lem, corrupt police (as revealed in a sensational 1971 investigation), and dif-ficulty keeping streets and subway cars clean (one episode of the show was set in a typically grimy one that broke down) and you had the nation's largest city teetering on the edge of insolvency.[10] Much of New York was literally going up in flames during the early 1970s, especially in the outer boroughs of Brooklyn and the Bronx, where arson for the sake of collecting insurance money on old buildings was a common practice. Under such circumstances, Archie and Edith's surname of Bunker was poetically apt.

The early 1970s were also a turning point for a reason that would not become clear until decades later: it marked the peak of real median income for men, adjusted for inflation, in U.S. history. To some extent, the retreat from this high point was hidden, not only because it was grad-ual, masked by the availability of overtime (businesses sought to avoid hiring more people), but also because of the influx of women into the work-force. Women's wages—typically lower than those for men working the same job—helped relieve the strain families were feeling.[11] In the years that followed, one of the key sources of that pressure became increasingly obvious: the willingness of workers in other parts of the world to do what Americans did for less, coupled with their increasing educational and technological competitiveness.

This downward pressure on wages was intensified by more structural changes in the world economy. Until the mid-twentieth century, advanced economies were rooted in *manufacturing*, which is to say they focused on producing goods. By the late twentieth century, however, the world, led by the United States, was increasingly a *service* economy, in which providing information or performing tasks was more important. Service economy jobs could be lucrative. And they could be plentiful. But unlike classic blue-collar assembly-line jobs, they tended not to be both. Most service industry jobs were concentrated in low-wage sectors like retailing and hospitality, known as pink-collar work because of its gender connotations. This is one more way that Archie Bunker, a dockworker, was an artifact of a receding American tide—still very much present, but one whose days, as he and those around him sensed, were numbered. He would ultimately be spared a downward spiral of wage earning by using the equity in his house—a house he was able to buy despite never finishing high school—to invest in a neighborhood bar, ending the series as a member of the petite bourgeoisie. In many respects, the door closed behind him.

While it would take decades for the implications of this interlocking series of social and economic transformations to become fully apparent, the direc-tion of the country was clear enough. "I don't know a dream that's not been shattered or driven to its knees," Paul Simon muses in his classic 1973 song "American Tune." It's all right, his narrator says: "You can't be forever blessed." Days of rage in the 1960s were giving way to days of sorrow in the 1970s.

Questions of Progress

So while there were clearly alternating currents to the contrary, the early 1970s marked an unusual moment in American history, both in its vitality and in the wave of despair that swept much of the country. Of course, there had been bad times before—the Great Depression was a living memory for millions of Americans, reflected in the song "Those Were the Days," which opened each episode of *All in the Family*. But besides a stratum of intellectuals (and even among them only temporarily), there had never been a sense that the basic premises of American life were in question during the Depression or at earlier moments in U.S. history. Americans tended to think they lived in an opportunity society where the future promised to be better than the past, and where inevitable setbacks would ultimately prove temporary. This was becoming harder to believe in the 1970s. Partly that's because there had been so many changes—and so many disappointments—in the 1960s. But this sense of uncertainty was also a function of the shifting geopolitical tides. And so millions of people began to wonder: Is the American way of life—variously defined, but usually grounded in material prosperity in one way or another—truly sustainable? And if not, what could/should Americans be doing differently? For a moment, one that turned out in a number of ways to be temporary, the 1970s were a time when a surprisingly large number of people were willing to peer into a collective abyss.

This, then, was the world into which *All in the Family* was born. It was the product of a remarkable moment in American history. It was also the work of an unusual man who had been the product of an older, perhaps more stable country, but one unusually attuned to its contemporary currents. His ability to bring different generations and different perspectives together in vivid dialogue would result in not only an astoundingly popular television show, but also an important cultural artifact that remains both a landmark and a measuring stick of who we were and what we've become.

2

The Revolution, Televised

Origins of the *Family*

All great works of art—which is to say works of art that strike a chord in their own time and resonate long afterward—are products of applied excellence in any number of ways. But as essential as excellence is to artistic success, it's never sufficient. Another important factor, for example, is the state of the cultural marketplace at a given moment: the ability of creators to find audiences who value what they have to say and who can in turn sustain them. That marketplace, in turn, depends on still other considerations, among them the available technology of a given moment as well as the means and scale of transmission.

All in the Family was an extraordinary TV program, one remarkable for the confluence of talents—writers, actors, directors, and others—who coalesced in what can be regarded as a lucky outcome, given the unpredictability that surrounds trying to get any show on the air. But its success was rooted in history in two senses: the way the show tapped the cultural currents of the 1970s, as well as its moment in the history of television. The show premiered when its communications medium—a *broadcast* medium that dominated the American media landscape from the late 1920s to the late

1970s—was at the very apex of its power and influence. *All in the Family* also arrived at a moment when its genre, the situation-comedy, had reached an inflection point in its evolution in terms of what had come before and what would follow. These are developments worth exploring before examining the show in further detail.

Riding the (Air) Waves

When *All in the Family* premiered in 1971, modern television broadcasting was about twenty years old.[1] The immediate roots of TV were in radio. Radio, in turn, derived from the telegraph, a nineteenth-century innovation that involved sending an electrical signal between two points of a copper cable. The staggering achievement here—one we in the centuries since are prone to take for granted—was the conquest of time and space: the ability to communicate information instantly between people without anyone actually having to deliver it in person. This achievement, in turn, spawned others, principal among them an effort to remove that cable and transmit data wirelessly, a feat that became possible at the turn of the twentieth century and one that was invaluable for the shipping industry as well as modern navies seeking to share intelligence (and avoid crashes). We have come to know this communications medium as radio. The subsequent invention of a device called the audion by the technologist Lee De Forest allowed the human voice to travel via radio waves, which was a great leap forward in terms of transforming radio from a specialized tool of industry into one of mass communication.

Until the 1920s, however, radio was largely a matter of transmission between two points. People who were passionate about the medium—known colloquially as radio "hams"—would set up transmitters and receivers and connect with other individuals over large distances. But in the middle of that decade a clever engineer in Pittsburgh set up a radio transmitter on the roof of his house to pick up an outdoor concert that his neighbors wanted to hear. This marked a conceptual leap. Instead of two-way communication between two fixed points, this was a matter of projecting a single message to many listeners at the same time: *broad*casting. It was now possible to create large invisible communities who shared experiences simultaneously, fostering collective conversations that could flow across city, state, and national boundaries. This was something new under the sun. For the next sixty or so years, broadcasting would be the defining experience of twentieth-century civilization: *mass* media as the essence of modernity.

Over the course of the 1920s, broadcasting picked up tremendous momentum and led to the formation of two major radio networks, the National Broadcasting Company (NBC) and the Columbia Broadcasting System (CBS), both of which sought to produce entertainment that would attract continental audiences by literally and figuratively connecting local radio stations by supplying them with the same content. By the early 1930s, both networks had developed a commercial framework by which that content would be supported by advertisers that paid for programs in exchange for the opportunity to promote their products. This might take the form of a company (like Eveready batteries or Pepsodent toothpaste) sponsoring a show for which it received acknowledgment before each installment, or some form of patter worked into the dialogue of the content itself. This was a different approach from what one would find in Great Britain, for example, where the government (in the form of the British Broadcasting Corporation, or BBC) paid for content with revenue in the form of taxes on radios.

These economic models carried over to television. Actually, many of the technical foundations for television had been laid in the 1920s. The difference, of course, is that unlike radio, television is both visual *and* aural. Like movies, television depends on an optical illusion whereby our brains perceive movement in watching a series of rapidly shown images where none exists. Early attempts at television involved spinning disks studded with punctures through which light was projected. The alternating pattern of light and dark created images composed of dots (today we know them as pixels) shown in rapid succession. At first, these images were little more than shadows. But they steadily got better.

Despite the technical possibilities, television was slow to spread for a number of reasons, among them the Great Depression and World War II, when much of the talent and energy that might have been used for development of the medium was channeled into radar technology for military purposes. But with the arrival of peace—and an economic boom—the stage was set for a cultural explosion. Over the course of the 1950s, television transformed from a cultural novelty to the central focus of national life.

Shows of Force

This centrality took a number of forms, or, more specifically, programming formats. Many of these were carryovers from radio, though they evolved quickly in the new medium. News, of course, had always been important to radio and would be for television as well, since adding a visual dimension greatly enhanced the ability of an audience to understand events. But this was not necessarily a matter of TV always being bigger and better. Take sports, for example. A radio announcer could more easily describe a baseball or football game than a photo camera could capture it—one reason why boxing was an easier sport for television to cover. Similarly, while television resembled film in that it was a visual medium, TV simply could not reproduce the sense of scale that movies could, since shows had to be produced more quickly and more cheaply than an average feature film. Many early television shows showed more kinship with the medium of theater than that of cinema. Indeed, one of the pioneering TV shows at the dawn of the medium was *Kraft Television Theater* (1947–1955), an anthology of dramas that featured new plays and characters each week. *All in the Family* is very clearly a descendant of this TV-as-theater tradition, especially in its early years. While the show would occasionally venture beyond the Bunker home, the family living room was essentially a standing set where most of the show's action took place. The theatrical vein in television was also apparent in another radio carryover, the soap opera—so named for the companies that sponsored it—which took drama in a somewhat different direction by featuring recurrent characters and extended storylines, something that could happen when audiences experienced shows far more regularly and conveniently than going to a theater. Here, too, is a genealogical antecedent for *All in the Family*.

The difference, of course, is that *AITF* was a comedy, not a drama. But the show also drew on antecedents from radio. One of the most beloved shows of all time—one whose popularity rivaled, if not outstripped, that of *AITF*—was *Amos 'n' Andy*, which ran in various forms on radio and television from the 1920s to the 1960s. *Amos 'n' Andy* was a racist satire based on the nineteenth-century minstrel show, where white characters "blacked up" their faces and hands with burnt cork and mocked the language and pretensions of African Americans. Each week, listeners tuned in to learn the latest mishaps for a set of familiar characters whose foibles, misadventures, and (especially) malapropisms amused tens of millions of Americans from all walks of life. In short, *Amos 'n' Andy* helped lay the foundations for a television genre we now know as the situation-comedy, or sitcom.

But the relationship between *Amos 'n' Andy* and *AITF* is more direct, and more complex, than that of a general precedent. In some important respects, *All in the Family* represents an actual inversion of minstrelsy: where the general thrust of blackface was to mock the pretensions and foibles of black people, *All in the Family* instead satirized that of a white one, Archie Bunker—and his not inconsiderable ilk. One of the standing gags in minstrelsy was the mangling of the English language by black men who were, in the terminology of the time, "putting on airs" by trying to sound smarter than they really were, as when, for example, the *Amos 'n' Andy* character Lightnin' referred to the "bizness repression" in an episode following the stock market crash of 1929.[2] (As was often the case, there was an ironic truth in such errors, which occasionally suggested an ambiguity, even sympathy, in depictions of African Americans even as actors mocked them.) In like fashion, one of the most reliable tactics for eliciting laughter in *All in the Family* was Archie's failed attempts to use formal language, as in his frequent use of the terms "ipso fatso," "present company suspected," and the like. Gynecology became "groinocology," and feminism was referred to as "the women's lubrication movement." Archie would similarly mangle or splice truisms when making observations like "we better not kill those chickens before they cross the road," or noting that "patience is a virgin."

This sense of historical precedent was quite conscious and explicit in the two-part 1975 episode where Gloria gives birth to her son Joey on the night that Archie and his pals are mounting a minstrel show as a benefit for their men's club. By the mid-1970s, minstrelsy had become verboten in polite American society—Mike, the show's liberal voice of reason, is emphatically appalled when he sees Archie and his pals in blackface in the Bunker living room before their show—but could be depicted in this particular context because the conceit of a group of middle-aged white men blacking up was so obviously ridiculous and indicative of their cluelessness. The joke is further extended when Archie finds himself unable to remove his makeup after learning that his daughter is in labor, and shows up at the hospital in blackface. There's one more layer of intertextuality here still: the scene is clearly an allusion to the 1953 episode of *I Love Lucy*—a show screenwriters Bob Schiller and Robert Weiskopf wrote for before joining the staff of *All in the Family*—where Cuban bandleader Ricky Ricardo rushes to pregnant Lucy's side from his nightclub, wearing an indigenous Latin American costume and terrifying the nurses in the maternity wing. In effect, we have an appropriation of an appropriation of an appropriation (at a minimum). Such is the essence of American popular culture.

Situating Comedy

All in the Family's direct and indirect ties to *Amos 'n' Andy* and *I Love Lucy* suggest its pedigree as the quintessential sitcom. As its name suggests, the sitcom is about situations—a new job, a relative coming to visit, a lost cherished object, and so on. The fun comes from how familiar characters react to the novel situation. Initially, all the loose ends got tied up by the end of any given episode of a sitcom, making them modular: you can start watching at any time and pick up what was going on. Later, running plotlines became more common. But the key to success for the sitcom was, in effect, its open-air architecture: just go with the flow. This allowed sitcoms to build and sustain large audiences. Indeed, such shows were good examples of what was later termed the "multiplier effect": the phenomenon where something (like, say, a social media platform) becomes valuable *because* so many people use it. They helped foster a broad national culture that stretched across any number of demographic lines.

Most early sitcoms focused on the traditional family. Here, too, there were many precedents in radio that crossed over to television. *Mama* (1949–1957), based on a book and film, focused on a Norwegian immigrant family at the turn of the century; *The Goldbergs* (also 1949–1957), featuring the multi-talented writer-actor-producer Gertrude Berg, depicted urban Jewish life. Such shows suggest the degree to which the first generation of sitcoms was receptive to cultural diversity. This is one reason why, beyond its intrinsically funny situations, *I Love Lucy* was so important; rather than depicting a traditional family, it depicted an interracial couple's often hilarious struggle to come to terms with such White Anglo-Saxon Protestant (WASP) orthodoxy through the characters of Latino Desi Arnaz and his endlessly restless redhead gringa (house)wife.

The most obvious immediate antecedent for *All in the Family*, however, was *The Honeymooners*, which featured Jackie Gleason as bellowing bus driver Ralph Kramden and Audrey Meadows as his long-suffering wife, Trixie. Though it is rightly regarded as a landmark sitcom, *The Honeymooners* ran as such for only a single season in 1951; much of the show's lore rests on material that subsequently derived from specials and skits incorporated into later shows. But in its hapless, boorish, and yet somehow endearing protagonist, Kramden is very clearly an archetypal godfather of Carroll O'Connor's Archie Bunker. "I know I am doing some of the things you did," O'Connor wrote Gleason during *AITF*'s heyday. "I wish I had done some of the things you are doing," Gleason replied.[3]

By the late 1950s, however, the tenor of broadcast sitcoms changed, shifting away from an urban, ethnic, working-class sensibility toward a white, Protestant, middle-class one. To a great degree, this reflected the upward mobility of a broad swath of assimilated baby boomers whose parents and grandparents were immigrants that had survived the Great Depression and World War II with a sense of rising social ambitions for their children. One indication of such changes was the explosion of suburbia, a demographic shift reflected in the hit shows of the era. Sometimes, as in the case of *I Love Lucy*, doing so became part of the plot. Others, like *Leave It to Beaver* (1957–1963) and *The Adventures of Ozzie and Harriet* (1952–1966), took emerging middle-class norms for granted, fostering a stereotypical image of the 1950s as relatively simple and serene.

At the time, such shows seemed to offer a vision of sleek American modernity. They were, nevertheless, avowedly traditional in their portrayal of gender roles—as the very title of *Father Knows Best* (1954–1960) suggests. In one 1954 episode of *Ozzie and Harriet*, for example, an effort to give Dad (Ozzie) a night out on the town is simply disastrous: Harriet can't balance her checkbook, little Ricky can't do his homework, and Ozzie is absolutely miserable over being exiled from home despite his wife's good intentions. Whatever truth there may have been to such portrayals of middle-class life— surely they would not have been savored to the degree they were if they bore *no* relationship to reality—they sidestepped social problems, notably the burgeoning civil rights movement, in ways that seem striking in retrospect. But however true or false they were, these sitcoms created an image of the time that has proven durable to subsequent generations. Indeed, it was television more than any other communications medium that reinforced it.[4]

Laughable Comedy

By the late 1960s, however, the genial, respectable tenor of sitcom culture on television was increasingly out of touch with reality. To be sure, this was part of its appeal: in a time of war abroad and social conflict at home—discord, which like so much else, was broadcast over the airwaves each night in the form of evening news—the light amusement afforded by such entertainment was widely experienced as a balm from stresses that were both personal and political. Indeed, some of the most popular sitcoms in the 1960s were often downright fanciful in their scenarios, albeit in different ways. There were, for example, fish-out-of-water shows such as *The Beverly Hillbillies* (1962–1971), about a poor backwoods family that strikes it rich after oil is found on their property, leading them to relocate to Beverly Hills. *Green Acres* (1965–1971) offered the reverse scenario: fancy New York City couple relocates to ramshackle farm. Sometimes the sense of fantasy was more literal, as in the case of *Bewitched* (1964–1972) and *I Dream of Jeannie* (1965–1970), which featured women with magical powers in suburban settings. But whatever form they took, and whatever one might say about these shows, there were two important realities that characterized them: they were popular, and, thus, they were profitable—which is to say that advertisers were willing to pay top dollar for commercials that would run before, during, and after every episode.

For most of the postwar era, there were three major broadcast networks on the TV landscape (along with a plethora of local channels, many of which ran old sitcoms as part of their programming): CBS, NBC, and ABC, a network created in the 1940s as part of an antitrust settlement with NBC that was something of an also-ran in the 1950s and 1960s. Each of these networks had contracts with hundreds of television stations—affiliates, to use the term of art—that broadcast their content across the continent. Of the three, CBS was widely regarded as the most successful—the so-called Tiffany network. This was less a matter of its sitcoms (*The Beverly Hillbillies*, a CBS show, was hardly highbrow fare) than its reputation in news and drama, which included a commitment to programming that was not necessarily for-profit—some of it government mandated as the price of its otherwise free license to profit from the airwaves. But whatever their relative status in the TV pecking order, executives at all three networks were aware that times were changing—and were trying to respond with shows that would attract younger audiences on which their futures would ultimately depend. After all, in 1965, 41 percent of the U.S. population was nineteen years old or younger.[5]

This was an issue in another way as well. By the early 1970s, it was beginning to dawn on programmers and advertisers that mere *quantity* of an audience was not necessarily a marker of *quality* from a marketing point of view. Mass was beginning to matter less than class: Americans with larger disposable incomes, and a disposition to buy things, were the most compelling segments of an audience population. Such people tended to be young, not only because young people were often financially supported by their families in an affluent American society and could thus make relatively more discretionary purchases, but also because young people were not yet habituated in their spending habits and were more willing to try new things, perhaps forming loyalties that might last for a lifetime. So shows that spoke to this constituency were more valuable, even if the audience for them was relatively smaller.[6]

The result of these structural shifts in the TV business was a tentative spirit of experimentation. One example of this was *Julia* (1968–1971), a weekly NBC drama about an African American nurse who actively tries to break out of racial stereotypes. Important harbingers in terms of comedy were *The Smothers Brothers Comedy Hour* (1967–1969) and *Laugh-In* (1968–1973), variety shows that edged into political humor that would be tame by later standards. These two strands of race and comedy would be fused by *The Flip Wilson Show* (1970–1974), which featured the famed African American comedian in a series of sketches and recurring characters such as Geraldine, a sassy southern black woman portrayed by the cross-dressing Wilson.

As a programming genre, sitcoms lagged in adapting to social change. One relatively bold move was the debut of *The Mary Tyler Moore Show* in 1970. Moore was already well known to television audiences for her role as a suburban housewife on *The Dick Van Dyke Show* (1961–1966), so when she reappeared as a single woman in Minneapolis pursuing a career in TV news, she registered social change at face value. Yet even here there was hedging: there had been talk of Moore's character having a divorce backstory, but the show's creators compromised with CBS and settled for a broken engagement. Still, there was no question that this marked a new direction.

Prince Lear

The Mary Tyler Moore Show was a respectable show about a respectable woman. But would it be possible to go further? To do something truly edgy? Depict people who were *less* than respectable without explicitly condemning them as such? To talk about things that had never been part of the sitcom universe? And if it *were* possible to do this, *who* would be interested in broadcasting it? And who would be interested in *watching* it? These were questions that Norman Lear was interested in answering.

Over the coming decade, Lear would emerge as a pioneering figure in the history of broadcast television, a maverick who broke countless taboos. But he was very much a product of the medium and had been present at its creation. Lear was born in New Haven, Connecticut, on July 22, 1922, to a Jewish family whose members lived, as he liked to say, "at the ends of their nerves and the top of their lungs."[7] Lear's father, Herman, served a three-year prison term for fraud when Norman was a child, and periodic financial upheaval was part of his early life, which was also marked by frequent strife between his parents—his memories include his father's frequent demand that his wife "stifle herself," a term that would later become part of Archie Bunker's verbal repertoire. Lear has repeatedly noted that Archie's character was indeed modeled on Herman—like Archie, he ruled his roost from a beloved armchair and would resort to casual bigotry in describing his son as "the laziest white kid he ever met," a line that would make it into the pilot episode of the series—but his memoir makes clear that the Lear family was one of pronounced striving for upward mobility, albeit in ways that crossed ethical lines.[8]

For the length of his life, Lear yearned to imagine an alternative history to the one he inherited. He did so to the point of fabrication, telling a story for years that his grandfather wrote regularly to the president (presumably Franklin Roosevelt) with a salutation that began "My dearest darling president." "I just needed that father figure," he confessed in a documentary released when he was ninety-four years old. Of Herman Lear, he said, "I don't know if it's good for me to have forgiven him and forgotten him, though I don't know that I've done either."[9]

Lear's moral fervor was heightened by the crisis of the 1930s, and in particular his experience as a Jewish boy in an age of rampant anti-Semitism. He describes listening to the radio broadcasts of famed "Radio Priest" Father Charles Coughlin, which were filled with hate-filled invective against Jews. When World War II broke out, Lear was eager to join the fight. "I wanted to be known as a Jew who served," he explained. "I wanted to bomb, I wanted to kill."[10] He served in the air force during World War II as a radio operator on B-17s, flying dozens of missions over Germany in 1944–1945. On some of those missions, his bomber was protected by fighter planes manned by the famed Tuskegee Airmen, a cadre of elite African American pilots, an experience that appears to have influenced Lear's subsequent racial attitudes.

After the war, Lear joined the masses of Americans who sought to claim the fruits of victory. He married for the first of three times, fathered the first of his six children, and worked briefly as a press agent and for his father in a failed appliance company. Yet his restlessness, ambition, and talent were distinctive. Hankering for a career in show business, Lear set out for Hollywood, where he hooked up with his cousin's husband, Ed Simmons. Through a combination of luck and persistence, they landed a series of gigs writing material for comedians, notably Danny Thomas (himself a broadcast pioneer). This in turn led to invitations to write for television, among them for the hottest act in entertainment in the early 1950s: (Dean) Martin and (Jerry) Lewis. Martin and Lewis built an entertainment empire that spanned live performances, movies, and television. By the mid-1950s, Lear and Simmons had become among the best-known and highest-paid writers in the business, though that business was also one of big paydays followed by anxiety-inducing layoffs. The two would eventually strike out on their own, and Lear began collaborating with a series of other showbiz people, among them the director Bud Yorkin, with whom he would form an outfit they dubbed Tandem Productions. The duo would share a series of duties in developing projects, but Lear was typically a writer/producer and Yorkin a director. As such, they went on to make a number of television shows and movies, among them the 1964 Frank Sinatra vehicle *Come Blow Your Horn*.

Until this point in his career, there was little evidence that Lear saw himself as a maverick. To be sure, he was very aware of his minority status as a Jew, one that shaped his sense of himself even in an entertainment business that had plenty of them. He grew up imbibing the talents of Jewish comic radio giants such as Eddie Cantor, Jack Benny, Fred Allen, and George Burns (whose comic sidekick was his Catholic wife, Gracie Allen).[11] As a student at Emerson College in Boston during the early 1940s, he regularly visited burlesque shows, a working-class form of entertainment with strong sexual overtones that included striptease. Lear later described burlesque as "my acting, producing, directing, and casting school,"[12] and it furnished the basis for the hit 1968 movie *The Night They Raided Minsky's*, which he co-wrote and produced. The movie was a valentine to the world of his youth, skillfully blending black-and-white with color photography and lovingly re-creating stage routines by seasoned pros such as Jason Robards and Bert

Lahr under the direction of William Friedkin, soon to go on to renown as director of *The French Connection* (1971) and *The Exorcist* (1973).

Such formative entertainment experiences shaped Lear's earthy sense of humor, but not an especially critical one. He came of age in an era of assimilation; as he noted of his wartime service in 2014, "We were far more *in* love with America and far more connected to the *idea* of America than we are now."[13] One needs only a few moments in reading an interview with Lear or hearing him talk to experience his sunny disposition; a sense of optimism seems to have buoyed him throughout his career and animated a sense of personal as well as collective progress.

There was a vein of mild satire in some of Lear's work. He wrote and directed the 1967 film *Divorce, American Style*, which takes a lighthearted approach to the subject—its focus is the burden of alimony, but all's well that ends well when the unhappy couples decide to reunite. He also directed the 1971 film *Cold Turkey* (it had actually been made a couple of years earlier but drifted for two years in turnaround), about an Iowan town's struggle to give up smoking for thirty days in exchange for a $25 million prize offered as part of a publicity gimmick by a tobacco company. Residents manage to pull it off; in an ironic comeuppance, the president of the United States confers his congratulations in the form of a missile factory that spews black smoke. But there was little direct political commentary here, and insofar as *Cold Turkey* is notable for any sense of social transgression, it's as the first mainstream American movie to include farting as the source of a joke. Actually, the principal reason why it's interesting a half century later is its mediocrity, despite the talents of comic actors such as Dick Van Dyke (playing against type) and Bob Newhart.[14] Thus, it's a telling indication of just how good, and perhaps how fortuitous, *All in the Family* was by contrast.

But Lear's social conscience was there, waiting to be tapped. In later reconstructing his interest in African American life, for example, he described taking trains from Hartford to Manhattan as a child, gazing at apartments in Harlem and picturing the lives of its residents, as well as recalling his wartime sense of shame at the way black GIs were treated in a segregated army. As a young man he regularly shot off telegrams to members of Congress.[15] Yet until the late 1960s, this sensibility wasn't reflected in his work. "I've wondered why the political activist in me took four decades to fully surface," Lear reflected at the end of his life. "I think it had something to do with money. Not dollars per se, but the feeling of comfort and safety that flows from acquiring enough of them."[16] A series of factors had come together by then:

Lear had achieved financial security; the nation was undergoing dramatic changes; and a bold move could bolster his career. These elements coalesced when he seized on a television project that captured his imagination.[17]

Near *Death* Experience

It was actually a British show. Its roots were in a single episode of a BBC anthology series, *Till Death Us Do Part*. First broadcast in 1965, the show featured a working-class character named Alf Garnett (Warren Mitchell), his weary wife Else (Dandy Nichols), and their daughter Rita (Una Stubbs). Alf holds reactionary views and clashes with his son-in-law Mike Rawlins (Anthony Booth), a staunch socialist lacking much in the way of a work ethic. *Till Death Us Do Part* ran as a miniseries in 1966, was made into a movie in 1968, and ran as a sitcom until 1975. It was Yorkin, living in London at the time, who brought the show to Lear's attention circa 1967, reacting to Lear's notion that there could be an American show there as "another one of Norman's fantasies."[18] Larry Gelbart, the writer and producer who would later go on to produce *M*A*S*H*, also lived in London at the time and was similarly fascinated—and similarly skeptical. "You didn't watch it; you were riveted to it," he later remembered. But he said he recalled "never once having the idea or the vision or the inclination to say, 'This would be great in America.' Because it was *unthinkable* that that could ever invade our land, and *Lucy* . . . you know?" Noting that as a taxpayer-funded enterprise, Britain's BBC ran on a different economic model than American television, Gelbart described *Till Death Us Do Part* as "a good case to be made for what happens when you don't have to worry about the terrible two A's: affiliates and advertising."[19]

But Lear saw possibilities—and seized them. "Oh my God, my dad and me," he later reported. "I was flooded with ideas and knew I had to do an American version of the show." Lear would later enumerate his own ideas for the characters: "I wanted him to have far more humanity [than Alf]. I wanted him to have a daughter, and I wanted the daughter to love her dad. I wanted his wife to love him, whoever he was, *whatever* he was."[20] Though Yorkin thought it would be a miracle if they ever got it on the air, he went along with the idea. Lear secured the rights and persuaded ABC, the network in last place in overall ratings, to commission a pilot episode for a show to be titled *Justice for All*.[21]

That title was a pun: in Lear's inaugural script, the main character's name was Archie Justice. There was an initial thought of making him an elevator operator, but Lear settled on making him, like Alf Garnett, a dockworker (from the start Archie would also have a second job as a cabdriver).[22] Lear considered Mickey Rooney—the legendary entertainer whose career stretched back to the age of silent film and vaudeville, when he was a child star—for the part of Archie and discussed it with him as potentially shrewd casting against type. But Rooney turned him down. "They're going to kill you, shoot you dead in the streets," he told Lear.[23]

It may seem odd that Lear would pursue an actor like Rooney, whose persona over the course of a long life was sweetness incarnate (he played a lovable, boyish character named Andy Hardy in a series of hit movies, and partnered repeatedly with the young Judy Garland). But this was a deliberate decision. "It was very important that Archie have a likeable face, because the point of his character was to show that if bigotry and intolerance didn't exist in the hearts and minds of the good people, the average people, it would not be the endemic problem that it is in our society," he later explained. (As we'll see, there were those who objected to this premise.) "I rarely saw a bigot that I didn't have some reason to like. They were all relatives and friends."[24]

Even as he was exploring his prospects with Rooney, Lear already had his eye on actor Carroll O'Connor. The Manhattan-born O'Connor, like Archie, had grown up in Queens, a fact that might explain his affinity for the character. But O'Connor's class background and political views were significantly different from those of his signature character. For one thing, O'Connor had a solidly bourgeois upbringing; his father was a lawyer and his mother a schoolteacher, and he attended college at the University of Montana at Missoula.[25] It was only during a visit to his brother in Ireland that he took up acting at the University of Dublin. After struggling to establish himself upon his return to New York, he scored a breakthrough by landing a part in a 1954 stage production of the James Joyce novel *Ulysses* with the storied actor Burgess Meredith, who would become a lifelong friend. (Meredith would become most famous as boxer Rocky Balboa's trainer in the smash series of *Rocky* films.) Over the course of the next fifteen years O'Connor built an acting career that ranged from Shakespeare to Hollywood, comedy to drama. Lear described the experience of hearing O'Connor read for the part and knowing he had found his man: "It was like Justice Potter Stewart's oft-quoted definition of pornography: 'I know it when I see it.' Carroll hadn't reached page 3 before I wanted to run into the street shouting for joy."[26]

The part of Archie's wife—initially named Agnes before it became Edith—was settled relatively quickly. Lear admired the stage and screen work of Jean Stapleton, particularly in a stage production of *Damn Yankees* on Broadway, and had cast her in *Cold Turkey*. Stapleton specialized in playing what the television critic David Marc described as "downscale, middle-aged, 'neighborhood' women" and Lear thought she would be a good match for O'Connor's Archie. The result was "a sitcom marriage on the scale of the Ricardos."[27]

The other two major roles were for the Bunkers' daughter, Gloria, and her husband, who at this point was named Richard (later to be Mike). They were played by actors Kelly Jean Peters and Tim McIntire. Peters played Gloria as a bit of an Irish moll; McIntire was a full-fledged hippie.

Dangerous Potential

The pilot episode for *Justice for All* was shot on September 29, 1968, before a live audience in New York.[28] The plot was simple: with Archie and Edith off at church, newlyweds Gloria and Richard, who lived with the Bunkers, have a rare opportunity to have sex in an empty house and head upstairs. But an impatient Archie pushes Edith to leave church early, and they return home to find the lovebirds coming back downstairs tucking in their clothes. According to Lear, the audience "roared" at the taping, as did ABC executives who watched the results. But the network brass was skittish—particularly after one test screening where the entire audience left the screening room, leading one executive to say, "We in senior management are going to pretend this pilot never happened"—and the show in fact never aired.[29] Executive Leonard Goldensen, who was working for the network at the time, persuaded his colleagues to defer deciding on the show until after exercising ABC's option to ask Lear to produce a second pilot. Lear refused to make requested script changes to soften Archie's character, but he did bring in two new actors (Candy Azzara and Chip Oliver) for the parts of Gloria and Mike. He also put Archie and Edith together at the piano to sing the song commissioned for the series, "Those Were the Days" (where indeed they would be at the introduction for every subsequent episode). In fact, Lear changed the name of the show from *Justice for All* to *Those Were the Days*.

Bud Yorkin, who had been off making another movie for Tandem Productions, came back and co-directed the episode with Lear, which was shot in Los Angeles on February 10, 1969. The network included a disclaimer at the start of the show: "For Mature Audiences Only."[30]

The timing was not propitious. In the weeks following the taping, CBS canceled *The Smothers Brothers Comedy Hour*, which had become increasingly controversial in its criticism of the Johnson and Nixon administrations, particularly over the Vietnam War. (Ironically, the decision to cancel was made by CBS executive Robert Wood, the same man who would later greenlight *All in the Family*, over frustrations regarding the show's content—a struggle that would soon begin with *AITF*.)[31] The programming situation at ABC was particularly touchy because in the same month the second pilot was taped the network launched a new show, *Turn On*, a sketch comedy that was considered so tasteless in its sexual innuendo that it was canceled after a single episode. Extant clips are downright creepy.[32]

But the issue was deeper than a particular broadcasting environment; it went to the very heart of television as a broadcast medium. While the political culture of the nation was changing, television remained the most conservative of the major mass media. Compared with a novel, a music album, or even a movie, all of which are discrete works of art with discrete budgets, television shows were open-ended, recurring, and expensive works to produce, made at the behest of sponsors, which would not buy advertising for shows they feared would compromise the appeal of their products. In such a climate, ABC decided to play it safe: the network declined to pick up the show.

Lear wasn't too disappointed: he was surprised to learn that he and Yorkin had been offered a three-picture deal by MGM—by most measures, the apex of a Hollywood career for a producer—that would cement his place as a prestige player in Hollywood. He was negotiating the deal when he heard from Yorkin, who had been at CBS pitching a different project when outgoing president Mike Dann asked about the ABC pilot. "Funny but impossible to air," Dann had heard. Yorkin screened it for him, and his laughter was loud enough to attract Fred Silverman, a young executive from a neighboring office who would go on to have an outstanding career as a programmer at ABC. Dann and Silverman agreed that the recently promoted new president, Robert Wood, needed to see the show. Wood agreed that it was terrific and asked Lear to bring it to CBS.[33]

It's worth noting that *All in the Family* lacked one key fan at CBS: the network's founder William Paley. "Paley hated the show. *Hated* it," Silverman later recalled. "He thought it was vulgar, it was coarse, and really, really disliked it." But Silverman noted that Paley, who was nearly seventy at the time, "couldn't overrule the whole network. Or he'd have an awful lot of unhappy people." The show, it seemed, must go on.[34]

This was a surprising development, not only because of the inherent conservatism of broadcasters but also because CBS was enjoying great success as the network of the status quo. Its string of comedies pitched to rural audiences—among them *Petticoat Junction* (1963–1971), *Mayberry R.F.D* (1968–1971), and *Hee Haw* (1968–1993)—were in Nielsen ratings top twenty in 1969–1970. But network researchers were also aware that younger viewers, on whom the network's future depended, were likely to be more interested in more adventurous fare. David Marc has pithily encapsulated the debate within CBS headquarters at the time: "A bird in hand, conservatives argued. Demographics in the bush, marketing visionaries replied."[35] Counterintuitively, the latter prevailed—not just with *All in the Family* but also in launching *The Mary Tyler Moore Show* (1970–1977) and *M*A*S*H* (1972–1983)—resulting in continuing dominance for CBS well into the new decade.

For Lear, the network's enthusiasm was enough to lead him to forgo the movie production deal and commit himself fully to television. But there were still obstacles as he moved forward over the course of 1970. Research conducted for CBS that year indicated that *All in the Family* tested below average: the numbers said it was likely to fail.[36] Carroll O'Connor, who was living in Rome at the time, was among those who doubted the show could actually last. "The thing is a sure disaster," he told his agent, "but the explosion will get us a lot of attention." Hedging his bets, O'Connor secured a pledge that Lear pay for a round-trip ticket so that he could return home if the show crashed.[37] The network, also seeking safety, asked Lear to rewrite the pilot, which he refused. Executives then suggested he run a different episode than the pilot first. Lear refused that too; he asserted that the first two plots (Archie and Edith returning from church, Archie and Mike writing letters to President Nixon) were purposely slight so that audiences could familiarize themselves with the characters. The first of many battles was waged over language ("we ask that homosexual terminology be kept to a minimum," read one memo), and there were concerns over audience reaction.

Lear, in observing a focus group through a one-way glass wall, noted that participants howled with laughter while watching the show, even as they indicated their disapproval with the devices they had been issued to register their opinions. "Unlike my friends at CBS I understood and was elated by the audience's reaction," Lear later reported. "Who, sitting among a group of strangers, is going to tell the world that they approve of Archie's hostility and rudeness? And who wants to be seen as having no problem with words such as *spic*, *kike*, *spade*, and the like issuing from a bigot's mouth?"[38] (Here we will note, not for the last time, the frank recognition of—sanction for?—pervasive bigotry in everyday American life.)

Yet even amid the obstacles and handwringing, plans for the show, which underwent a few key tweaks, moved forward. The parts of Mike and Gloria were once again recast. Two years earlier, Rob Reiner, son of Lear's close friend and comedy legend Carl Reiner, had wanted the part, but Lear felt he was too young. But it now seemed plausible to cast him, and after a successful audition he was awarded the part in minutes. John Rich, a director Lear cast to helm many of the coming episodes, suggested that Lear have a look at Sally Struthers, who had recently appeared on the Smothers Brothers' show. "She auditioned with Rob and it was another bolt of lightning," Lear remembered, later describing Struthers as "a little pool of light." (Ironically, one actor who didn't get the part was Penny Marshall, who would later be Reiner's real-life wife.)[39] One further change was made as well: the name of the sitcom became *All in the Family*.[40]

In yet another attempt to play it safe, CBS ordered thirteen episodes of *All in the Family*, or half of a full season. The network's brass decided the show would be a midseason replacement to take over the slot of a faltering series, which turned out to be *To Rome with Love* (1969–1971), about a widower college professor (John Forsythe) who relocates his family from Iowa to a school in Italy. A note in *TV Guide* warned viewers what was to come: "This series will explore American prejudices by looking at one of those of one middle-class family—if viewers can take the heat. There's plenty of abrasive language and subject matter to keep the cards and letters pouring in."[41] The network issued its own advisory in text that appeared before the opening notes of the show's theme song: "The program you are about to see is *All in the Family*. It seeks to throw a humorous spotlight on our frailties, prejudices, and concerns. By making them a source of laughter we hope to show—in mature fashion—just how absurd they are."[42] The network also sent warning notes to its affiliate stations and asked for forbearance as the network moved in new programming directions. As an additional measure, CBS hired extra telephone operators to handle the expected surge in calls.[43]

Over at the *New York Times*, a preview of the show, and the likely reaction to it, was skeptical. "Is it funny, for example, to have the pot-bellied, church going, cigar-smoking son of Middle America, Archie Bunker, the hero of *All in the Family*, fill the screen with such epithets as 'spic' and 'spade' and 'hebe' and 'yid' and 'polack'?" asked reporter Fred Ferretti, in a review that appeared the day the show would make its debut. "Is it funny for him to refer to his son-in-law as 'the laziest white man I ever seen'? Or to look at a televised football game and yell, 'Look at that spook run . . . It's in his blood'?" Ferretti's own view was clear: "The answer, I say, is no." Ferretti said he actually liked the pilot of the show, which he had been allowed to see the previous week. But he felt the final product was too sensationalistic in its bigotry, though he recognized that audiences may think otherwise. "It will be an interesting 13 weeks for CBS, and for the viewing public," he concluded.[44]

At 9:30 P.M. on Tuesday, January 12, 1971, following episodes of *The Beverly Hillbillies*, *Green Acres*, and *Hee Haw*, the (third) pilot of *All in the Family*, "Meet the Bunkers," hit the airwaves.[45] It would indeed be interesting.

3

Fuzzy Reception

Meeting the Bunkers

As it turned out, the reception wasn't what they were expecting. It was more like a nonreception.

The first episode of *All in the Family*, "Meet the Bunkers," begins relatively quietly, with Mike Stivic, played by Rob Reiner, coming through the door of 704 Hauser Street in Queens. (In retrospect, there's some irony in this, in that so many future episodes would hinge on Archie's more blustery entrances.) Reiner's version of Mike, wearing a denim shirt and trousers, was something of a happy medium between his two predecessors in the show's pilots: his visual persona was less of a liberal stereotype than the beaded, peace sign–bearing Tim McIntire, but more obviously left-wing than Chip Oliver's more straightlaced Mike.[1] He makes clear to Gloria that he's in the mood for love, since they have the house to themselves. (Struthers, for her part, positions her character somewhere between Kelly Jane Peters's earthier portrayal and Candy Azzara's chaste one.) But Gloria, preparing for her parents' twenty-second wedding anniversary celebration, to take place in the dining room, rebuffs Mike by pointing out that they don't in fact have the house to themselves: their friend Lionel is upstairs fixing Archie's television set. From the very start of the first episode—even before we meet Archie himself—we see that he will have an African American foil.

Lionel, played by Mike Evans, was also a matter of improved casting over the actors who preceded him in the two pilots, combining a sharp wit with a mild manner. When he comes downstairs he greets Mike by asking him what the white liberal socialists are up to these days. In the ensuing conversation, Lionel notes that Archie likes it when he speaks in an exaggerated black dialect, redolent of minstrelsy, in telling him of his ambition to become an electrical engineer. Mike, appalled by Archie's crudity, asks why Lionel goes along with it. Lionel shrugs; he says telling people what they want to hear is the easiest way to get what he wants. Amid all broad racial humor to follow, this matter-of-fact line is the most haunting, a reminder of the ways African Americans have always navigated—and continue to navigate—white racism by pragmatically indulging fantasies rather than rejecting them.

The sparks really start to fly when Archie and Edith return home earlier than expected from church. Archie, irritated by the pieties of the minister (dismissing him as living in an "ivory shower," the first of his many malapropisms), yanked Edith out prematurely, something she tries to treat stoically as they take off their coats, expressing gratitude that Archie came to church at all. They encounter a lip-locked Mike and Gloria, which appalls Archie: "Used to be, the daylight hours was for the respectable things in life." A series of charged conversations between Archie, Gloria, and Lionel follow, typified by a line that encapsulates his vision of society: "If your spics and your spades want their share of the American Dream, let 'em get out there and hustle for it just like I done." When Archie responds to Mike's protests that his father-in-law had it easier than people of color, Archie replies by noting he didn't have anyone agitating or protesting on his behalf, leading Edith to note that he didn't have to, because he got his job through his uncle. (Jean Stapleton's Edith was more tart here than she would later be.) So it was that the dynamics of the next decade would be established: outrageous statement followed by remonstration and riposte, the tension eased by the jokes of third parties who break the deadlock.

Ideology aside, there are two riveting aspects of the sitcom that are apparent immediately and have only become more so with the passage of time. The first is the mesmerizing quality of Carroll O'Connor's Archie. Everything about him—his gait, his working-class accent, and, above all, his astoundingly plastic face, something repeatedly exploited by close-ups, a concession the show makes to the medium of television in what is other-wise a largely theatrical experience—commands one's attention.

The other thing that jumps out at you is how almost unbelievably unpleas-ant Archie is: most of us would consider him a toxic personality and try to get away from him. It's made clear at the outset that for Mike, Archie is the price he pays for food and lodging while he goes to college. Though she loves her father, this is true for Gloria as well, who works to support Mike in the hope that the couple will achieve independence and upward mobility by leaving the nest. Edith's devotion to Archie is harder to understand. He repeatedly tells her to stifle herself and calls her a "dingbat," and one has to wonder to what degree she really is stupid, a prisoner of her patriarchal cul-ture, or both. Jean Stapleton's initial reading of Edith becomes sweeter over time—and, increasingly, she plays the role of anchor of the family and the show as a whole. But in this first episode, actor and part are overshadowed in the face of O'Connor's toweringly negative Archie. In retrospect, it's amazing that millions of people willingly subjected themselves to it week after week.

Weak Signals

It was far from clear that they would. "*All in the Family* is either going to be an instant smash, or an instant disaster," opined a reporter for the *Hollywood Reporter*.[2] But it turned out to be neither. The principal challenge facing the show was not hostility but indifference. From a viewership standpoint, the signals were decidedly mixed. For all the concern that CBS had about a neg-ative reaction, which prompted the network to have additional phone operators on standby, there were only about a thousand calls, with over 60 percent of them positive; and other anecdotal information suggests the show had more fans than critics. Another encouraging sign was the results of a poll that CBS commissioned in those early weeks showing that a major-ity of respondents, which included members of minority groups, were not offended.[3]

However, the initial indications from the all-important Nielsen ratings were not good. The overnight report indicated that *All in the Family* got only 15 percent of the viewing audience, ranking in fifty-fifth place after its first week. Ratings from early February showed *AITF* scoring an average of about 10 million viewers a week—huge numbers today, but decidedly anemic for 1971, where a typical show was seen by twice as many viewers and the best-rated show got three times as many. It managed to move up to forty-sixth place in mid-March before falling back into the fifties again.[4] Given the cost of production and a survival-of-the-fittest mentality in a finite prime-time schedule, the future of the show was cloudy at best. O'Connor's demand for a round-trip ticket home to Rome as a condition for signing on to the cast was beginning to seem prescient.

Reception of the show among critics was a somewhat different story. On the one hand, there was a steady stream of raves. A preview story in the *Los Angeles Times* called it "the happiest thing to hit commercial TV since the coaxial cable" (within a decade, of course, coaxial cable would be transforming the television landscape). *Variety* called it "the best TV comedy since the original *The Honeymooners*" the night after the pilot aired. The following month, Jack Gould of the *Times* was cautiously encouraging: "Some of Archie's words may chill the spine, but to root out bigotry has defied man's best efforts for generations and the weapon of laughter just might succeed. The possibility entitles *All in the Family* to a chance." Cleveland Armory, the influential critic for *TV Guide*, was more effusive, describing it as "the best thing on commercial television," going on to say that it "opens up a whole new world for television and has already made the old world seem so dated that we doubt that any new program, from here on in, will ever be the same again." Even members of the black intelligentsia found good things to say about it. "Archie Bunker is real," wrote Pamela Haynes for the (African American) *Los Angeles Sentinel*. "Far from protesting, members of minorities slandered by Archie should rejoice at this non-cosmetized portrait of the 'master race.'"[5]

On the other hand, there were plenty of negative reactions to *All in the Family* as well, some issuing from lofty perches. Writing two weeks after the show's premiere, *Times* writer Stephanie Harrington dismissed the show as "vulgar and silly. And after the disgust-at-first-shock wears off, the vaudeville clinkers passed off as humor are totally predictable, both in themselves and as means of conveying the show's moral: All prejudice—racial, class, sophisticated against unsophisticated and vice versa—is bad."[6] In *Time* magazine, reviewer Richard Burgheim asserted that the series "proves that bigotry can be as boring and predictable as the upthink fluff of *The Brady Bunch*."[7] The black television journalist Tony Brown was more direct, calling *AITF* "shocking and racist." And a week after the *Los Angeles Sentinel* ran Haynes's rave of the series, Whitney Young of the Urban League weighed in on its pages to decry it "as a new low in taste," asserting that "while the show tries to satirize bigotry, it only succeeds in spreading the poison, and making it—by repetition—respectable."[8]

Such commentary was not limited to the print media. "I have to say, I have to feel, that the laughter hurts," said Rabbi Meyer Heller of Temple Emmanuel of Beverly Hills, speaking about *All in the Family* as part of a panel discussion on the longtime CBS Sunday morning talk show *Look Up and Live*, produced in association with the National Council of Churches. In an installment titled "Laughter: Hurt or Heal?" Meyer, reflecting mainstream elite opinion, went on to say, "The repetition of these stereotyped terms that we thought had died tend to be hurtful, harmful to the public good." (Lear's reply: "I've heard all these epithets. If they had died, where had they gone and where had they gone to? Do you really believe that *All in the Family* resurrects them from death?")[9]

Another person who did not count himself as a fan: the president of the United States. As we now know, Nixon routinely (and secretly) recorded his conversations in the Oval Office, and so it is that we know his reaction to *AITF*, which he denounced as "glorifying homosexuality. . . . I think the son-in-law goes both ways, like the daughter and all the rest."[10]

Two of the most visible assaults came from *Life*, a magazine nearing the end of a half century as the quintessential newsweekly magazine in an age when such publications were staples of middle-class life. "Something fresh must be acutely missing if CBS's recent *All in the Family*, a minstrel show that's big with bigotry and revives half-forgotten hate words, is hailed as a breakthrough," wrote one reviewer. The other attack came from John Leonard, widely regarded as the most influential cultural critic of the era. Writing in *Life* that March, Leonard denounced *All in the Family* as "wretched," resting on what he called "a double-edged lie. Cutting one way, it tells us that workingmen are mindless buffoons. . . . Cutting the other way, the lie tells us that Mr. O'Connor's Archie is, anyway, charming. Forgivable."[11] Leonard seemed close to locating Lear's Achilles heel: that he was too clever by half. An air of glibness could sometimes hang over the producer's work, something that became a little more apparent over time, especially in his post-*AITF* career.

Gentlewoman's Disagreement

It was Leonard's latter point—that *All in the Family* could lull you into condoning racism—that figured into the most substantial attack on the show. It didn't arrive until months later, once again in the *Times* (and here it should be noted that the nation's paper of record giving so much space to the show is something of a statement in its own right). It came from Laura Z. Hobson, the prolific writer best known for her 1947 novel *Gentleman's Agreement*, which was made into a film that won an Academy Award for Best Picture that year, starring Gregory Peck as a magazine writer who goes undercover as a Jew and discovers the potency of anti-Semitism in American life. In a long essay on the front page of the Sunday Arts & Leisure section on September 12, Hobson noted that in the twenty-four years since *Gentleman's Agreement* had been published, she maintained a personal vow not to comment publicly on the issue of bigotry in American life.[12] But now, at age seventy-one, she felt compelled to register her objection to the show, especially since it had gained significant traction by that point. Hobson's complaint, as she herself described it, was a counterintuitive one: *All in the Family* was not offensive *enough*. In telling ways, the show pulled its punches: Archie would use terms like "Hebe" or "Yid" but never the harsher "kike." He would say "spade" or "jungle bunny" but never "nigger."[13] (This a time when it was still permissible to print the word in a major national newspaper.) The effect of such choices was to tame racism—and, however unwittingly, legitimate it:

> Clean it up, deterge it, bleach it, enzyme it, and you'll have a show about a lovable bigot that everybody except a few pinko atheistic bleedin' hearts will love.

> Well, I differ. I don't think you can be a bigot and be lovable; I don't think you can be a black-baiter and lovable, nor an anti-Semite and lovable. And don't think the millions who watch this show should be conned into thinking that you can be.[14]

As we've already seen, Hobson's perspective runs directly contrary to that of Lear: the very premise of *All in the Family*, as far as he was concerned, is that the only way to confront racism is to situate it in the context of everyday life and relationships, the way it typically appeared, amalgamated with all kinds of other emotions and characteristics that people—very often people we love—might have. "This wasn't a terrible human being," he wrote of Archie in his memoir. "This was a fearful human being. He wasn't evil, he wasn't a hater—he was just afraid of change."[15] It's easy to see the logic of Lear's argument. It's also easy to see why Hobson would find it objectionable: that by personalizing bigotry you make it hard to see, and combat, for what it really is. A necessary sense of moral outrage gets dulled.

Lear's response was, in effect, that he was providing a corrective to the view that Hobson was presenting. In an op-ed response to her that was published in the *Times* the following month, he accused her of being selective in her language as well, noting that she never used the term "schwartze," a specifically Yiddish racist term, implying that she was pulling punches of her own in refusing to recognize that however oppressed they may have been, Jews can be haters too. But the problem, he argued, is not that he was dulling sensibilities but rather that his critics were by denouncing versions of racism that were so dramatic as to seem remote, and thus irrelevant, to real life as most people experienced it. "I believe I know how Ms. Hobson likes to see her bigots portrayed in the mass media," he wrote. "I know because her generation has provided dozens of stereotypes for my generation—in movies, books, magazines, radio, etc. I grew up with them."

A bigot is a white man who says "nigger!" to a black man's face, forcing him to move aside so that he may pass, and spitting as he does.

A bigot is a vigilante who lynches a black man, sometimes castrating him first.

A bigot is a white sheriff who rapes a black woman in the back of his squad car.

We've had these bigots through the years—one-dimensional stereotypes—ad nauseam.

How many of us have ever known a man who has raped a black woman in a squad car? Then how do we relate to him? How do we see a little of ourselves in him? On the other hand, most of us have known people who drop words like spade; and people who with a sly smile have tossed a yenta into the conversational waters to see if it would float.[16]

It seems important to acknowledge the legitimacy of both perspectives here. Indeed, it seems impossible to fully grapple with racism and its legacies without recognizing what might be termed the ventilation and eradication approaches—and the tension between them. If they seem incompatible, so too do many human experiences: the love and fear that animate romance; the intimacy and dehumanizing violence of soldiers in combat; the sense of the sacred and the profane in religious experience. The issue, then, is not whether one is more honest than the other, but rather the care and sense of context with which they're deployed. Clearly, elite opinion on *All in the Family* split on the effectiveness of its ventilation strategy.

The subjectivity of such judgments was something that a number of reviewers of the show recognized, especially after the first wave of reviews. "There's a basic principle at work in our exposure to the mass media known as selective perception," noted one writer for a small California newspaper in February 1971. "It simply means we are inclined to read into a message that which is compatible with our existing attitudes, opinions, and beliefs. So where *All in the Family* may be designed to parody social illnesses, it may in many instances be reinforcing them with the attitudes being displayed and demonstrated by the Bunker family." A series of academic studies about the show conducted at the time came to no firm conclusions about its impact on viewers.[17]

Lear agreed that *AITF* functioned as a kind of national Rorschach test—to a point. While it was clear at the time, and ever since, that he was aiming for a degree of calibration that would allow multiple points of view to be recognizably and fairly represented, he understood himself to be purveying a distinct position that was not infinitely elastic. "As much as Archie reminded his viewers of fathers, uncles or neighbors, I don't recall a single letter that said, 'I see a lot of myself in Archie,'" he later wrote.[18]

He may not have been looking hard enough. "I wish there were more Archie Bunkers," an Oregon storekeeper said at the time. "You can't just change their ways, that's all. Like me, they're asking me to go along with all these new ways today, but I just can't see it. Me and Archie—it's too late for us." (As is often the case, racist views are cast in terms of loss by those who express them.) A railroad switchman exulted in the sitcom's bracing candor. "What is great about that show," he said, "is that . . . it's just like you feel inside yourself. You think it, but old Archie, he *says* it, by damn."[19]

O'Connor understood that the character he portrayed was seen as more than an object of ridicule. Speaking many years later, he recalled a conversation with a television writer who was skeptical of what he was doing. He related the conversation as dialogue:

"You think you're kidding the character" [the writer told him].

"Yes, I think we're making a fool out of Archie Bunker. And that's how we're going to repay his racism and his bigotry. We're going to make a fool out of him."

"You *think* that's what you're doing. You're really playing to a crowd of people out there who are indeed Archie Bunker."

That turned out to be true. But the other thing proved to be true also. We did make a fool out of him and everybody saw him made a fool.[20]

Though it may have been complex and/or ambiguous, Lear understood the show to be making a bold and valuable statement. "For twenty years—until *AITF* came along—TV comedy was telling us that there was no hunger in America, we had no racial discrimination, there was no unemployment or inflation, no war, no drugs, and the citizenry was happy with whomever happened to be in the White House," he wrote. "My view is that we made comedy safe for reality." He added, "That reality included black people."[21]

Family Moment

It's not clear how much the critical discourse surrounding *All in the Family* mattered in 1971. Certainly, it didn't in the short run; well into May, ratings for the show were anemic at best. But as Memorial Day approached, things started to change. Word of mouth began to build; one magazine writer noted that teachers were asking CBS for study guides about the show.[22] A key boost came in the form of the Emmy Awards, and in particular a highly placed fan: Johnny Carson, host of *The Tonight Show* and one of the most influential figures in the television industry. Carson, who was hosting the ceremony that year, suggested what became the show's opening: a skit with the Bunkers sitting down in their living room to watch the broadcast. Edith, characteristically, talked about her excitement and how lovely everyone looked. Archie winced and denounced "all them Hollywood liberals." The only reason he's watching, he explains, is the hope that Duke (John) Wayne, "the only real man in that crowd and a honest to God American, might show up." (Carson himself jokingly referred to Lear as "a nice guy for a Hebe.")[23] The actual Emmy proceedings that followed provided another shot in the arm in the form of three awards: Outstanding New Series, Outstanding Comedy Series, and a statuette for Stapleton for her role as Edith. (Watching her acceptance speech is a jarring experience; she inhabits her role on the show so vividly that you almost can't believe her measured, sophisticated real-life persona.)

Such high-profile recognition was exceptionally timely, coming as it did at the end of the television season, inaugurating a summer when the networks typically broadcast reruns of their successful shows. This was especially true given that *AITF* had initially debuted in January, not the previous September, when it might have gotten lost amid a full slate of competition, and still had a few new shows left while most others were in reruns. "If the show had not begun at midseason, the chances are it would have disappeared after its initial thirteen-week run," Lear explained. "But when the other two networks' first-run programming ended, a percentage of their audiences finally tuned into CBS to see what they'd been reading and hearing about, and our ratings started to climb." Anticipating such a scenario, Silverman shrewdly insisted on running the series through the summer, demonstrating the acumen that would soon make him the most celebrated programmer on television.[24]

All in the Family now made its move. On May 25, the *Times* reported that the series had reached the number two slot in the Nielsen ratings, second only to the Emmy telecast where it had been so prominently featured. By the start of the 1971–1972 television season, *AITF* had become the most popular show on television, a perch it would hold for the next five years. Only one other sitcom, *The Cosby Show*, would match it. But *AITF* was not merely a ratings winner; it was precedent-smashing in terms of the breadth of its audience as well as its content. Bud Yorkin was stunned to learn in 1971 that the series had attained a 70 share in the coveted New York market—70 percent of all televisions in the city were tuned in to the show. In this context, Hobson's piece, which appeared at the start of the show's first full season, was a rear-guard action against a burgeoning phenomenon. By early 1972, it was routinely drawing over 50 million viewers on a weekly basis. At the Emmys that spring, *AITF* swept the field: actor, actress, supporting actor, supporting actress, comedy series, and a host of others. Carson, again performing hosting duties, dubbed the awards ceremony "an evening with Norman Lear."[25]

The show's impact was evident in other ways as well. In the wake of its success, CBS cleaned house with its traditional lineup, canceling mainstays such as *The Beverly Hillbillies* and *Hee Haw* (which would continue in syndication on local stations around the country). Lear would be in the vanguard of a new wave of shows with a social and political and/or social edge. These would include *AITF* spin-offs such as *Maude* (1972–1978) and *The Jeffersons* (1975–1985), but also sitcoms such as *Sanford and Son* (1972–1977), *Good Times* (1974–1979), and *One Day at a Time* (1979–1984), which significantly expanded the racial and gender horizons of what was depicted on television. (More on these shows in chapter 10.)

But this was all in the future. In the years to come, *All in the Family* would become an institution. Perhaps paradoxically, its impact flowed from what in the end was a startlingly intimate experience. "The episodes were written and produced as plays, with people talking and behaving in real time, like a piece of theater," Lear explained almost a half century later. "Much as a baker sets his dough in the oven, we set down these little plays of ours before an audience of 250, whose laughter, occasional tears, and applause, like heat to bread, caused our play to rise."[26]

It's now time to look at why—to explore in more detail what the show did, and how it achieved its flavor.

4

Producing Comedy

Making *All in the Family*

Of all the popular arts, television may well be the most collaborative. In fact, all artistic enterprises are group efforts. The solitary writer needs an editor and a publisher—for starters—if a finished work is ever to see the light of day, and comparable supporting players are essential even for the most do-it-yourself minded musicians, coders, or fashion designers. Of course, there are other media—theater and movies come to mind—where teamwork is obviously of the essence. But television outstrips them all in the density of participation required to make a show work.

There are a few reasons for this. One is technological. A TV show typically makes all the demands one would expect of a theatrical production on either side of the stage, plus the full complement of cameras and related devices, along with the people to manage them. One could say the same of a feature film (which indeed may have a more elaborate technical apparatus behind it), but here we come up against another challenge distinctive to television: time. A well-funded movie production typically has a schedule measured in weeks. A TV show, by contrast, has an annual production schedule that lasts for months—and if the show is successful, that schedule will repeat year after year. And while moviemakers answer to financiers, production companies, studios and distributors (who may overlap), a TV production—especially a network TV production—will also have to contend with the demands of corporate network executives, advertisers, and/or government regulators (in the form of censors, for example, who are much more active than in the film business, which admittedly does have ratings that can be a major influence on content). And then there is the bottom line of ratings. A book, movie, or song gets released and either succeeds or fails. A TV show is subjected to an ongoing referendum in the form of viewership numbers, which will affect its duration, if not its content.

For all these reasons, a TV show—even a successful TV show—is a volatile proposition. (Indeed, it's sometimes success that *makes* a TV show a volatile proposition.) The pressures to produce, whether simply in meeting a deadline or in maintaining quality, can be immense. Coordinating schedules for actors becomes increasingly difficult, especially as they become more successful and new opportunities, sometimes as a result of a show's renown, begin to emerge. And competitive pressures from other shows make it hard to sustain high ratings. While there are incentives for shows to last, especially in terms of lucrative syndication deals in local and international markets that become viable if a show runs long enough, few make it that far, whether because audience interest isn't there or collaboration breaks down.

All in the Family was an unusual television show in any number of ways, one of which was its longevity. While there are shows that ran longer than its nine seasons (*The Jeffersons*, an *AITF* spin-off, ran for eleven), its durability was notable for its time, as well as before or after. While it's never really possible to entirely account for the length of any show's run, in the case of *AITF* it appears that everyone involved recognized they were a part of an extraordinary undertaking that continued to feel special as it unfolded. In short, the show lasted because it was good.

Conservative Form, Progressive Content

In trying to account for why it was good, it's helpful to consider an intriguing tension, even paradox, which characterized the show. Which is this: while the *content* of the sitcom was daring, even subversive, in reworking and stretching the genre, its *form* was quite traditional. Its basic architecture rested on a sturdy foundation that dated back to the origins of television as a medium, and its creators had deep ties to those origins, whether as a matter of experience or allegiance.

The key figure here, of course, was Norman Lear. Lear had lived through the golden age of radio and began his career at the dawn of the television age. His formative influences included George Burns, Milton Berle, and Fred Allen, all of whom came out of the same (urban Jewish) cultural matrix that he did. Lear's first jobs in the industry were writing for Danny Thomas and then for Dean Martin and Jerry Lewis, with whom he honed his comedy chops. Lear was fond of citing Allen's joke about early television: "It is called a medium, because it is neither rare nor well done."[1] But the pioneers of television were often geniuses at pouring old cultural wine into new technological bottles, especially when it came to humor. *All in the Family* would later rise to fame on the strength of its topical commentary, but the delivery of its rapid-fire jokes—as a matter of pacing, facial expression, and physical comedy, among other elements of craft—owes at least as much to vaudeville as to anything on television at the time.

Vaudeville, of course, was a stage medium. And so, for all intents and purposes, was early television. Although the most obvious point of comparison for TV was film in terms of both being shot on camera, edited, and so forth, early television was subject to considerable logistical and cost pressures that placed a premium on shooting shows in tightly circumscribed spaces. Shooting on location, for example, was prohibitively expensive. Some of the earliest landmark programs of the 1950s, such as *Texaco Star Theater*, which began in radio during the late 1930s before migrating to television from 1948 to 1956, were stage shows. (In the 1975 episode "Mike Faces Life," Mike, Gloria, and Edith nostalgically sing the theme song from the show.) Others, such as *Playhouse 90* (1956–1960), were more specifically stage dramas broadcast to national audiences.

From a procedural standpoint, much about television production had changed by the time *All in the Family* debuted in 1971. Multiple cameras, videotaping, and even the use of film had all been adopted as technology and facilities improved. To be sure, *AITF*'s production crew availed itself of such state-of-the-art resources. But at heart, the show was a twenty-four-minute teleplay shot mostly on a set representing the Bunker family home (more on this in the next chapter). There were occasionally other settings—Archie's favorite watering hole, Kelsey's Bar, was one, along with forays into police stations, Laundromats, and the kitchens of the Jeffersons and Lorenzos—but the show was a resolutely interior experience that was theatrical in multiple senses of that term.

Perhaps the most important way in which the show was theatrical was the role of its audience. Unlike most other sitcoms, *All in the Family* was video-taped live, in real time, at a CBS facility in Beverly Hills that seated approximately 300 people. According to the series historian Richard P. Adler, this was because Lear, who was experienced with this approach, believed it worked best, but also because it was cost-effective: the price of each taping was significantly less than filming, an approach that had become more widespread since Desi Arnaz adopted it for *I Love Lucy* (1951–1957). After reading through the script for a show on Monday, rehearsing it on Tuesday and Wednesday, and blocking it out in the theater on Thursday, each episode was typically shot twice on Friday evenings: a so-called dress rehearsal at 5:30, followed by another performance at 8:00 P.M. Writers were on hand to edit dialogue that didn't work, and scenes were often spliced between the two performances before the final product was broadcast. That broadcast included a single commercial break; Lear successfully argued against the three acts CBS initially demanded.[2]

As with mounting a play, such an approach could foster an air of feverish intensity, an experience that Lear dubbed "joyful stress" in the section of his memoir focusing on *All in the Family*. "We live dangerously, then our audience tells us what is possible," John Rich, who directed most of the episodes in the first four seasons of the show, explained at the time. It's notable that Rich, who enjoyed a long career as a film and television director, began his TV career as a stage manager for *The Kraft Television Theater* (1947–1958), an anthology drama series. "When we're working before an audience, if we stop and back up, we lose momentum. We do our repair work afterward." A *Time* magazine story compared this approach to that of out-of-town try-outs for a Broadway production. "We're doing a play a week and we're trying to be entertaining every minute," Rich explained. "We don't have a Hartford or Boston for tryouts."[3]

The actors fed on this vibrancy. "It was like doing theater, and I was very comfortable in that," Jean Stapleton remembered decades later. "That laughter just feeds you." Carroll O'Connor agreed, though he noted that audience laughter could sometimes slow down the show. (It was at his request that the live tapings ended in *AITF*'s final season, though audiences were shown episodes and their reaction was edited into the final broadcast.) Rob

Reiner used a musical analogy to capture the improvisational spirit of the enterprise. "It was like great jazz players," he said.[4]

There was one important respect, however, in which the collaborators on *All in the Family* exploited a visual technique grounded in the medium of television: the close-up. Simply put, the show would not be half as funny as it was without the tight, lingering shots of actors' reactions to each other. This was especially true for O'Connor, whose remarkable mien captured endless shades of disdain, perplexity, and frustration. But Stapleton was very good at this as well—her utter ingenuousness could be priceless in revealing what she was thinking. (There would be a long, vacant pause on her face before she said "Oooohh" in recognition of the subtext of whatever was being said.) For the most part, *AITF* was shot in a naturalistic fashion that didn't call attention to itself, as befits a show that aimed for the intimacy of theater. But this exception to the rule lent the show a tremendous sense of energy as well as intensifying its comic effect.

Perhaps the greatest asset *AITF* enjoyed over its long run was the quality of the scripts. Lear got the ball rolling at the start of the series, but *All in the Family* was anchored by a large stable of writers who provided a steady stream of storylines, dialogue, and institutional memory that maintained a continuity of tone and detail over nine seasons. The longtime *Washington Post* TV critic Tom Shales notes that among the most important was Milt Josefsberg (who had written for Jack Benny, Lucille Ball, and Bob Hope) as well as Bob Schiller and Bob Weiskopf, veteran writers for *I Love Lucy*.[5] Most scripts were group projects, but there were also regular teams within the rosters as well. One good example was the collaboration among Bernie West, Mickey Davis, and Don Nicholl, who at various points wrote, edited, and directed episodes. (They eventually created a production company to produce other series, among them *The Jeffersons*, for Lear.)

One pivotal figure in this web of collaboration was Reiner. Though a young man—he was only twenty-four years old when the series debuted—he came to *AITF* with an impressive pedigree as the son of Lear's friend and colleague Carl Reiner, a television impresario in his own right. A writer, director, and producer of wide renown, Reiner Sr. was best known for launching *The Dick Van Dyke Show* (1961–1966), many of whose episodes were directed by Rich. (Rich had the difficult decision of choosing between a new show featuring the star of that series, Mary Tyler Moore, and *All in the Family*; he chose the latter.)[6] Rob Reiner had already launched a career

as an improvisational actor when he came to *AITF*, which became an appren-
ticeship, as he used his downtime to learn about production techniques
that would later become part of his repertoire when he launched his career
in the 1980s as a Hollywood director. But however fresh his blood might
have been in the mix of figures producing *AITF*, Reiner carried forward the
same DNA from the early days of television, making him a generational
bridge in shaping the show's sensibility. Reiner was a particularly important
figure in mediating relations between Carroll O'Connor and Lear. "I got
caught in the middle sometimes," he noted, trying to resolve conflicts by
pushing past them, focusing on the work.[7]

Carroll O'Connor, of course, was the fulcrum on which the show rested,
and his talents were undeniable. These extended beyond acting into script
revision, a practice he exercised actively. In reading over accounts of the
show's history, it's clear that he was a force to be reckoned with.

O'Connor's Bunker Mentality

There's no doubt that Carroll O'Connor and Archie Bunker were very different people. In their politics, for example, the two were at opposite ends
of the spectrum. O'Connor was vastly more intelligent than the character
he played, as testified by the actor's ability to so fully imagine him—and the
lack of evidence we see in the show for Archie's ability to inhabit points of
view other than his own. O'Connor could also demonstrate impressive self-
knowledge. But in retrospect it's clear that in at least one respect the two
figures had one important trait in common: cantankerousness. And in this
regard, the actor exceeded his alter ego in his insistence on bending others
to his will.

One can see O'Connor exhibit irascibility in ways that have nothing to
do with his work on the show. He opens his 1998 memoir, *I Think I'm Outta
Here*—a title with more than a hint of truculence to it—by excoriating a
theater critic for the *San Francisco Chronicle* who panned *A Certain Labor
Day*, a play O'Connor wrote and in which he starred the year before the
book was published. (The reviewer called it "a heartfelt bungle.")[8] "My howl
over the demented assault in San Francisco might have been left for an
inclusion in a later segment [of the book], but I said to myself *Put it up
front. It's a vengeful and ignoble outburst and reveals what you're really like*,"
he writes in the prologue. One suspects a good editor would have tried,

albeit unsuccessfully, to talk O'Connor out of putting forth such a diatribe, if not cutting it entirely. One might also regard the dearth of coverage of his role as Archie in the book as another indication of contrariness that denied most readers the very reason they would want to read it: there are a mere ten pages devoted to the show in the 321-page paperback edition.[9]

Multiple observers agree that O'Connor played a hands-on role in terms of the way his character was written—"I don't care what joke you give him, Carroll O'Connor will rewrite it," remembered one actor[10]—and O'Connor complained on multiple occasions that he was never given the writing credit he felt he deserved (when asked, he explained that most of his contributions took the form of revisions on set or in notes he prepared at home during production).[11] "Our 'Archie' writers were the cleverest draftsmen in television and what they delivered every week was the very special product they were hired to write," O'Connor noted three decades later with a strong undercurrent of passive aggression, as his use of the term "draftsmen" suggests. "But I refused to play the naked joke, to do the setup-punchline routine, and asked them to recast jokes as characteristic thrusts and rejoinders, and rework sketch material to the emotional dimensions of a short play. They often balked and more than once threatened to quit, but I too more than once threatened to quit."[12]

Indeed, he did quit, and on more than one occasion. The first time was in 1971, when O'Connor objected to the way his character reacted to the birth of a baby in an elevator ("The Elevator Story," first broadcast in 1972), calling the script repulsive and unplayable. "Carroll fell to pieces and began to cry. He couldn't go on, hated the show, couldn't bear me, and cried to a point that made me realize that this behavior, this degree of testing, had to end here," Lear later wrote. "If he won this battle, the creative team would be throttled, and the show I believed in would die anyway." O'Connor failed to appear for work on two occasions in shooting the episode, but ultimately turned up and finished it, to widespread acclaim.[13] He later went on strike in sympathy for the electricians union in 1974, which created some upheaval (leaving, as Isabel Sanford later remembered of her role as Louise Jefferson, opportunities for other characters to have more speaking time).[14]

O'Connor made his position clear to the outside world as well. "I'm the star of the number-one show on TV," he told *Playboy* in 1972. "If I were somebody like Jackie Gleason, they'd all be out on the street," he said, recalling an argument with John Rich about a scene that called for Archie to find himself under the mistletoe with Louise Jefferson. (Unlike O'Connor,

Gleason had actually created and produced *The Honeymooners*.) "I couldn't imagine how anybody would set up this kind of argument with a big star like Jackie or Lucy [Ball]. Why were they persisting in this thing when they knew Carroll O'Connor didn't want it? I called my agent that night and said, 'Be prepared to get me out of this show at the end of the season.'" When the interviewer asked if O'Connor was "abusing the star's prerogative to throw his weight around," O'Connor replied by saying "Not abusing it. Using it rightfully—and properly." He was still complaining six years later, telling *People* magazine, "I do not make nearly as much as stars of some other, less highly rated shows."[15]

O'Connor's most serious protest occurred in July 1974, when he filed suit against Tandem Productions, seeking back pay, clarification of his salary, and, reputedly, for his name to go above the title of the show in its opening credits. Lear, for his part, obtained a court order barring O'Connor from performing elsewhere. The future of the show hung in the balance at the start of the fifth season. Writers came up with a multi-episode scenario of Archie heading to a conference in Buffalo and failing to check in at home, causing great anxiety for the family. Amid speculation that his death would be written into the show—Jean Stapleton mused on the possibility of Edith venturing into an interracial relationship—O'Connor broke the suspense by showing up for the final episode in the sequence to wild cheers from the studio audience.[16]

The biggest source of tension seemed to be that between O'Connor and Lear. Lear described O'Connor as "relentlessly contrarian"; O'Connor chafed at what he regarded as Lear's controlling stance toward Archie's character ("he hated to tamper with a joke").[17] Interestingly, however, each seemed to look back on their relationship with some regret. "Norman and I soon perceived we didn't like each other much and I was nasty to him on occasions," O'Connor reflected thirty years later. "I should have kept my cool. But you make these mistakes, you know." Lear, for his part, recognized that O'Connor's tweaks to scripts could be brilliant. "If Carroll O'Connor hadn't played Archie Bunker, jails wouldn't be a 'detergent' to crime, New York would not be a 'smelting pot,' living would not be a question of either 'feast or salmon,' and there would never be a medical specialty known as 'groinocology.'"[18] Lear did not see O'Connor during his final illness—there were lingering financial disputes, and Lear, who felt remorse for not doing so, also suspected he would not be welcome at O'Connor's bedside. After his death in 2001, Lear paid a visit to his widow, Nancy, who showed him a complimentary note he'd written O'Connor that the actor kept on his desk until the day he died.[19]

O'Connor wasn't the only source of friction in the *AITF* family. Sally Struthers sought release from her contract in 1975, hoping to do more work in feature films; she lost in arbitration.[20] But the truth of the matter is that any television collaboration, almost by definition, is a volatile enterprise. And yet in the second half of the 1970s, the series did achieve some stability. Lear by that point was juggling multiple projects and was less of a hands-on figure, reducing the friction between him and O'Connor (he "was glad to see less of me, as I was to see less of him," the latter remembered).[21] In the words of the series chronicler Donna McCrohan, "Storm clouds gathered, burst, abated. The skies cleared. *All in the Family* went on." McCrohan cited the appointment of Mort Lachman as executive producer as a turning point, as was the arrival of director Paul Bogart. The show had a number of directors after Rich left, but got a second lease on life when Bogart came aboard with the start of the sixth season. He helmed almost one hundred episodes.[22] This phase of the show's life was marked by more varied settings and more fluid camera work that showed even the most familiar elements of the Bunker home from fresh angles.

By the end of the decade, however, most of the principal figures were ready to move on—with the ironic exception of O'Connor, who persuaded a reluctant Lear to carry the Bunker family saga forward with *Archie Bunker's Place*. By that point, *All in the Family* had accumulated over 200 episodes—a huge number by contemporary standards, when a season of a series may consist of as little as six, and rarely more than thirteen, episodes. By contrast, *AITF* typically had twenty-four episodes per season—an output difficult to imagine now.

It's time to look at those episodes in more detail.

5

The Character of Home

Chez Bunker

Seven hundred and four Hauser Street is a fictive two-family house located in Queens, New York. But its specific location in that borough of New York City is a bit contested. There is in fact no Hauser Street in Queens—though there is a Hauser Boulevard in Los Angeles near where Norman Lear's production company was based. In the later years of the show, there are multiple references to the house being located in the Queens neighborhood of Astoria,[1] but Lear was uncertain when queried about this in 1993.[2] There's less doubt about the physical structure, featured in *All in the Family*'s opening credits, which include a montage that begins with an aerial shot of the Manhattan skyline before gradually descending into Queens and concluding, at ground level, before what is presumably the Bunker home. That house was—and remains—located at 89-70 Cooper Avenue in the Glendale section of Queens, which became something of a pop culture shrine for decades after the show went off the air (though not much anymore).[3]

Etymologically speaking, "Hauser" is an interesting choice of name for the setting of *All in the Family*. Very clearly, it closely resembles the word "house" in English. But "hauser" has other connotations in German as well as Yiddish as "housekeeper."[4] There's an irony here in the combination of

Teutonic and Jewish terms, reflecting both the Bunkers' WASP heritage and the diversity that may well be the essence of the American character. There's another irony as well: like its many predecessors in the sitcom tradition, *All in the Family* has a domestic setting, reflected in its very name. But the show is also notable for its subversion of that tradition, turning the pieties of the genre on its head in emphasizing conflict and ignorance rather than harmony and wisdom—without forsaking the sense of cohesion and underlying strength that's also part of that tradition. "Hauser" is a masculine noun in German, but at the end of the day (and daily life *is* the great subject of the sitcom), Edith and Archie are housekeepers, pillars of their family and community.

Such niceties aside, the important and obvious fact of 704 Hauser Street is that it's in Queens—not in Manhattan or a leafy suburb but in an outer borough of the great metropolis of New York City. Of all the city's boroughs, Queens has long been regarded as the most prosaic. Brooklyn had a cherished cultural identity as a separate city for most of its 400-year history; the Bronx, while a byword for urban poverty for much of the last century, nevertheless has a gritty cache familiar to many who know little else of Gotham lore. Staten Island, by contrast, is a place apart, notwithstanding its municipal status (one that to this day maintains a Bunkeresque white, working-class demographic, albeit more of an Italian one that Archie routinely dismissed as "dago" whenever he encountered it).

But Queens is something of a liminal zone. Technically, it's a county (Brooklyn, its counterpart on Long Island, is King's County, befitting the colonial origins of both—the queen in question is Henrietta, the seventeenth-century wife of Charles I). The western half of the borough was absorbed into greater New York City in 1898, while the remaining communities formed suburban Nassau County, which is now among the most affluent in the United States. Queens, by contrast, remains a stronghold for the city's—and the nation's—working class. If Queens were a city in its own right, it would be among the largest in the United States, its population approximately the same size as that of neighboring Brooklyn. But for the last century, Queens has had a transitional character between Manhattan and Long Island (a term that, as commonly used, does not include Brooklyn or Queens, even though both boroughs are on the island). The sometimes benighted character of Queens was captured vividly in some of the settings, among them the notorious "valley of the ashes," of F. Scott Fitzgerald's 1925 novel *The Great Gatsby*, which was published around the time

Archie, a Queens native, was born—and indeed would have come straight from the milieu of its hapless minor character, George Wilson.[5]

Queens has long been among the most demographically diverse locales in the world. (About the only place that can compete with it is the East End of London—not coincidentally, the setting of *All in the Family*'s inspiration, *Till Death Us Do Part*.) Of course, the meaning of the word "diverse" has changed over time. A century ago, when the Italians and Irish were routinely described as "races," the migrant flood from Manhattan—to this day commonly referred to as "the city" even by those from other boroughs—was of largely European descent. After the Second World War, subsequent waves originated from elsewhere, notably Africa, Latin America, and Asia. Not surprisingly, the arrival of such people figured into many *All in the Family* episodes, notably those featuring the black Jefferson family. But befitting the show's Janus-faced character, Italians, Poles, and the Irish still had relatively chiseled identities now commonly lumped together into the category of "white," just as distinctions among Protestants, Catholics, and Jews are now regarded as "people of faith" in contrast with a largely secular multicultural elite. Meanwhile, distinctions between Haitians and Dominicans, mainland and Taiwanese Chinese, and Jamaican and Nigerian blacks have become more apparent even to the least culturally savvy outsiders. The melting pot may be cracked, but the spices still simmer as the flavors change.

Classifying the Bunkers

Just as the word "race" has had meanings that remain both stable and shifting, so too for the word "class." There's no doubt that the Bunkers are working-class people and that 704 Hauser Street—whether located in Astoria, Glendale, or just about any other Queens locale—sits in a working-class neighborhood. (An exception is Forest Hills, the affluent hamlet from whence the man who literally embodies Archie, Carroll O'Connor, hailed.) One indication of this is the similarity of 704 Hauser to the homes around it, all of which, as the opening montage makes clear, are packed close together. Another class marker is the accent of the characters that populate the neighborhood. Few people today have the distinctive patois of Archie and Edith—perhaps most vividly captured in their pronunciation of "toilet" (terrlet)—but anyone who listens to them, then or now, will not fail to recognize their downscale origins. No less than the world of *My Fair Lady*—the 1956 Broadway musical based on the 1913 George Bernard Shaw play *Pygmalion*—one's voice remains an important indicator of class status, and it's Archie's intonation and his frequent malapropisms that mark him as working class more than any other attribute.[6]

But class is more commonly associated with levels of consumption, and here it should be noted that the working class of *All in the Family* enjoys a lifestyle that may well be enviable when compared with that of later generations. This duality—absolute downscale identity coupled with relative material affluence—is central to understanding the Bunkers in their milieu and their relation to our own time.

For starters, the Bunkers are homeowners, not renters. The couple lived with Edith's family after their wedding circa 1948, rented an apartment shortly after that, and bought 704 Hauser in 1955, presumably to accommodate their daughter Gloria. "It was you who made this house a home," Archie tells her in the 1975 episode "Mike Makes His Move," where we learn much of this information. "It was your husband who made it into an all-night diner," he adds, one of his frequent digs at Mike's appetite. The Bunkers took out a twenty-year mortgage that they finished paying off in 1975, something they commemorated by hosting a mortgage-burning party (a once-common custom that has since faded) in the episode when Mike and Gloria finally move out.[7] It is this liberation from making mortgage payments that would enable Archie to purchase the bar that would dominate his final seasons on television. While that doesn't necessarily mean they can retire in style, Archie and Edith nevertheless appear to have achieved a level of stability that seems enviable then *and* now. In the words of the TV critic David Marc, "The mere fact that the Bunkers live in a detached single-family dwelling is enough to bestow on them the middle-class status of alright-niks."[8] Indeed, the Bunkers may well have thought of themselves as middle class—that remarkably elastic and evasive term that helped forge a myth of cultural consensus in postwar society.

Not that the Bunker home is anything special. Actually, its lack of special-ness is a measure of the artistry of *All in the Family*'s art director Don Roberts, who supervised the production design of dozens of television shows in the 1970s and 1980s. Roberts crafted a brilliantly realized set for *AITF* that captured the complex class character of the Bunker family and its cultural milieu. Its focal point was the front door of 704 Hauser, a frequent point of entry for all the show's characters, who step into a seamless living room / dining room. The brown floral wallpaper is faded, bordering on shabby. (It would be replaced over the course of a couple episodes in 1977.) A swinging door that's the source of much comedy separates the dining space from the kitchen, which is similarly workmanlike, with a cheap Formica breakfast table that furnishes the setting of many conversations. A staircase near the front door leads to a pair of bedrooms for Archie/Edith and Mike/Gloria and a rarely seen—but frequently discussed—bathroom. (It became the basis of a 1977 episode, "Fire," that resulted from Archie's faulty installation of a fuse.) There's also a basement that becomes the setting for a memorable episode when Archie finds himself locked in for a weekend (and in a drunken state faces a rescuer he believes is God—and who happens to be a black man). And finally, an unseen attic is referred to as a possible refuge for Lionel when he has a fight with his father in the 1974 episode "Lionel the Live-In." Many of the props, like the elephant on a side table, or the family photo by the living room telephone, were familiar fixtures for viewers. In something of an inside joke, Edith talks to Archie in one of the final episodes while watering a fern he's never noticed that she notes has been there for nine years.

The estimable television historian Horace Newcomb captures the spirit of the Bunker home in a 1974 analysis: "The furniture is not the plush modern with which television viewers have always been familiar. It is old, worn, without style. The comforts are those of use, rather than design, and the easy chair sits before the [frequently malfunctioning] television set waiting for Archie to occupy it. The dining area is in the living room. Upstairs the bedrooms are bastions of privacy, but as in any crowded situation, privacy is often ignored. The bathroom—there is only one—is another point of contention, and serves both as a battleground for the two families in the home and as a symbol of Archie's social prudery."[9] Indeed, one of the most reliable triggers of laughter for studio audiences watching tapings of *All in the Family* is the offstage sound effect of a flushing toilet, oftentimes as an ironic commentary on conversations taking place in the living room.

Part of what makes such moments comic is the way the Bunkers strive to maintain a sense of domestic respectability. Though it's rarely noticed by any of the characters, Edith is a remarkably tireless housewife: she's almost always on the move. We often see her in the kitchen, but her daily routines also include shopping and budget responsibilities. In one episode when Archie is hovering at home because his union is on strike, Edith recites a litany of weekly chores (vacuuming, window cleaning, etc.) that Archie finds exasperatingly detailed, though he himself will be vacuuming before the strike is over. She answers the phone one day with a rare wry joke that she's working because it's the maid's day off.

Of course the fact that Edith *is* a housewife is yet another indication of the relative affluence of the American working class in the second half of the twentieth century. Though such an identity would be increasingly dismissed as oppressive and repugnant by feminists then and since—Edith's daughter Gloria among them—it was often an aspiration for millions of women hoping to trade the imperatives of alienated labor for someone else into the more rewarding work of making a home for one's family—in short, Edith is a "hauser" too. The crucial premise for this role was a sufficiently high wage level for working-class men to support the institution of housewifery for their spouses. The decline of working-class men's wages and participation in the labor force, which have proceeded in tandem since the early 1970s, made such a sexual division of labor impossible, even if it remained desirable. (More on this in chapter 7.)

Precarious Perch

It's important to note that however enviable the relative situation of the Bunkers in the 1970s, the family was nevertheless stalked by economic insecurity. Archie's primary occupation is that of a dockworker—and shipping was among the first industries to be transformed by automation. Thus, his character would have no choice but to recognize that his job would ultimately disappear, even if such a fate wasn't imminent. But he has more immediate sources of uncertainty as well, which include anxiety that he will be pushed aside in favor of younger men (the plotline of the 1973 episode "Archie Goes to the Hospital") and labor unrest, the focus of a 1974 string of four episodes titled "The Bunkers and Inflation." The very title of those episodes points to another source of economic stress, grounded in rising prices resulting from the energy crisis (it was an attempt to adjust the thermostat at 704 Hauser that got Archie trapped in his basement in the 1973 episode "Archie Locked in the Cellar"). At one point in the inflation episodes, Edith, who reluctantly seeks paid employment, reveals to Archie that the family's savings are almost exhausted. And at the start of the final installment, Archie frets that he may have to take out a second mortgage. Here and elsewhere, pending crises are averted, but future worries are hardly banished.

There's one demographic wrinkle associated with 704 Hauser Street's location that bears mention here: the fact that the Bunkers lack an automobile. In some contexts this would be an actual indication of poverty. (In the early 1940s, the Soviet government began showing the John Ford film *The Grapes of Wrath* to its citizens to illustrate the ravages of the Great Depression, only to stop when it became apparent that Russian viewers were amazed that the impoverished Joad family had a car.)[10] But in large stretches of New York City, a car has long been widely considered an unnecessary, even downright onerous, proposition given the availability of mass transit.[11] Not that the subway is a pleasure; Archie isn't alone in the routine complaints about difficult commutes that pepper many episodes of the show. The most obvious and easy alternative for more affluent city residents before the age of Uber was taking a taxi, and here it's telling that Archie moonlights on nights and weekends as a cabdriver to help make ends meet. Such a job would inevitably mean he would be leaving the more familiar precincts of Queens for regular runs into and out of Manhattan.

In short, Archie has jobs, not a career, at least until the eighth season of 1977–1978, when he finally achieves a dream of running his own business (and even then he keeps his cab-driving gig). This, therefore, means a sharp divide between work and home. Such a divide tends to be sharper for working-class people than for the elite, who tend to have careers rather than jobs. For working-class people, home tends to be a refuge from the ravages of work and a haven from an often heartless world.[12] Of course, this isn't always true—and it certainly isn't always true in the world of *All in the Family*. But the notion that it *should* be, that it *can* be, is the crucial premise on which much of the show's comedy (and pathos) rests. As such, 704 Hauser is the essential fifth major character of the show.

Family portrait: Publicity still for *All in the Family*. From left, clockwise: Jean Stapleton as Edith Bunker, Rob Reiner as Mike Stivic, Sally Struthers as Gloria Stivic, and Carroll O'Connor as Archie Bunker. The show entered the network stealthily as a midseason replacement on January 12, 1971, in a nation in the middle of a cultural transition. It would go on to become a defining artifact of an era loosely known as "the sixties"—and its legacy in the seventies. *(Photofest)*

Endowed chairs: Living room props from the *All in the Family* exhibit at the Smithsonian Institution's National Museum of American History, where they've been on display since 1978. "The popular but often-controversial show dealt directly with difficult topics such as race, ethnicity, changing social mores, and the women's liberation movement," reads the placard included in the exhibit. "It was a funny show," a father explained to his son on a recent August afternoon. "Almost fifty years ago now. History." *(Photo by Jim Cullen)*

Smart set: Production photo from *The Black Angel*, an NBC television show from 1945. Like all new communications revolutions, television drew on earlier media, especially theater, in formulating its cultural conventions. Living rooms would become ground central for countless sitcoms—*All in the Family* notable among them. *(Photofest)*

"Black" humor: Tim Moore and Jester Hairston strike a characteristic minstrel show pose in the television version of *Amos 'n' Andy*, which ran on CBS from 1951 to 1953. The show, a sequel to the hugely successful radio program created by Freeman Gosden and Charles Correll, peddled a century's worth of racist stereotypes in minstrelsy, arguably the most popular form of entertainment in the nineteenth century. *All in the Family* was an inversion of the minstrel show in its recasting Archie Bunker as the archetypal idiot whose malapropisms revealed ironic truths.

In the name of the father: Jim Anderson (Robert Young) presides over an evening at home in the family living room set of *Father Knows Best* (1954–1960). The show embodied the mythology of the nuclear family in the postwar age, one *All in the Family* would deconstruct with a prototype of dumb dads that would dominate for the next half century. Shown from left: Lauren Chapin as Kathy Anderson, Elinor Donahue as Betty Anderson, and Jane Wyatt as Margaret Anderson. *(Photofest)*

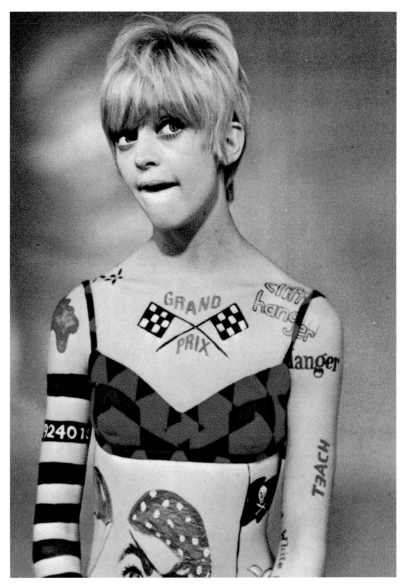

Tattoo taboo: Goldie Hawn makes an appearance on *Rowan & Martin's Laugh-In* (1968–1973). The variety show was among the first network offerings to bring a countercultural sensibility to the deeply conservative medium of broadcast television. *(Photofest)*

Colorful figure: Norman Lear in his 1970s heyday. Genial, irreverent, and insistent, his optimistic sense of transgression literally changed the face of television. *(Photofest)*

Direct approach: Norman Lear directs Carroll O'Connor and Jean Stapleton (with Sally Struthers and Rob Reiner in the background) on the set of *All in the Family*. The success of the show was a product of multifaceted contributions of multiple players—and some creative friction between O'Connor and Lear. *(Photofest)*

Skeptical start: Still from the pilot episode of *All in the Family*, first broadcast on January 12, 1971. Note Edith's expression of resigned detachment; Jean Stapleton would soon significantly change the way she played the character. *(Photofest)*

Home entertainment: Edith has fun in the 1974 episode "The Longest Kiss" while neighbors George Jefferson (Sherman Helmsley), Louise Jefferson (Isabel Sanford), and Irene Lorenzo (Betty Garrett) look on. The living room of 704 Hauser Street was the great crossroads of *All in the Family*, where a variegated cast of characters shared the stage with the Bunkers. *(Photofest)*

Trans-formation: Archie converses with Beverly La Salle (legendary San Francisco drag queen Lori Shannon), unaware of the character's sexual identity, in one of a number of episodes featuring Beverly's character in *All in the Family*. The show was far ahead of its time in depicting—and engaging with issues surrounding—gender nonconforming people. *(Photofest)*

Enter, left: Bea Arthur makes her debut as Maude Findlay on the "Cousin Maude's Visit" episode of *All in the Family* on December 11, 1971. Less than a year later she would be the star of her own sitcom, *Maude*. The show, a wry satire of limousine liberalism, would run for six seasons. *(Photofest)*

Comic aim: Archie Bunker in a characteristic pose—his chair, his living room, his wife Edith by his side. Exasperated by one of her digressive anecdotes, he performs one of his periodic pantomimes that culminate in mock suicide. Archie is a raging sexist who loves, and depends on, his spouse. As such, the character was central to Norman Lear's artistic and political vision. *(Photofest)*

Close relationship: Mike and Archie in a characteristic pose. Their often bitter antagonism sparked the friction that sustained *All in the Family* through the nine seasons. Mike was both smarter and wiser than his father-in-law, but his foibles—and his economic dependence on Archie—made many of their matches an even fight. *(Photofest)*

Generating strength: Edith counsels her daughter Gloria in one of her periodic moments of distress. Over the course of *All in the Family*'s run, Gloria herself became a (feminist) mother who ran a household of her own. *(Photofest)*

Deck hands: Mike and Gloria enjoyed a companionate postfeminist marriage with a shared liberal outlook. But like many of his peers, Mike was not quite a liberated man, and tensions between him and Gloria periodically surfaced—and intensified—during later seasons of *All in the Family*. *(Photofest)*

Uptown: Louise and George Jefferson (Isabel Sanford and Sherman Helmsley) in their luxury Manhattan apartment during an episode of *The Jeffersons* (1975–1985), the most successful of the *All in the Family* spin-offs. Norman Lear said he created the show in response to critics who complained that other sitcoms in his broadcasting empire, like *Sanford and Son* and *Good Times*, indulged in racist stereotypes. *(Photofest)*

All in another family: A still from the aborted reboot of *Roseanne* in 2018. The show was canceled following offscreen racist remarks by the show's star, Roseanne Barr, a decision that deprived viewers from making independent assessments of the provocative questions the sitcom raised in an increasingly fractured culture. *(Photofest)*

Attuned: Archie and Edith perform "Those Were the Days" in the opening credits of *All in the Family*. Few women today would identify with Edith's vocation of housewife. But she—through the medium of Jean Stapleton's talent—endowed it strength, depth, and, ultimately, dignity. *(Photofest)*

6

Not Bad for a Bigot

The Making of Archie Bunker

The premise for *All in the Family* rests on a hazy historical illusion embodied in its opening song—namely, that it sounds older than it actually is. "Those Were the Days" was written by Charles Strouse (music) and Lee Adams (lyrics), longtime collaborators best known for their work in the musicals *Bye Bye Birdie* (1960) and *Annie* (1977). Norman Lear worked with Strouse and Adams on *The Night They Raided Minsky's*, the 1968 movie he wrote and produced, and commissioned them to write a theme song for the new sitcom he was creating as that film reached fruition. As its title suggests, "Those Were the Days" sounds deliberately old-fashioned, even though it was brand new—it was, in effect, a fake historical artifact. The song, whose title at one point was going to be the title of the sitcom as well, opened every episode of *All in the Family*, including the three pilots, though there were variations in how it was performed; most of the time it was played with Archie and Edith singing the lines in turn, as well as together, while Edith plays the piano.

"Those Were the Days" begins as a simple exercise in nostalgia, fondly recalling the heyday of big bands in the 1940s, when Glen Miller ruled the airwaves. But there's some historical slippage here. Miller's heyday was the

63

early 1940s, when, in fact, Archie and Edith were young. The musical style of the song itself, however, harks back to an earlier time, the golden age of Tin Pan Alley at the turn of the twentieth century. And some of the lyrics land squarely between those points, like "Mister, we could use a man like Herbert Hoover again." Hoover assumed the presidency in 1929, around the time Archie turned five years old. So he could hardly have been conscious, much less approving, of Hoover's Republican brand of politics. The ensuing lines, however, seem to leapfrog over the Hoover years—which is to say the early days of the Great Depression, when Hoover's popularity went into a nosedive from which it never recovered—into a political sensibility that was more widespread during the second half of the twentieth century than during the first half: "Didn't need no welfare state / Everybody pulled his weight." The next line, "Gee, our old La Salle ran great," refers to a line of automobiles that went out of production in 1940. In short, "Those Were the Days" is a temporal mess.[1] It's all over the historical map.

Which is why it works so well. Because, strictly speaking, Archie Bunker doesn't really make much historical sense either. The odds are high that a guy like him *did* need the welfare state: it was the greatest thing to ever happen to the white working class of his childhood, when it became a lifeline for millions of Americans trying to hold on amid a terrible economic crisis. Labor unions, unemployment insurance, social security—each of these pillars of the welfare state directly aided the Archie Bunkers of the world, who were far more likely to be Roosevelt Democrats than Hoover Republicans. That ideological orientation was also likely to last beyond Roosevelt's New Deal as well. As a World War II vet, Archie would have been eligible for the GI Bill, which would have allowed him to purchase 704 Hauser Street on much more attractive terms than he would have otherwise been able to do. While we can't be sure about any of this—and we all know that people's political identifications (or, for that matter, their musical tastes) aren't always predictable—simple logic suggests the only thing in the song that's consistent with his character is his affinity for Glenn Miller; this assumes, of course, that his racism would not prevent him from appreciating Miller's jazz idiom, whose musical source was African American. Then again, racists have a long history of loving black culture.

In an important sense, however, all these nuances are beside the point, because in the world of *All in the Family*, there are really only two times: then and now. And the dividing line between them—or, to use the parlance of the time, the (generation) gap between them—was clear: the 1960s.

Archie's whole life in the show is based on a rejection of the sixties, which is to say an unusually rapid period of social change in which it seemed that the nation had undergone a radical break in continuity. Archie's hostility to this change is something most contemporary viewers can readily grasp; in part we see ourselves on the other side of the chasm from where he stands—the one he's rejecting. But a richer understanding of Archie's character, and a deeper understanding of the show's achievement, can be gained from unearthing Archie's backstory in the bits and pieces we learn over the years of the show's run and how they situate him, and us, in an admittedly twisting, but nevertheless unbroken, historical stream.

Bunker Mentality

That backstory is reasonably clear, notwithstanding some ambiguities and a few contradictions. The man we come to know as Archie Bunker began his life as Archie Justice before Norman Lear decided this was too obvious and changed it to Archie Bunker after the first pilot. "Bunker" is indeed a better and more evocative name, one that suggests entrenchment and hostility to an alien environment. And "Archie" evokes the word "arch," as in extreme (archrival), as well as in strong and central (as in the center of a curved structure that supports substantial weight).[2]

Archie was born in the spring of 1924 (Gloria at one point notes his birthday falls between the astrological signs of Taurus and Gemini). There's some confusion about his family composition. In the 1976 episode "Archie Finds a Friend," Archie describes himself as an only child; but early in the second season he notes he has a sister, Alma, and a brother, Phil. There's also another figure, his estranged brother Alfred, who surfaces for a couple of episodes in the final season of the show.[3] Fred (his nickname), played by actor Richard McKenzie, has a very different ideological outlook than Archie, and appeared to be his father's favorite—a source of resentment for Archie even as we learn he took the fall for his brother's childhood misdeeds.

Geographically speaking, Archie is a Queens boy. Exactly *where* in Queens is not entirely clear; in one of the final episodes, we learn that his father had a house in Woodside, but Edith notes earlier in the series that he attended Flushing High School, which is about six miles east of Woodside. In the *AITF* sequel series *Archie Bunker's Place*, Archie says he grew up in Long Island City, which is located at the extreme western edge of Queens. But this is all inside baseball (a sport Archie played in high school and for which he has a lifelong attachment; he's a fan of the Mets, who play in Queens). Viewers in the 1970s would have understood, with greater or lesser degrees of clarity, that he's an outer borough guy—with all that implies.

A child of the Depression, Archie experienced poverty. We get a vivid glimpse of his childhood in the classic 1978 episode "Two's a Crowd," written by *AITF* mainstay Phil Sharp, in which Archie and Mike find themselves locked inside the storeroom of Archie's tavern and drink away their boredom. A slurring Archie tells Mike about his schoolyard nickname, "Shoebootie," a moniker he acquired because he wore out a shoe at a time when his father, a brakeman on the Long Island Railroad, was unemployed, and the family couldn't afford a new pair. So his mother found him a boot to wear to school, prompting mockery from his classmates (which grew worse when they learned his formal name was Archibald). Archie notes that the only kid who didn't join in the jeering was a black boy named Winston. Mike expresses surprise that a black kid would like him. To the contrary, Archie replies that Winston beat the hell out of him. Why was that, Mike asks. When Archie waves off an answer, Mike presses him. "Because he said I said he was a nigger," Archie replies. "Did you?" Mike asks. "Sure," Archie responds. "That's what all them people was called in those days. Everybody called them niggers. That's all my old man ever called them. What the hell was I supposed to call them? I didn't know the difference. What was I supposed to do—call them a wop? [Wop was a dismissive term for undocumented Italian immigrants—"wop" was an acronym for "without papers."] I couldn't call them a wop because wop is what we called the dagos."

When Mike asserts that Archie's father was wrong to use this racial slur, Archie heatedly rejects any criticism of Bunker Sr. He describes his father's efforts to clothe him, bring him candy, and play baseball with him. And yet, without a trace of self-conscious irony, he also describes his father's powerful hands—something Archie knows because his father broke one of those hands hitting him. He also reveals that his father once locked Archie in a closet for seven hours "to teach him to do good." Archie ends his little speech pointing a finger at Mike. "How can any man who loves you tell you anything that's wrong?" he asks.

The point of this tragicomic exchange—"Son of a bitch, wasn't that good," Lear later recollected in watching it again—is clear enough: Archie Bunker is a product of his environment, and that environment was one of deprivation and abuse that in turn made him abusive.[4] It's worth noting, however, that Archie has partially overcome his father's example: whatever his considerable faults, there's no indication that he ever physically assaulted anyone. Thus, he represents a finite triumph over environmental determinism. It's also worth noting that affluent people with good childhoods can be at least as racist as anybody else. Nevertheless, this scene is compelling in the way it depicts what the sociologists Jonathan Cobb and Richard Sennett called "the hidden injuries of class" in their book of the same name—a book, coincidentally, first published in 1972, when *All in the Family* began its cultural ascent.[5]

In our time, working-class people are sometimes depicted as bigoted because they're afraid of losing their relative sense of privilege—what W.E.B. Du Bois famously called the "psychological wage" of whiteness, a form of cultural currency Archie is all too willing to pocket.[6] But as often as not, their behavior is driven not so much by a matter of embracing the perquisites of white supremacy as it is by a fear of returning to shameful feelings and experiences they know all too well. The adult Archie is offensive, but the child Archie was a clueless white victim who inflicted pain on a black child who in turn understandably retaliated by beating him up (a perhaps rare case where a black child *could* retaliate). A scene like this one hardly depicts Archie in a positive light. But it does make his behavior, and that of millions of other Americans, coherent in a way that may temper any instinct we have to censure him: an important, and potentially dangerous, artistic position, which is why it initially evoked such strong opposition—and perhaps also why the prominence of that opposition to the show faded, because the racism it depicted was so widely shared, so terribly ordinary.

Learning Curves

In any case, Archie survived his childhood. He did so with a deficient education: like millions of Americans before World War II, he never finished high school; he left in his final semester to get a job to help support his family, a confession he makes to Edith after they have a fight in the 1972 episode "Archie and Edith Alone." In the 1973 episode "Archie Learns His Lesson," Archie studies for a general equivalency degree in pursuit of a promotion— and, to Gloria's disgust, takes for granted that he should take crib notes on his hand to make sure he passes. (He does, but is passed over for the promotion.)

Archie, then, is an ignorant man. This is true in a factual sense, but he reveals his lack of sophistication in other ways too. The trait is foundational to his character in terms of how the other characters, and the audience, see him. His ignorance is a matter of crude opinions, like his certainty that Jews are more intelligent, and Africans more athletic, than everyone else. It's also a matter of unintentionally humorous mispronunciations (the tax firm of H&R Crook, his denunciations of feminist "Gloria Steinway," the running joke of his difficulty remembering people's names, and, when corrected, responding by saying "whatever"). And, especially, it's evident in his inability to understand that other characters see through his efforts to portray himself as more enlightened than he really is. This was shown most famously in the 1972 episode "Sammy's Visit," where Sammy Davis Jr. responds to Archie's protestations that he's not prejudiced with an ironic peroration that ends, "If you were prejudiced, you'd walk around thinking you're better than anybody else. But I can honestly say, after spending these marvelous moments with you, that you ain't better than anybody." Sometimes, Archie says things that are truer than he seems to realize, as when he bats away a suggestion that he and Edith reveal to their niece that their alcoholic father wants to reclaim her by saying that "lies is what holds families together." Such ignorance, of course, is what makes Archie's bigotry permissible to depict, and why network censors allowed lines like "tighter than a Jew's purse": the understanding is that we laugh *at* Archie, not *with* him.

As noted in chapter 3, the truth is more complicated, for a number of reasons. The first is that we as audience members can never be sure we *are* laughing at him—are other people secretly in sympathy with Archie? Are we? And how broad is the term "we"? The presence of the pointedly named George Jefferson—his name an amalgam of George Washington and Thomas Jefferson—is a black character (brilliantly realized by Sherman Helmsley) who in some ways is a racial mirror of Archie, and one who occasionally finds moments of ironic convergence with him. He's a minority character in more ways than one, but, in the moral logic of the show, an indispensable one.

The second ambiguity in Archie's character is that for all his mangled locutions and crude opinions, he can be remarkably quick-witted. You might say that this isn't really about crafting him as a three-dimensional character—indeed, you could argue that his quickness actually detracts from his realism in the name of the sitcom writer's imperative to keep the jokes coming. But there's a consistency to Archie's rapier-sharp jabs that suggests that there are a few things that he understands very well. Naturally, he wields humor most aggressively against Mike. "You've seen the latest unemployment figures?" Mike asks him in a characteristic attack on the Nixon administration in a 1974 episode on the stagnant U.S. economy. "I'm looking at an unemployment figure right now," Archie replies with a stare, pointedly reminding Mike that Archie is supporting him so he can go to college instead of working for wages. In the 1978 episode in which Mike is offered a professorship on the West Coast, Archie describes California as "the land of fruits and nuts. Every nut's a little fruity, and every fruit's a little nutty." He makes a meta-textual aside in one of the final episodes of the show when he observes, "Entertainment is a thing of the past. Today we have television." Though unfair, these jokes are clever and tart. They're also wholly reflective of Archie's otherwise limited character.

But the biggest obstacle in simply dismissing Archie as an irrelevant old fool is suggested by the key role he plays in his family as the core breadwinner. Here again his name is apt: Arch (which is what Mike calls him) as keystone. He serves that role in his family as the main breadwinner, supporting his wife, his daughter, and his son-in-law. But Archie is a solid citizen in other ways too. The most obvious example of this is his status in World War II—"the big one," as he likes to call it. Archie was eighteen when he entered the air corps in 1942, which served as an aerial branch of the U.S. Army until it gained the status of an autonomous branch of the military as the air force in 1947. He served in Italy, earning a Purple Heart comically: he took shrapnel in one of his buttocks, a repeated source of jokes over the course of the series.

Archie's return from overseas, which coincided with his mother's death, allowed him to resume a courtship with Edith Baines that had begun when she was in high school. Not that this was easy for him to do; many members of her family objected to Archie—one such character, Edith's cousin Maude, would feature in a few episodes and get a show of her own—and Edith's mother at one point whisked Edith off to Atlantic City in the hopes of fostering a breakup. He nevertheless won her hand, and the two wed. After lodging for a while with Edith's family they got an apartment (and a cat, Gus, with whom Archie had a relationship of mutual hatred). A family connection on Edith's side allowed Archie to land a job as a dockworker, one that earned the couple enough money to buy their house and raise Gloria. It was a quintessential postwar story. The rest, you might say, is (television) history.

Archie is a dour, unpleasant figure who can exhaust those around him with his misanthropy. But he does have instinctive, unfeigned loyalty for God, family, and country—as he understands them. Nothing is more consistently explicit in this regard than his patriotism. In the first of the four "The Bunkers and Inflation" episodes of 1974, Archie raises a glass and offers "a toast to the good old U.S. of A., where everybody gets a slice of the pie. All you have to do is work, and in the end you'll get it." To which Mike replies with a double entendre: "That's right, Arch. That's where you're gonna get it: in the end."

Archie issues his most memorable, and oft-quoted, paean to his country in a 1976 oration Mike dubs "Archie Bunker's Bicentennial Minute," a reference to short commentaries that popped up on television during the nation's 200th anniversary: "Listen here, professor. You're the one who needs an American history lesson. You don't know nothin' about Lady Liberty standing there in the harbor, with her torch on high, screamin' out to all the nations of the world: 'send me your poor, your deadbeats, your filthy.' And all the nations sent them in here, and all of them came crawlin' in here, like ants, the Spanish P.Rs. from the Caribou in there. Your Japs, your Chinamen, your Krauts and your Hebes, and your English fags. They all come in here, and they're free to live in their own separate sections where they feel safe and they'll bust your head if you go in there. That's what makes America great, buddy!" There's an added layer of irony in the speech, given that what prompts it is Mike's concern that he will not get a teaching job in Minnesota that he covets because one of the candidates is an African American who will get preferential treatment (the Supreme Court decision *Bakke vs. Board of Regents*, upholding the legality of affirmative action, would be issued the next year). If there's one thing that trumps politics for Archie, it's family: he doesn't want his daughter and grandson to move away. He'll show his commitment to his family with more gravity in the 1977 episode when he rejects overtures to join the Ku Klux Klan after he learns the Klan plans to go after Mike over a letter he wrote to the editor of a local newspaper.

Archie's version of American history is, to put it mildly, selective. Note, for example, that he has nothing to say about the Americans who didn't immigrate here voluntarily. And it tends to be simplistic in the sense that his respect for authority can sometimes override any consideration for whether that authority is legitimate. So it is that Archie maintained a fierce loyalty to President Richard M. Nixon (Archie repeatedly refers to him as Richard E. Nixon) long after he resigned in disgrace.

Immoral Majority

Actually, Archie's attachment to Nixon is indicative of the sea change in American politics that occurred around the time *All in the Family* premiered. As noted, the young Archie should logically have been a Democrat. We're in fact never told about Archie's voting record prior to the 1970s, though he does complain at one point of his childhood that "all we had was the Great Depression, Eleanor [a lightning rod for liberal causes] and a bad team in Brooklyn" (the Dodgers, who would be replaced by the Mets). Many youthful Democrats in the early postwar years—among them Nixon's replacement for Archie's affections, Ronald Reagan—began to reconsider their party loyalty when FDR's successor, Harry Truman, was attacked for being soft on Communism as the Cold War with the Soviet Union heated up. It seems likely that Archie was a supporter of Republican president Dwight Eisenhower in the 1950s, as indicated by an offhand 1975 remark in his kitchen that "nothing makes sense in this country since General Eisenhower was sleeping in the White House." Yet even many white working-class voters who voted for Ike in 1952 and 1956 remained Democrats, who continued to maintain their party loyalty in local and state, if not national, elections well into the 1960s.

Even more than the Cold War, the development that really catalyzed party realignment was the civil rights movement. Until the 1960s, the Republicans portrayed themselves—with some legitimacy, given that the Democrats in the South were the party of the Ku Klux Klan—as "the party of Lincoln." In the 1960 presidential race, Richard Nixon could portray himself plausibly as more of an ally to the movement than John F. Kennedy, at least until the Kennedy campaign shrewdly intervened to have Martin Luther King freed from one of his many imprisonments at the time. Civil rights really became a Democratic cause beginning with the administration of Kennedy's successor, Lyndon Johnson of Texas, whose push on this front dovetailed with his famous War on Poverty, which created so-called Community Action Programs to press for reforms in the nation's cities. This was, as Johnson well understood, a politically fraught stance that cost him support, especially among Democratic machine politicians such as Richard Daley of Chicago and Sam Yorty of Los Angeles (the topic of a conversation between Archie and Henry Jefferson in the 1973 episode "Henry's Farewell"), who resented and resisted the arrival of activists that sought to rearrange power structures in their cities. One result was accelerated white flight from cities to suburbs—and the growing movement of white voters from the Democratic to the Republican parties. Archie embodies that shift, one that had been gradually but largely completed in much of the country by the time the series opens. Indeed, the process was so substantially complete that it was increasingly hard to remember that guys like him were once Democrats.[7]

There is one remaining loose end in the portrayal of Archie's character: he's portrayed as resolutely (mainline) Protestant, albeit a nonpracticing one. Indeed, a key plot point in the pilot involves Archie abruptly yanking Edith prematurely from an Episcopal church service in irritation over liberal pieties of the Reverend Felcher, a figure more referred to than seen over the course of the next nine years, though he does make an appearance in the 1971 episode "The Saga of Cousin Oscar," a relative who dies while visiting the Bunkers. Archie routinely refers to Reverend Felcher as "Reverend Fletcher," is repeatedly corrected, and never gets it right. His Protestantism is more a matter of culture than doctrine or piety. But his religious affiliation doesn't really work on any level. That's because Archie's Episcopalianism, and the way it plays out, is the result of a power struggle between Norman Lear's and Carroll O'Connor's visions of the character.[8]

Lear made it abundantly clear on multiple occasions that notwithstanding the immediate inspiration for the character of Alf Garnett of the British series *Till Death Us Do Part*, he patterned Archie on his father. Herman Lear was a Jew, but the main elements Lear took from Herman were his casual racism (Archie's description of Mike as "the laziest white man I ever met" in the pilot episode comes straight from Lear's childhood memory of his father describing him); his dismissive attitude toward his wife, whom he called a "dingbat" and told her to "stifle" herself; and his tendency not to worry too much about the ethical niceties of a given situation.[9] It was very important to Lear's larger design that such traits not be essentialized as part of any cultural minority but rather as ones that could and did characterize anybody, a point he tried to underline by making Archie part of what was still a WASP majority. "I refused to pin the bigot in Archie on any specific ethnicity or religion," he later explained. So it was, for example, that Archie routinely put down Catholics ("the pope is like the civil service: they're in there for life," he says in the 1973 episode "Edith's Conversion," comparing what he regards as two irredeemably corrupt bureaucracies) alongside his jibes at other constituencies in American society. One recurring character on the show was Father Majeski, a Polish priest whom Archie visits in that episode over his concerns that Irene Lorenzo's sister, a nun, is trying to evangelize Edith.

But Archie's anti-Catholicism is the least convincing part of his character, in large measure because the animus against Catholics had largely faded after the election of Kennedy in 1960. A bigger problem is that Archie seems more Catholic—specifically Irish Catholic—than he does Protestant. As the television historian David Marc notes, "There is very little other than the name of Bunker that is Yankee about Archie."[10] Partly this is a matter of traits etched deeply into his character by the show's writers, which include sexual prudery and an instinctive respect for authority that has long engendered fears of authoritarianism among skeptics of Catholicism. But more decisively it's because of O'Connor's dominant influence on the character, a major dimension of which can literally be read at face value: he's a Mick if ever there was one. "That face screams Irish!" Lear recalls hearing repeatedly. "So why fight it, use it!"[11] But fight it Lear did, in what amounts to one of the few times he allowed ideology to trump character on a show that was often exquisitely calibrated. He nevertheless recognized he at best fought O'Connor to a draw. "Archie's physicality and personality were all Carroll, but his emotional being and belief system came from me," he later noted. "That was the basis of our quarrels."[12]

Perhaps because he's so deeply intimate with the profane, Archie also has a deeply instinctive—indeed, to the point of superstitious—sense of the sacred. He will occasionally make biblical references in his twisted way (he alludes to Lot's wife of the book of Genesis, who was turned into a pillar of salt after gazing back on the wicked city of Sodom, by telling Edith that she'll be turned "into a pillow of salt") and routinely gets angry at Mike, an avowed atheist, over his dismissiveness toward conventional Christian morality. But the most substantial revelation of Archie's bedrock religious faith comes in the 1976 episode where he's outraged that Mike and Gloria are not going to baptize their son Joey, and neither Edith nor their minister—the Reverend Tommy Chong, who happens to be covering for Reverend Felcher, and who Archie refers to as "Charlie Chan"—is willing to contravene their wishes. So he surreptitiously goes to church and performs the rite himself. In addressing God directly, Archie explains that he understands he hasn't been to church lately, but feels it was imperative to come for the sake of Joey, because "I don't want my little grandson to grow up without religion in this rotten world of yours." Belatedly realizing that he's just insulted the deity, he tries to backpedal: "We all know you did the best you could," he says, noting that

God only had six days. However misguided or objectionable his behavior—Mike, when he finds out, will never forgive him for this, referring repeatedly to it for years to come—Archie clearly acts on a deeply held principle, one he holds at some personal cost. "I hope that took, Lord," he says after performing the rite, "because they're going to kill me when I get home."

Fatherly Racism

Whatever the internal tensions or contradictions that mark Archie's character—which are nevertheless credible in the sense that tensions or contradictions can be said to characterize all of us—there is considerable coherence to his persona, a consistency that marks his behavior with other people. This of course is most evident in his interactions with racial minorities, which can be summed up simply: Archie is a white supremacist.

But racism is something that comes in different forms and takes its contours in specific contexts. Which is to say that Archie is a racist of a particular kind: a racial paternalist. He doesn't much mind Other people, as long as they know their Place, and since he's inclined to take his own racial superiority for granted, his proper role in society should be one of serene benevolence rooted in his own sense of self-esteem. That this self-esteem is misplaced is one of the chief comic engines in *All in the Family*.

The problem, of course, is that Archie lives in a world where his paternalism is increasingly, and embarrassingly, outdated. His typical reaction to this is not malice—a different form of racism that's more visible and volatile than bemusement and frustration. "I accept that we live in a country where democracy has got us by the throats," he laments to Edith near the end of the show's run, explaining why he doesn't want a black family to move in to the house formerly occupied by the Jeffersons (as well as Mike and Gloria, who have also moved on up by that point). "I admit that people got a right to be where they want to be. But why does that have to be next door to me?"

Unlike the other members of his family, Archie doesn't really have friendships with people of other races, the most impressive of which is that between Edith and Louise Jefferson (who tolerates Archie because he's the price she pays for Edith, carefully steering clear of him and his offensive remarks the best she can). But he does seem capable of having, and maybe even craves, a sense of connection with members of racial minorities, albeit on his own terms. This is most obvious in his relationship with Lionel, whom Archie regards with some warmth. Lionel seems to return this warmth, though insulates himself from Archie's racism with mild, ironic jokes at Archie's expense that Archie generally fails to recognize as such.

The possibilities, and limits, for an authentic interracial relationship on these terms come into vivid focus in the 1972 episode "Lionel Steps Out." That episode opens with Archie's niece Linda, an airline stewardess based in Baltimore, having stayed with the Bunkers for the last couple of weeks. (Linda is the daughter of Archie's brother Fred, referred to but unseen in this episode.) Linda is going to spend her final night in New York by going out dancing—with Lionel. This is not immediately obvious to Archie, who goes out for cigars, or Edith, whose reaction when she finds out is initially one of shock. "Oh," she says. And then "Ooooh." And "Ooooooooh." Edith explains that her first thought upon learning this is wondering what Archie will think. In this regard, Edith is an interesting barometer of how unsettling interracial relationships, even of the mildest sort, were even among relatively unbigoted whites at the time. "It's just so strange," Edith admits. "I guess I'm just not used to it." She can and does adapt quickly, however. Archie, of course, is a different story and erupts into rage impressive even by his standards. (Lionel's uncle Henry, who has been summoned to Chez Bunker, amid living room tumult that also involves Mike, Gloria, Linda, and Lionel, is also angry: "No more cream in the coffee!" he tells his nephew.) Archie demands to talk to Lionel alone in a kitchen table conversation. What follows is an unusually frank racial exchange. "I'm very disappointed in you, Lionel," Archie begins. He's sincerely, however misguidedly, hurt. "I thought you was one of the good ones. I thought you was my friend. I mean, I had you in my house here—and I mean the front door as well as the back. You sit here at my table. You break bread with me and all of that. And then you go and do a thing like this? Thank you very much, Lionel" (he concludes caustically).

Lionel begins responding to Archie in his usual mode of irony: "Awww, you don't have to thank me, Mr. Bunker. I'd do it again but she's leaving tomorrow."

Archie brushes off the joke. "Let's cut the funnies out. This is very serious. You know what I'm saying to you. I'm saying that youse guys oughta stick with yourselves."

Lionel again parries him by saying something he knows Archie doesn't mean: "You mean guys oughta stick with guys?"

"You know what I'm talking about, Lionel. I'm saying whites oughta stick with whites and coloreds ought to stick with coloreds."

Lionel leans back and sighs: now even he wants to put the joking aside. He stands up. "Look, Mr. Bunker," he says, "it's been a year and a half now since we moved into this neighborhood. I was just 19 then and I got a big kick outta you. But I'm pushing 21 now and I'm not getting that big a kick out of it anymore."

Archie tries to cut him off: "All right, put a lid on all of that, Lionel."

But now it's Lionel who's angry. "I'm not finished," he says, cutting Archie off. "We've been friends, and we can go on being friends. But when it comes to black and white and all the other wonderful thoughts you have in between, put a lid on *that*, Archie." Disgusted, he returns to the living room—to audible applause from a studio audience that often likes to flatter itself with its enlightenment by virtue of signaling its approval of those who stand up to Archie.

Which, in truth, is not all that hard to do. ("Don't let Archie bother you," Edith tells another character late in the show's run. "He barks, but he doesn't bite.") Lionel and Linda make clear to all parties that their relationship is their own business. When Archie summons his niece despite Edith's protestations that he should leave her alone, Linda puts him in his place. "Good night, Uncle Archie," she tells him. He persists, but Linda gets the last word. "All I've got to say to you is goodnight, Uncle Archie." And this is pretty much the spirit of the show: Archie, and the retrograde values he embodies, can be—should be—ignored.

This is an important message, albeit a limited one. The truth is that racists can't always—shouldn't always—be ignored. In a way, this is a lesson Lionel learns when he decides Archie's racism is no longer a laughing matter. The problem, of course, is that bigotry of the Archie Bunkers of the world is not always something that's all in the family; it's one that infects public discourse through structures of racism that make it hard for the Lionels of the world to do many other things beyond dating white women. This problem is more evident in the public discourse of the twenty-first century than it was in the twentieth, but it's never been far from most black people's consciousness. It's not exactly that *All in the Family* is blind to structural racism; we do see and hear about it in passing, and Mike will repeatedly note it over the course of the series. Nor is the reality of racial and ethnic violence entirely ignored, as indicated by the Klan episode referred to earlier. There's also a chilling one involving a Jewish Defense League–like militant whose anti-Arab rhetoric Archie likes but who ends up getting killed by a car bomb just outside the Bunkers' front door. But these are secondary themes in a TV show that is, after all, a sitcom. Its ideological thrust probably also reflects confidence on Lear's part that the march of progress will eventually make such problems as much of a relic as Archie Bunker is. If so, the passage of a half century suggests such confidence was misplaced.

Engendering Sexism

One might make many of the same observations regarding Archie's relationship to gender that one can with race. Here, too, he's a paternalist. This is true in the most literal of senses: he consistently addresses his adult daughter Gloria as "little girl" for the entire show (which, in fairness, she shows no sign of disliking). Indeed, Archie's paternalism can be downright endearing. The best example of this is his relationship with Teresa, the Puerto Rican hospital worker who briefly boards with the Bunkers. They meet when Archie is about to undergo surgery for gallstone removal, and he is predictably irritated by what he regards as her inattentiveness while conversing on the phone (she sizes him up quickly, fairly, and effectively). In the aftermath of his recovery, which followed a spell of unemployment, the Bunkers have a cash-flow problem and decide to rent out Mike and Gloria's old room. When, in a later episode, she coincidentally responds to a want ad and shows up at the Bunkers' door, looking for a place to stay near the hospital while she studies for medical exams, Edith is delighted and rents her the room on the spot. Archie, of course, is a good deal less pleased, and there will subsequently be tiffs over Teresa's musical choices, her English, and the like. Archie does register, however, that Teresa has a volatile boyfriend from whom she's trying to get some distance, so when there's a loud knock on the door, he assumes that the Latino man standing there is a threat and sucker punches him in the solar plexus (he's her brother; he's not badly hurt). Teresa, charmed by Archie's protectiveness, subsequently dubs him "Papi," a term of endearment, and a gentle poke in the ribs in its own right.

As with race, Archie's back gets up when women assert equality. Exhibit A in this regard is Irene Lorenzo; she and her husband, Frank, become the Bunkers' neighbors in 1973. (Irene is ably played by Betty Garrett; Frank by the wonderful character actor Vincent Gardenia, who appears in other roles in *All in the Family* before his turn as Irene's husband.) Irene is Irish and Frank is Italian—joyously, outlandishly so—but the two reverse traditional gender roles in that he's the cook and housekeeper, while Irene is a handy-woman who can, among other things, fix the broken Bunker telephone (and, as Archie learns to his chagrin, play a mean game of billiards). Archie is upset when, after cheerfully recommending Irene for what he assumes will be a clerical job down at the docks where he works, she ends up getting hired as a forklift operator. He has little choice but to tolerate this, or his (correct) suspicions that there are sarcastic subtexts in her conversations with him—"Was that a shot?" he repeatedly asks. The even-tempered Irene wisely never answers; like Louise Jefferson, she focuses her attention and affection on Edith, Mike, and Gloria.

Archie's retrograde approach to the sexes extends to those who don't exhibit gender-conforming behavior. His sneering hostility to gay men is perhaps his most glaring and sustained form of prejudice; he refers to them as "fags" and makes crudely mincing gestures throughout the show's run. This bigotry surfaces as early as the fourth episode of the show, when Archie darkly suspects that Mike and Gloria's friend Roger is gay (rejecting their protestations that his sexuality is irrelevant to their friendship). The core joke of the episode is that Roger turns out to be straight, while one of Archie's drinking buddies, a former professional football player, turns out to be gay. Archie will never really grapple with alternative sexuality until the sequel sitcom *Archie Bunker's Place*, when the recurring character of Fred, a gay waiter, becomes part of his everyday life.

One of the more amusing—and, eventually, tragic—plotlines of *All in the Family* looks at gender nonconformity from a somewhat different angle. In the 1975 episode "Archie the Hero," Archie comes home from a shift driving his cab crowing because he successfully administered CPR to a passenger who fainted in the taxi (he learned the technique by reading a poster over many sessions sitting on the toilet at work). The twist is that the person Archie assumes is a woman is in fact Beverly La Salle, a cross-dresser who performs at a local club. Archie is deeply embarrassed by this, and in a compassionate gesture Beverly denies to a reporter that Archie was the one who saved her. (Edith, for her part, strikes an instant and deep bond with Beverly.) Beverly would return for two more episodes—one in which Archie uses her to play a joke on his friend Pinky, and another in which she is murdered in a hate crime that shakes Edith to her foundations (more on this in chapter 7). La Salle, adroitly embodied by Lori Shannon (aka Don McLean), was a three-dimensional character who became part of the Bunkers' orbit, and is a good example of the way the show was ahead of its time in handling important subjects with humor, sophistication, and political awareness. Shannon, who was a well-known comic and cabaret performer in San Francisco, could be considered the first character on the transgender spectrum to appear as such on television.[13]

The most important gender relationship in Archie's life is of course with Edith, and in this regard he really does have an intimacy that's missing from other demographic encounters. Perhaps because that sense of distance is missing, he's less a paternalist than a tyrant. This is not simply a matter of Archie's dismissive put-downs of Edith, which include the epithet of "dingbat," his frequent demand that she stifle herself, or his increasingly elaborate routines when she tells run-on stories (which include pantomimes of his loading a revolver and shooting himself in the head, hanging himself, or poisoning himself in self-administered acts of mercy while enduring her tedious narratives). It's also reflected in his incessant demands that dinner be ready when he walks in the door, that his clothes be laundered as per his instructions, and that she be absorbingly attentive when *he's* the one with stories to tell. He is, in short, the quintessence of the male chauvinist pig. Which is something his own daughter frequently points out—and at different points in the series makes her heatedly angry.

But this irreducible reality co-exists alongside a series of others. We'll put aside for the moment why Edith puts up with this abuse, or what she may get in exchange for it (these are topics for the next chapter). The point at hand is that Archie does materially provide for Edith in ways that allow her to do other things beyond the housekeeping that she loves, such as volunteer at a nursing home. In his better moments, the gruff Archie will express his understated but unmistakable affection for her: "You know something Edith? You're a pip. A real pip." Archie is also, notwithstanding moments of temptation, devoted to Edith. In the 1976 episode "Archie's Secret Passion," he panics when she invites an old high school flame of his over for dinner (though their encounter was so forgettable that Edith has to supply the supposed paramour the details Archie told her of what happened all those years ago, which the woman then recounts to Archie to create the flattering illusion that she remembered). In the single most implausible plot development in the whole series, a physically attractive middle-aged waitress (veteran actor Janis Paige) falls for Archie, and he almost has a tryst with her—the two kiss before Archie puts a stop to it. She returns two years later when Archie's partner Harry unwittingly hires her to work at their bar, eager to resume their relationship. But Archie again holds the line.

There are two important dimensions to Archie's marriage to Edith that bear noting. The first is that from the very beginning, Edith has more power than may be immediately apparent, and she's not afraid to assert it when she deems it necessary. We get the first indications of this in the first season of the show, when Edith gets jury duty, parries Archie's demands that she get out of it, and goes on to be the lone holdout for acquittal in a murder case where it turns out the accused is innocent. In a very different fashion, we learn that Archie's bluster is a good deal less effective than it seems when Edith undergoes menopause and becomes the moody one for a change. (Archie is so rattled by the experience that he fearfully asks if she's having menopause again whenever she gets angry in the years that follow.) Edith can get her way when she really wants it, as when she demands Archie abjure a Knicks game with Mike and instead go with her to celebrate their twenty-fifth wedding anniversary in Atlantic City. She's also capable of standing up for herself when she feels wronged. In the 1972 episode "Archie and Edith Alone," he insults her altruistic impulses after he realizes that she let him win at cards, disparagingly calling her names like "Saint Edith" and "Edith the Good." Edith demands, and eventually gets, an apology from him. In the 1973 episode "Archie the Gambler," Edith is furious to learn that Archie has resumed his addictive behavior of betting on horses and gives him an ultimatum: quit gambling or quit the house. He capitulates. Edith's most direct challenge to Archie's authority occurs in the 1975 episode "Edith Breaks Out," when he demands that she stop volunteering at an assisted living facility because he wants her to be a full-time housewife. Edith refuses and prevails in the end by informing Archie she will no longer volunteer—management at the nursing home is so pleased with her work that they've hired her instead. So it is that even this most traditional of housewives enters the paid workforce.

The other key point regarding Archie's relationship with Edith is that it's not static. His general trajectory over the nine seasons of *All in the Family* (and into *Archie Bunker's Place*) is one of a general mellowing of his character. The locus of his evolution is in his marriage, where he is increasingly affectionate and open about his dependency on Edith. At the end of the three-part series in which Archie struggles to overcome unemployment, he turns to Edith before they turn in for the night and asks, "Do you, Edith Baines, take Archie Bunker to be your lawfully bedded husband until you can't take him no more?" Archie also recognizes that Edith's ability to bend him to her will is more than a matter of resolving deadlocks but involves actually shaping his behavior. Angry to learn that, despite his wishes, she has facilitated an African American couple moving in next door, Edith tries to reassure him that it will be just fine. "Listen, you know damn well there are certain things about me that you ain't never going to change," he tells her in angry exasperation. "But you're asking me to make out like I'm gonna!" Edith beams at him. "That's *riiiight!*" she says, a revealing flash of wisdom beneath her often literal-minded conversation (she had just reassured Archie that their new neighbor Polly's husband simply can't be another George Jefferson because his name is Ed). A standing Archie slumps over his chair in despair, Edith strokes him affectionately, and the camera fades out.

By the end of the series, Archie has attained a genuine appreciation for Edith and the pivotal role she plays in his life. In the final episode, "Too Good Edith," Edith takes her adoptive niece Stephanie to the doctor for a vaccination, but the doctor notices a bruise on Edith's leg and quickly realizes she has a serious case of phlebitis. He orders her to stay off her feet, an injunction Edith ignores because Archie needs her to make food at home for the upcoming St. Patrick's Day Party at his bar. She overdoes it and collapses on the stairs, prompting an emergency visit from the doctor, who lashes out at Archie for ignoring the dangers of Edith's medical situation. This is a plausible accusation—the doctor was a childhood friend of Gloria's and knows Archie all too well. Indeed, it would be very easy to imagine the Archie of the early seasons of the show telling Edith to simply tough it out and obey his wishes. And, in truth, he really should have been attentive to Edith's difficulties, which were clear enough even if she didn't disclose them. But Archie is shocked, and sincerely grieved, to learn of Edith's illness. He instantly drops any push to get the party going at the bar. The last scene of the series features Archie at Edith's bedside. His final line in *All in the Family*: "I ain't nothin' without you." When, at the start of the second season of *Archie Bunker's Place*, Edith dies offscreen, Archie is shell-shocked (ironically, one of the people who try to help him and his niece Stephanie through the grieving process is none other than the black neighbor Edith recruited for the Jeffersons' old house). The scene where Archie breaks down after finding Edith's slipper in their bedroom is the most heart-rending moment of the Bunker saga.

Archie Moves On Up

As important as his marriage is in the making of Archie Bunker's character, there are other indications of his evolution as *All in the Family* progresses. One shouldn't exaggerate this; he's still railing against "Buddha, the pope, Marx and Lemons" as well as "godless gooks" through the final season of the show. But he nevertheless demonstrates some capacity to act—or, perhaps more accurately, not to overreact—when confronted with new facts on the ground. Perhaps the most striking indication of this is the 1976 episode "The Draft Dodger," when Mike's friend David joins Archie's friend Pinky for Christmas dinner at the Bunkers. President-elect Jimmy Carter had announced his plan for limited amnesty for those who escaped the draft, which would take effect the following year. David is a draft dodger; Pinky lost his son in the Vietnam War. Archie has been carefully (albeit clumsily) trying to steer the conversation away from Pinky's son when he learns that David avoided serving in the military. He predictably blows his top—until he watches as Pinky reaches out and shakes David's hand in an effort to put the deep wounds of the war aside (the studio audience applauds heartily). Archie, who gets up and leaves the table, is flummoxed by Pinky's act, which is actually progress for him. "I got to work this out," he says to Edith, who tries to coax him to return by arguing that he should follow Pinky's lead. She then adds two crucial words to her plea: "for me?" This brings him back, hesitantly. "When dinner's over, I still gotta work this out," he tells everyone at the table. This is hardly a clear resolution to the conflict, but the very fact that it's an open question rather than a closed one suggests Archie's real, if limited, capacity for growth. It will appear, more clearly and decisively, in a Season 9 episode when he learns that Stephanie's deceased mother was Jewish and gives her a Star of David necklace. His receptivity to the unstinting love the child has been giving him has softened his hard heart.

Most of the discussion of Archie's development as a character focuses on how he grapples with his prejudices. But it makes sense to close this discussion in effect where it began: by looking at Archie on his own terms rather than evaluating him on the basis of how he deals with others. Archie is of course a bundle of prejudices and resentments. But like most people, he has his aspirations too. And in the eighth season of the series, he reaches for his brass ring: the opportunity to become his own boss. He achieves an American Dream of running his own business, and ends the series having achieved upward mobility by moving from the working class to the petit bourgeoisie when his favorite watering hole, Kelsey's Bar, becomes Archie Bunker's Place.

It isn't a pretty process. When Archie visits Kelsey in the hospital at the start of the two-part 1977 episode "Archie Gets the Business," his old friend makes clear he's ready to retire and will sell the bar to the first person who can come up with the requisite $40,000. Archie in effect steals the place out from its bartender, Harry, who also wants to buy it but can't come up with all the cash (he eventually comes in as a partner once it becomes clear that Archie can't succeed without his talents). Archie can come up with the money, but doing so requires him to mortgage the paid-off 704 Hauser Street—a plan that Edith vociferously opposes. So Archie forges her signature on the loan application. Interestingly, it's Mike who quietly comes to Archie's defense when a deeply agitated Edith realizes what's happened. He helps her understand how important buying the bar is to Archie's self-esteem—his manhood, really—and she decides to forgive him. While one can question the plausibility of Archie as a business owner (this is, after all, a man who routinely bungles figures as frequently as he mangles words), Harry is around to steer the ship and Archie Bunker's Place turns out to be a reasonable financial proposition for a man who will never be rich but who will live out the remainder of his years, and the American Century, in relative comfort. As George Jefferson, who has since moved on up to owning a chain of drycleaners and living on the Upper East Side, wryly observes after Archie boasts that he too is a businessman, "It's nice to see a white man make it every once in a while."

And though, in a great many ways, Archie Bunker is Yesterday's Man, there is one way in which he's ahead of the curve. His incomprehension and rejection of liberalism, embodied most fully in his daughter and son-in-law, in effect make him the butt of a great historical joke at which much of the audience for *All in the Family* was happy to laugh—Archie Bunker buttons ("America's Foist Family") and other campaign paraphernalia surfaced in the 1972 and 1976 presidential campaigns.[14] The liberal left has always regarded itself as the vanguard in American society, the articulators of an emergent common sense which the majority will follow. Indeed, *All in the Family* was an active part of that process in the way it depicted race, gender, and other issues in the 1970s. But in an important respect the joke would prove to be on the liberals. Archie makes a favorable passing mention of Ronald Reagan as early as 1972 and tells Mike in 1976 that he favored Reagan over Ford in the 1976 Republican primaries. "And you're going to get Reagan in '80, wise guy!" Most liberals considered that prospect laughable right through most of the 1980 presidential campaign, but Reagan won decisively: the Archie Bunker vote proved larger than a great many Americans expected. It would last longer than a great many Americans expected. Can anyone doubt that Archie would have voted for his fellow Queens native Donald Trump in 2016? Trump, for all his incoherence and departure from the Reagan coalition, is nevertheless part of a coalition that extends back to Archie Bunker in thumbing his nose at the secular pieties of the left.

The post-Bunker project of the American right has been understood by its champions as a restoration of lost but valuable truisms of the world before the 1960s: those were the days. As far as liberals and progressives have been concerned, the conservative quest has not been a matter of restoration but rather nostalgia: a longing to impose a world that never was. The truth of modern conservatism is somewhere in between. The lack of certainty where—and the striking success of *All in the Family* in inhabiting that ambiguous space between—makes it a great work of art. And a valuable artifact in revealing the deceptive simplicities of American history.

7

A Really Great Housewife

The Character of Edith Baines Bunker

History is a process of remembering and forgetting. Most people proceed through their lives on what academic historians call "presentist" terms—they care about the past insofar as it clarifies their immediate circumstances, and they tend to measure and judge the past by the prevailing metrics and moral standards of their own times. As they grow older and realize that those metrics and moral standards shift beneath their feet like tides at the seashore, they may be more willing to consider the ways in which newly revealed facts (or, more commonly, newly rearranged facts) change perceptions, and may find themselves rediscovering that which receded from view now seems important, even pressing. So it is that the past keeps changing.

The process of forgetting is more elusive. Remembering happens gradually or forcefully, but arrives in one's consciousness as a realization. Forgetting, however, is something you don't notice. It tends not to happen all at once. You may for one reason or another be reminded of that which you've overlooked, acknowledge it, and then refocus your gaze until it disappears from your field of vision entirely. It may re-emerge as circumstances change—or not. This is a necessary and inevitable process; both as individuals and societies, it is not possible to remember everything. In part, that's because we have to make choices of one kind or another, and there's no point in dwelling on what's left behind. Indeed, there may be necessary healing involved, as old adversaries put aside their differences—and pass away, making room for new ones.

Here's something that as a society we're in the process of forgetting: what it meant to be a housewife. Most people have a reasonably good idea what the word means, though it's usually denoted in other ways, like "stay-at-home mother" or "homemaker"—terms that implicitly contrast such a status with women whose labors take the form of wage earning, because most adult women are, whatever else they may be, employees of some kind. "Housewife" has a dowdy, even disreputable, air. It's something few girls today want to be, nor something her parents—especially her mother—want her to be.

There are some very good reasons for this. One, of course, is ideological: the rise of feminism, a force that looms large over many plotlines in *All in the Family*. Another, not wholly separate from it, is economic. The steady surge of women in the paid labor force in the second half of the twentieth century was to a significant extent a reflection of the relative decline in men's wages, a falloff whose impact was softened by the addition of a second paycheck. Even if women *wanted* to be housewives today, relatively few could afford it. Those that are tend to be affluent—and typically outsource many of what were once the core tasks of that occupation with nannies, housekeepers, takeout, and a host of labor-saving devices.

This is a curious state of affairs. Housewifery was once commonly regarded as honorable and widespread. Now it's not either. In 2018, the *New York Times* reported that no more than 2 percent of high school girls since 1985 said they wanted to become homemakers, even if most went on to say they still wished to be mothers.[1] Given this remarkable decline, it's worth taking a moment to trace how the concept of housewifery emerged before considering the case of Edith Bunker—what she represented, how the values she embodied have receded, and the challenge of appreciating her role in *All in the Family*—as well as the role of homemaking in the world at large.

It's essential to note that while the association between women and domesticity is centuries old, at least in the West, the specific role of housewife has some fairly specific historical contours. It's a creation of the Victorian era, which is to say a product of the industrial revolution. Before the mid-nineteenth century, work—in the broadest sense of that term—was centered in the home, which, more often than not, meant a family farm. Men and women often worked side by side (or, at any rate, on the same piece of property, whether or not they actually owned it), and while there was typically a sexual division of labor, there was also a certain permeability in the line between work, family, and domestic life. The rise of factory labor fostered a new and sharper sexual division of labor, in which men worked in factories while women worked at home—or, at any rate, this was how it was remembered. In fact, women and children also worked in factories, among other settings. But there's no denying the reality that home and work became less integrated than they used to be.

And this, in turn, fostered the formation of a new ideal—one typically accessible only to elite women and those of a newly emergent middle class—of what gender historians have subsequently named separate sphere ideology: an idealized vision of family in which men and women each had specific gendered roles. Generally speaking, men were responsible for provision and protection, and women for nurturance and moral grounding. These roles could overlap, especially in the realm of child rearing. Women could also sometimes play an important, if circumscribed, role in public life, providing valuable social capital in their communities. Much of that social capital has since been lost because fewer women now have the time or inclination to sustain institutions like the League of Women Voters, parent-teacher associations, and other institutions that provide crucial glue in the nation's civic life.[2]

Again, the framework here was an ideal more than a reality, and as such was never universal. But it's one that became plausible and attractive to a widening circle of Americans in the twentieth century as wages began to rise and a new stratum of white-collar office jobs offered at least a veneer of respectability for a growing segment of the U.S. population. As a man who worked on the docks and drove a taxicab, Archie Bunker lacked this middle-class respectability. But because he worked in a sector of the labor market that was unionized, his wages were high enough to support a wife and child—a wife who could work in the home and raise that child full time. This is what it meant to be a good provider, and what allowed Archie to compete in the marriage market (a market in which he was decidedly lacking when it came to any number of other attributes). "To be a good provider was a kind of holy grail for me," Lear later explained of his vision for Archie, a vision grounded in the Great Depression, when such men were hard to find.[3] A big part of the reason why this mattered is because men like Archie made being a housewife a legitimate *aspiration*, one realized by millions of women in the middle third of the twentieth century. That some of them found the role confining, even oppressive—a reality captured by Betty Friedan's classic 1963 polemic *The Feminine Mystique*—is without question. But this view was never universal among midcentury women and was not embraced by Edith Bunker. Even well into the twenty-first century, when the economic foundations of the old gender order have shifted decisively, many men and women still find themselves longing for a world when men were the primary economic providers.[4]

Edith's Mysterious Choice

Edith's backstory in *All in the Family* is less sharply etched than Archie's but is reasonably clear—if not in factual terms, then certainly in affective ones. She was born as Edith Baines in 1927, but it's unclear where; most of her extended family is based in New Jersey at the time of the show, a place Archie mocks almost as much as he does her kin, none of whom seem to like him. Wherever she was born, Edith was in Queens by the time of her adolescence. She attended the fictive Fillmore High School, where she apparently overlapped with the older Archie; this is a bit puzzling because he's on the record as attending Flushing High School, though it's possible he switched schools before dropping out. He was overseas by the time she graduated in 1943 and was writing her love letters by then. After he returned from the war, Edith worked at the Hercules Plumbing Company in 1946, a job she recounts in characteristically numbing detail to one of her classmates at her thirtieth reunion. It's unclear exactly when she married Archie, but it appears to be about two years later. Gloria was born eleven months after that, by which point she appears to have settled into what would become her vocation as a full-time housewife.

The picture one gets of Archie's childhood is one of deprivation and abuse. Edith's, by contrast, appears to be one of deep and wide affections. She never seems to run out of cousins, uncles, or aunts to talk about or visit, and her ability to play the piano suggests at least the trappings of middle-class respectability (her mother was apparently disappointed that she didn't turn out to be much of a dancer, a clue that her life wasn't entirely a charmed one). Such advantages may help explain her exceptionally sunny temperament, though that's at least to some degree an independent variable—plenty of affluent people have miserable personalities, and plenty of people with miserable childhoods have sunny personalities. Still, it does seem that a deep stock of happy memories has helped Edith go through life with an enviable disposition.

The big mystery—really the biggest of the entire show—is just what she sees in Archie. Edith's parents didn't approve of him, nor do any of her relatives, among them the formidable Maude, who appear in various episodes over the years. Then and now, many a viewer can fairly flinch at the way he treats her—his sexist sense of entitlement, his routine put-downs, his appalling insensitivity to her needs and interests—and see that he doesn't deserve her.

To put it bluntly, the simplest explanation for Edith's attachment to Archie is that she's stupid. Certainly, there are many signifiers indicating Edith's lack of sophistication: her accent, her slowness to get a joke, her tendency to cite magazines like the *Reader's Digest*—an uneducated person's idea of refinement—as a source of authority. (She's also fond of *Marcus Welby, M.D.*, a popular television show of the 1970s that starred Robert Young as a doctor who dispensed bromides along with prescriptions.)[5] Archie, by contrast, reads lurid publications like the *National Enquirer*, which he sees as a source of news the liberal elite tries to hide. But Edith has a middlebrow instinct for self-improvement that sets her apart from Archie, only one of a number of ways that she seeks, and knows, things that he doesn't.

A second explanation for Edith casting her lot with Archie has to do with the aforementioned marriage market. Again to be blunt: Edith is lacking in the most obvious competitive resources. She doesn't come from money. She isn't well schooled. She's pleasant-looking but hardly arresting. The same could be said for Archie in all these cases, of course; but as noted he does have a capacity for hard work that he could trade for a spouse. Archie may well have been the best Edith could do from an economic standpoint. But did she really have to marry such a jerk? And did she have to be so cheerful in tolerating him? Even Gloria, whose very existence depended on it, is regularly appalled by her mother's willingness to take Archie's abuse.

A third explanation—initially perhaps the least convincing, but increasingly compelling the more one watches the show—is that Archie and Edith are bound by mutual erotic magnetism. This is something the longtime television and print journalist Sander Vanocur noticed in a 1976 piece for the *Washington Post*: "A strong sexuality cements their relationship. It is a sexuality based on the deepest kind of love."[6] This is a point that Carroll O'Connor in particular emphasized in his wrangles with writers on the show, sometimes objecting to their penchant to use the couple's prudery as a source of cheap laughs.[7] To be sure, both Archie and Edith share a sense of furtive embarrassment about sex, in marked contrast to Mike and Gloria, and both couples have awkward conversations about sexual problems at different points in the show. One of the longest-running jokes in the series involves Archie's tendency to misinterpret affectionate gestures from Edith as unwanted sexual advances. But both were part of a generation for whom marriage was the only legitimate basis for sexual intercourse, and the bonds they forged at that formative moment prove durable, especially since neither has much in the way of alternative prospects when the show airs, with both characters well into middle age, though, like Archie, Edith also has an ardent suitor whose advances she kindly but firmly declines in the 1978 episode "Love Comes to the Butcher."[8] The affection between Edith and Archie, sexual and otherwise, becomes more evident as the series proceeds.

For all its receptivity to any number of sexual arrangements, *All in the Family* is finally a paean to the Bunkers' heterosexual monogamy. One affirmation of this comes in a backhanded form in the 1972 episode "The Bunkers and the Swingers," in which Edith responds to a personal ad in a magazine she found on the subway calling for "mature lonely couples seeking new friends." Gloria and Mike realize the implications of the text in a way Edith does not, but are too embarrassed to spell it out to her and are in a hurry to leave for the ballet. Because of a misunderstanding about the date, the swingers—played by veteran *AITF* trouper Vincent Gardenia and Rue McClanahan, soon to have a supporting role in the *AITF* spin-off *Maude* and a starring role in *Golden Girls*—arrive earlier than expected. It's important to note here that the writers of the show emphasize the goodwill, generosity, and humor of the couple, who mistakenly believe Edith and Archie are spouse-swappers, setting up a classic comic scenario of misunderstanding that would result in a 1973 Emmy Award for Outstanding Writing in a Comedy Series. It falls to Louise Jefferson, who has dropped by to borrow a casserole dish, to explain to Edith what's going on when Edith shows her the ad. When Archie finally realizes what's happening, he responds with unforgiving hostility. But it's McClanahan who steals the show with a remarkably nuanced piece of acting in which she reveals a vein of sorrow in the couple's search to do something to save their marriage. The Bunkers, however, are on firmer ground.

Edith, then, does appear to have her reasons for casting her lot with Archie. But other mysteries remain about the character. This seemingly most transparent of figures is finally the most intriguing of them all, and the mystery deepens when one looks at the origins of the role and how Edith made her way to the screen.

A Gift for Happiness

In Norman Lear's memoir, *Even This I Get to Experience*, it's clear that the driving engine of what became *All in the Family* was Archie: his roots in the personality of Lear's father, Lear's desire to capture and represent the world-view of a bigot, and Lear's struggles with Carroll O'Connor over the shadings of Archie's character. Edith, while important, was secondary. Lear worked with a prominent casting director, Marion Dougherty, to find the four leads, but knew on his own that Jean Stapleton, a well-established stage and screen character actor with whom he had worked on his 1971 feature *Cold Turkey*, would be a good prospect. Stapleton and O'Connor had worked together in an episode of the 1962 TV drama *The Defenders* (she played a hotel worker who testified against O'Connor's character, a murderer), and the two knew and respected each other, even if they weren't particularly close. It became clear that the two enjoyed unusually good chemistry, and got their parts long before the roles of Mike and Gloria were settled. Stapleton, more than many of those involved in the show early on, was confident it was going to work.[9]

Lear made clear to Stapleton that "my intention, first and foremost, was to entertain, not to raise eyebrows."[10] This is something she took to heart. Unlike O'Connor, she was not inclined to second-guess the writers, directors, and producers with whom she worked, toward whom she was tirelessly complimentary. And while O'Connor took an expansive interest in both representing and critiquing Archie's worldview—in his 1973 interview with *Playboy* O'Connor anatomized every aspect of his character from his diet to his views on capital punishment—Stapleton seemed to hold Edith at arm's length. Like O'Connor, she was very different in real life from the person she portrayed; but while there could be something downright obsessive in the Archie-Carroll relationship, Stapleton was very clear in her own mind that Edith dwelled in a world of make-believe. Though Stapleton became active in women's issues late in life, she described herself as apolitical for much of her career and never seemed particularly reflective in talking about her politics or her art (in her 2013 obituary, the *New York Times* described her as "a confirmed if not necessarily outspoken feminist").[11] Actually, there's something almost dispiriting about the way Stapleton talks about Edith in the extended interview she conducted with the Academy of American Television many years later. The words she uses to describe Edith— "compassionate," "not too bright," "a great sense of wisdom and heart"—seem downright prosaic.[12] One waits in vain for her to offer the key to the character and how she unlocked it.

What's a little jarring about this is how uncontrovertibly evident it was that, good writing notwithstanding, Stapleton played a decisive role in embodying one of the truly great characters in the history of television. It's mystifying how she did it; the daughter of an opera singer and a billboard salesman, Stapleton demurred when asked if her character was modeled on anyone in particular. But her transformation into Edith—the high nasal voice; the cantering gait; the slow but glowing smile, threaded with complexities that became richer with time—was simply wondrous.

It didn't happen all at once. In *Till Death Us Do Part*, Alf Garnett's wife Else (played by Dandy Nicholls) gave as good as she got in dealing with a cranky husband. Edith was never exactly caustic, but could be clear-eyed in cutting Archie down to size, as when in the pilot episode she punctuates a lecture Archie gives on the importance of pulling oneself up by one's bootstraps by noting that Archie himself got his first job through a family connection. But Stapleton and the writers felt their way toward a different approach for the character, Stapleton borrowing the high-pitched voice from a character she played in the 1958 musical *Damn Yankees*, and adopting a more oblique strategy for responding to Archie that was less a matter of fighting back than sidestepping his criticism.

What evolved was a character with a gift for happiness. This was evident in a number of ways. One was Edith's obvious pleasure in her daily routine, which included running to greet Archie when he came home at the end of his workday (that this was something he also enjoyed could be inferred from his displeasure whenever anything stopped her from doing so). Edith was also deeply fond of music, and in particular loved to sing. Indeed, she was prone to erupt into song any chance she got. What made this especially funny is that she was a terrible singer (Stapleton by contrast was a fine singer who performed in multiple musicals), something abundantly evident every week in the opening credits when she sang "Those Were the Days" and veered into the screeching, off-key line, "And you knew who you *weeeeeere* then!" Edith's musical taste comes from the American songbook; over the years of the show her repertoire included Johnny Mercer's "Glow Worm," Clarence Williams's "I Wish I Could Shimmy Like My Sister Kate," and "Zip-a-Dee-Doo-Dah," the Allie Wrubel–Ray Gilbert song from the 1946 Disney musical *Song of the South*. One delightful moment of the show occurred in the 1976 episode "Mike and Gloria's Houseguests" when she, Archie, Mike, and Gloria mark time during a blackout by breaking into a spontaneous harmonized version of the vaudeville classic "Down by the Old Mill Stream."

Perhaps the most entertaining moment of Edith's musical life unfolds at the opening of the 1973 episode "Archie and the Kiss," when she bounds downstairs and plants a big kiss on Mike's cheek for no apparent reason. Intrigued, he asks her why, and Edith responds by saying that it's because it's Henry Mancini's birthday—at which point Edith breaks into a cater-wauling version of his hit "Moon River." What follows is one of her charac-teristically digressive stories that culminates in a memory of Archie taking her to Radio City Music Hall in 1961 to see *Breakfast at Tiffany's*, in which the song was featured, and out for ice cream at Schraffts (once a prominent New York City landmark) in an evening that culminates in a kiss—a recol-lection at which Edith grows bashful. Mike is charmed, but the mood is bro-ken when an irritable Archie returns home from work and slams the front door. When Mike objects to the disruption, he slams it again. And when Edith comes out of the kitchen to greet him with the news that it's Henry Mancini's birthday, he slams it a third time for emphasis. But nothing will dampen Edith's good cheer.

A Socially Connected Woman

The most striking, and profound, manifestation of Edith's capacity for joy comes from her interactions with other people. It's here that Stapleton's acting—as well as the string of minor characters who shuttle through the Bunker home over the years—is decisive. Over and over again in *All in the Family*, one witnesses Edith *seeing* people, and their sheer pleasure in being recognized in a profoundly empathetic way. This is something that happened routinely on the show whenever Louise Jefferson or Irene Lorenzo dropped by. But the most comically moving illustration of the point is vividly made in the "Class Reunion" episode of 1973, when Edith and her cousin Amelia speculate about whether their classmate of thirty years ago, the great Buck Evans, will be attending. "God he was beautiful," Amelia says three different times in a discussion about the upcoming event. Edith herself had a crush on him. "They used to call me 'Who's that with Buck Evans?'" she notes. The joke—and it's literally a very big one—is that the Buck Evans who arrives at the event is virtually unrecognizable in his obesity and baldness. But not to Edith: "I'd know you anywhere!" she exclaims, the two beaming at each other. "Your eyes, your blue eyes are just the same. I can still see inside ya. Archie, ain't he beautiful?" (Archie, needless to say, is a good deal less impressed—and much relieved.)

The greatest examples of Edith's ability to connect with other people occurred at moments of death when she was on hand to help family, friends, and neighbors make an existential transition. There are three examples worth considering in some detail.

The first is a beautifully written 1976 episode, "Archie Finds a Friend," which focuses on Archie's endless fascination with get-rich schemes—in this case centering on the man who runs the local watch repair shop, Mr. Bernstein (Jack Gilford), who has developed a device to remotely ring doorbells. Archie is convinced that this is a million-dollar proposition—in large measure because Mr. Bernstein is Jewish, and Jews presumably are infallible when it comes to making money—and is eager to invest despite Edith's skepticism. When Bernstein visits 704 Hauser and learns of this, he offers Archie an easy out, but Archie won't hear of it. It turns out that the device has a glitch in the form of a grinding sound, which Bernstein leaves to fix and then returns having done so. They're all so happy that Bernstein, who has a heart condition, overdoes it a bit and has to sit down. It also turns out that there's another problem: the device now rings all the doorbells on the street. Bernstein, who is anxious, frustrated, and suffused with self-doubt—"Bunker, let's face it: it's possible that people like you and me were never meant to be rich"—apparently has a heart attack. Archie acts with unusual empathy to make him comfortable, while Edith calls Bernstein's doctor, who tells him that the situation is serious and that he'll be right over. She then goes over to comfort Bernstein, gazing at him kindly and telling him that the device is worthy and will eventually work well. "It's your dream and you gotta follow it," she tells him. Bernstein is moved by the depth of Edith's compassion. "Mrs. Bunker, for you I'd like to make the bells ring all over the world like Christmas Eve," he says to her. She leaves to get him something to drink, and in the interim he dies. This is something Edith understands before Archie does, and she now has to comfort him as he steps outside onto the porch. Edith notes they never learned Mr. Bernstein's first name; when she asks Archie whether he thinks he can fix the device, he says he isn't smart enough. The episode ends with Archie using the device to trigger all the doorbells in the neighborhood as a tribute to Bernstein.

A second example of Edith's capacity for empathy—one that triumphs over her ignorance—is evident in the 1977 episode "Cousin Liz." She and Archie have checked into a hotel for the funeral of her cousin, a schoolteacher who never married but lived for twenty-five years in a house with another teacher named Veronica, who organized the funeral. Edith is Liz's closest living relative, and as such Archie hopes that maybe the Bunkers will come into a little money, a hope that rises when he learns that a silver tea set in the house is worth thousands of dollars. Veronica pulls Edith into her bedroom and explains that she would very much like to keep the tea set as a memento, as she and Liz used it frequently. Edith resists; it's an heirloom that has been in her family for a hundred years. As she goes on to recount this history in typical detail, Veronica turns away in obvious pain, leading Edith to cut off her story midstream. Veronica tries to explain to her that she and Liz were fond of each other, *very* fond of each other, loved each other very much—and Edith simply doesn't get it. "It was like a marriage," Veronica says, trying again. "A marriage? It couldn't be. I mean you and cousin Liz was both—" whereupon Edith finally grasps that her cousin and Veronica were lovers. It's a long, painful realization, full of Edith's "ohs," reminiscent of her discovery that Archie's niece Linda and Lionel had gone on an interracial date.[13] But her shock fades as she processes this unexpected information.

"I wonder why she [Liz] never mentioned it," she muses.

"Do you think we would have been allowed to work as schoolteachers?" Veronica replies. The question of whether gay people should be allowed to work with children was a source of major controversy in the 1970s; a crusade against it was led by the antigay activist Anita Bryant. At the time the episode aired in the fall of 1977, there was a proposition on the ballot in California to bar gay people from teaching. It was rerun the night before the election; the bill was defeated. The episode later won an Emmy for its script. "Oh God. That's one of my favorites," Lear said three decades later.[14]

Edith can't fathom why Liz and Veronica's sexuality would be relevant to their profession. "It doesn't affect the brain, does it?" she asks, genuinely puzzled. Veronica chuckles at her ingenuousness.

Edith moves on to the emotional implications of what she's learned. "Oh, Veronica, I wish you hadn't told me about this."

Veronica understandably interprets this remark as an expression of distaste about the lesbian relationship. "So do I," she replies, disgusted, getting up to walk away.

Edith, realizing that she's unintentionally offended Veronica, pulls her back.

"Oh no. I didn't mean it like that. I mean it's so sad. It must have been terrible loving somebody like that and not being able to talk about it," Edith says, intuiting the emotional cost of a closeted gay life. "You can have the tea set. I mean, it belongs to you. You're really her next of kin."

The obstacle of course will be Archie. He grasps more quickly than Edith does that Liz was a lesbian, but can't understand why that means Edith shouldn't get the tea set. "Because she deserves it," Edith explains. Archie resists, and threatens to take Veronica to court for the right to the tea set—something Veronica says won't happen because she can't afford the risk that she'd be outed in a legal proceeding and lose her job. It's at this point that Edith remonstrates with him heatedly, her pleas culminating with the statement, "Archie, I can't believe you'd do anything that mean." Called to his better angels, Archie relents. "You always say the one thing that forces me to make the wrong move," he complains as they leave (though Archie pockets the sugar tongs from the tea set, figuring he can use them for ice cubes).

A Stubborn Goodness

Edith's ability to instinctively fuse empathy and morality was never more evident than in the 1979 episode "Edith Gets Fired." Here she pays a hospital visit to a critically ill patient from the nursing home where she works, who has just recovered from a near-death experience. The woman, however, is disappointed she didn't die. A widow, she saw her husband beckoning to her as her life ebbed away, and is now marooned among the living, where her fearful daughter won't come visit. She explains to Edith that she loves and forgives her child. When Edith asks whether there's anything she can do, the woman responds by asking Edith to hold her hand. Understanding what's happening, Edith places both hands on that of the dying woman and decides not to summon a nurse. In the following scene, Edith is in an office, where, amid her daughter's weeping, the woman's son-in-law demands to know how she could have been allowed to die. The director of the nursing home fires Edith, which is a grievous personal loss: she loves her job. But the wisdom of her choice becomes clear when the daughter comes to her house to apologize for her husband, and learns that her mother was at peace with her and the world, a gift Edith gives her that the woman fully appreciates.

Edith's ethical compass is as strong as her emotional one, and serves her in similarly good stead. We see it, for example, in the 1971 episode "Edith's Accident," when she accidentally dents a car with a can of cling peaches and, to Archie's alarm, leaves a note on the car so that the owner can be paid for repairs. It turns out the car belongs to the local parish priest, Father Majeski (Bernard Hughes, who will make a couple appearances on *All in the Family*), which doesn't mollify Archie, who schemes to prevent an expensive repair bill, not realizing the hefty price he's quoted by a mechanic is actually for other repairs (Father Majeski ultimately refuses to take any money from Archie, appalled by his parsimony). Edith's honesty can also be quite funny, as in the classic 1978 episode "The Commercial," which takes places in a local Laundromat. An unsuspecting Edith is approached by an actor who offers her a princely sum of $50 for Archie's shirt. She agrees—a little reluctantly, as it's Archie's favorite Mickey Mouse souvenir from Disney World—and watches in horror as the actor tears it up and stains it with condiments. Her reaction is so priceless that the director of the commercial and the ad account executive who have been in hiding come forward to offer her a job for a detergent commercial on the spot. The problem is that it will be Edith's job to testify that the detergent is better than its competitors, and this proves impossible for her to do, to the dismay of the crew—and, especially, Archie, who senses gold in his wife's TV career, which he's eager to (mis)manage.

Edith's decency is more than an amusing quirk; it's also something that she actively asserts even when it displeases others. We see this in the first season of the show, when she resists peer pressure from fellow jurors and holds out to prevent the conviction of what turns out to be an innocent man. And while Edith may put up with all kinds of mistreatment from Archie, she draws a firm line when she believes doing so may hurt others. So it is, for example, that she goes forward with jury duty against his wishes. She can also be assertive when she needs to be. "You mean you're gonna disobey your husband?" an incredulous Archie asks when he learns that the Bunkers will not be inheriting cousin Liz's tea set. "Yeah," she replies. "Case closed." (The audience applauds.) When Archie asserts that Veronica and Liz will have to answer to God for what he regards as deviant behavior, Edith responds by saying "He's God. You ain't."

Edith's worldview is rooted in her religious faith—a faith with some fairly specific contours. As noted in chapter 6, Archie is a religious man after a fashion, but his vision of God is essentially authoritarian: religion is a source of order—not doctrine, ritual, or, for that matter, moral behavior. Edith, who attends church services regularly, has little interest in the trappings of faith either, but it's clear that her vision of God is one that offers comfort, strength, and guidance. She's ecumenical at heart, greatly enjoying the Catholic services she attends with Irene Lorenzo and her nun sister. God is a wellspring of love in her life—love she experiences and love she shares.

Imperfect Improvements

A character like Edith is easy to sentimentalize—or dismiss. Indeed, sometimes the characters of *All in the Family* themselves did, as when Archie contemptuously called her "Saint Edith" in a moment of irritation when she let him win at cards. But the writers on the show were aware of this perception and took active steps to complicate the character with situations and behavior that provided crucial ballast. In fact, Edith was not a saint. She could be exasperating in her digressions, and she could lose her temper, as she did when she slapped Archie in the face in the 1973 episode "Archie the Gambler" (the audience reacts with shock, shouts, and laughter when she does). The character of Edith is fully human and has very human reactions when faced with very human challenges.

Like, for example, the prospect of cancer. This was the focus of the 1973 episode "Edith's Christmas Story," in which Edith discovers a lump in her breast that may be malignant. She tries to keep it to herself but is so obviously distracted that Gloria senses something must be wrong, and so Edith tells her (Mike overhears). Edith is emphatic that Archie must not know. Her friend Irene tries to comfort her in a kitchen-table conversation, which leads Edith to express her fear that she may need a mastectomy, which frightens her because she's afraid that Archie will no longer find her desirable. Irene tells her that her fears are misplaced: a mastectomy will not be a big deal. "Believe me," she says, reassuringly.

"You don't know," Edith replies, a rare case of dismissiveness on her part as she gets up to resume her ironing.

Irene gets up to follow her. "That's just the point, Edith: I do know." Edith shakes her head, irritated by what she regards as Irene's presumptuousness.

Irene grabs her arm and speaks more firmly: "I know." In the ensuing conversation, Irene explains that she had a mastectomy six years earlier, and her marriage to her husband Frank did not suffer. This disclosure helps Edith face what's ahead. The plan to keep her pending surgical procedure a secret from Archie founders when Irene accidentally reveals Edith is having a biopsy, at which point Archie rushes to the hospital. "Jeez, you're my wife, no matter what happens," he says at her bedside, which Edith regards as the nicest thing Archie ever said to her (clearly, the threshold is low). The lump turns out to be a benign cyst, and Edith is fine—except that in her excitement about this outcome she jumps from an examination table and breaks her ankle. After the episode aired, there were widespread reports of a surge in mammogram appointments and requests for the episode from community service organizations.[15]

Edith faces a more immediate existential threat in the two-part 1977 episode "Edith's 50th Birthday Party," in which she finds herself alone in the house—her family and friends are gathered next door for a surprise party in her honor—when a rapist knocks on the door. He presents himself as a police officer investigating sexual assault until he sees the coast is clear and makes his intentions known. Edith may be sweetness incarnate in most situations, but she resists the assault with every means at her disposal. After an extended sequence of terror—a striking departure from the norms of the sitcom—Edith seizes an opportunity to run into the kitchen, pulls a cake out of the oven, and shoves the hot pan in the rapist's face, allowing her to escape. Her ordeal is not over, however, and amid her extended emotional upheaval it takes a while for Edith to finally do what she had counseled Gloria, who herself sustained a sexual assault in the 1973 episode "Gloria the Victim," to do: report the case to the police. The rapist is ultimately apprehended—and Archie never refers to Edith as "dingbat" again.[16] (Gloria's assault is discussed in chapter 9.)

One final example of Edith's human frailty is worth noting here. It involves Beverly La Salle, the transvestite who appeared in 1975 and 1976 episodes (see chapter 6). In yet another two-part Christmas episode—*All in the Family* seems to save its most socially impactful episodes for the holidays—Beverly returns in 1977 to take the Bunkers out to dinner, inviting them to attend her performance at Carnegie Hall. But when Mike walks Beverly to a cabstand before the show, the two are assaulted; Mike is hospitalized and Beverly is killed in a hate crime. Edith is shattered by this senseless act of violence and finds herself questioning her religious faith. Emotionally and physically listless, she has trouble going through the motions for Christmas dinner, clearly grief-stricken as Archie insists on saying grace. ("A. Bunker here," he begins his prayer. "As you know the Christmas season is once again at our throats.") Edith can't bear to go through the motions. "I can't, Archie," she says, getting up from the table. "My heart ain't in it."

Mike follows her into the kitchen, with Archie wondering what on earth an atheist will have to offer to a woman enduring a spiritual crisis. What follows is a conversation that clearly alludes to the 1973 episode "Games Bunkers Play," in which Edith helps Mike through an emotional crisis (more on this in chapter 8). "I'm sorry I spoiled Christmas," Edith tells him. "You better go back and eat your Christmas dinner." When Mike says he's not hungry, Edith does a double take: Mike's appetite is a running gag on the show. "You can't depend on anything no more," Edith says, a listlessly delivered joke that becomes yet another expression of despair.

"Ma, who you mad at?" Mike asks.

"I'm mad at God," Edith replies. She goes on to explain: "All I know is that Beverly was killed for who he was and we're all supposed to be God's children. It don't make sense. I don't understand nothing no more."

Mike asks Edith if there were any subjects she hated in school. A bit confused, she answers: algebra. "But you didn't drop out of school, did you?" he notes. "Maybe we're not supposed to understand everything all at once." He goes on to say that "if there is a God, you're one of the most understanding people he ever made." He then delivers the decisive line: "We need you." Mike kisses her, holds her hand, and leaves her to her thoughts.

This is apparently what Edith needs and she returns to the table, declaring she wants to say grace, which she does with another uncharacteristically dry joke by imitating Archie: "Dear God, E. Bunker here." She proceeds: "I'm sorry that I don't understand everything at once. But I am thankful."

She goes on to give thanks for Mike and Gloria and their grandson Joey. "You forgot somebody, Edith," Archie notes tersely. Edith duly gives thanks for Archie and then proceeds to a long list of people she's thankful for, which leads Archie to mockingly seek refuge by trying to stuff his head into the Christmas turkey. The episode fades out with Edith continuing what has become an incantation of gratitude. Norman Lear considered the episode "the best show we've ever made."[17]

A Woman of Power

The examples cited here have been ones where Edith has shown signs of human frailty, in part to illustrate that she is a three-dimensional character. But as often as not—and increasingly as *All in the Family* proceeded—she is a source of strength and wisdom for those around her, not in some unwitting or instinctive way but as a matter of considered judgment.

A good example of this wisdom is evident in the 1973 episode "The Battle of the Month." Gloria returns home from work on her birthday, feeling poorly because she is menstruating—probably the first time the topic had been broached in a sitcom, or, for that matter, any other broadcast television show. The situation is aggravated by Archie's insensitivity to hearing about it, which leads to a string of humorous euphemisms ("it's mother nature come to call"; "a visit from a friend"; or, in the case of an old acquaintance of Edith's who had eleven children, "the blessing"). Gloria grows angry at Archie for his relentless sexism, and angry at Edith, whom she calls "a doormat," "a zero," and "a nothing" for putting up with it—which results in a rare case of Edith feeling truly insulted and showing it. The family arguments escalate and by 3 A.M. have enveloped Mike and Gloria, who have erupted into a shouting match triggered by Mike's statement that he won't take Gloria's criticisms of him seriously because he knows she's on her period. She ends up hitting him, a moment Archie witnesses (and says was worth getting up for). Finally, in the middle of the maelstrom, Edith demands that everyone sit down and listen to her, a command that all obey. She proceeds with what initially seems another of her circuitous anecdotes, this one involving maple syrup, but it's actually a pointed story about how her parents had a trivial disagreement over breakfast that escalated into a vicious argument. They didn't speak for three weeks, and even after that their marriage was never the same. "So before you two start saying things to each other that you'll never take back, stop and think how much you really mean to each other." Whether it's the words or the emotional fervor with which she says them, Mike and Gloria do step back from the brink. Gloria, belatedly recognizing the power of her mother's maternal authority, praises her by saying she's something. Even Archie, in a rare moment of praise, seconds that emotion, calling her "something else."

Which brings us back to the main point here. Over the course of *All in the Family*, we see Edith Bunker as a woman, a citizen (we learn, by the way, that unlike her husband, she voted for Democrat Jimmy Carter in 1976), and an employee, as well as in many other social roles, especially that of friend. But the core of her identity—the source of power and satisfaction in her life—is that of a housewife. That few of us would choose such a role for ourselves with the same degree of alacrity should not blind us to the value of that identity in the past, and help us value those who uphold its fragments and legacy in the present. Edith's sense of awareness, and her importance, grows over the course of the series. But her identity remains grounded in what can fairly be called her vocation.

A vocation that, in the final season of the show, gets reaffirmed in a new way. Just as Archie gets a new lease on life by buying a bar toward the end of the series, Edith gets one by effectively gaining a second child. In the 1976 episode "Gloria's False Alarm," during which Mike is panicked because it (incorrectly) appears that Gloria is pregnant again, Edith reveals to Gloria that Edith's doctor told her it would not be safe to bear another child after Gloria was born. So when Edith's widowed alcoholic cousin Floyd brings his nine-year-old daughter Stephanie (Danielle Brisebois) to the Bunkers and asks them to take the child off his hands for a visit of suspiciously vague duration, Edith jumps at the chance, overriding Archie's resistance. By this point, Mike, Gloria, and Joey have relocated to California, and having another child in the house will allow Edith to resume her role as mother for a child who desperately needs one. (It may also help Edith compensate for the loss of her job at the nursing home.) The bond Edith and Stephanie forge is instinctive and powerful, and provides a graceful coda for the show. In the process, Edith prods Archie to embrace his own role as a surrogate father, in effect preparing him to be the primary parent when Edith herself would no longer be in the picture.

Letting Edith Go

Which, by the late 1970s, was something Jean Stapleton was increasingly eager to see happen. By 1978, the only member of the prime quartet of actors who had such interest in continuing with *All in the Family* was O'Connor (who, ironically, had been the most likely of them to complain and quit in the early years of the show), though CBS executives liked its strong ratings and advertising revenue and thus wanted to see it return that fall. But Lear was also among those who believed the show had run its course, particularly after Rob Reiner and Sally Struthers followed through on their plans to leave at the end of the eighth season in 1977–1978. "It seemed like a natural stopping place," he said.[18]

Out of deference to the network and O'Connor, Lear agreed to allow a final season of *All in the Family* in 1978–1979 to transition to *Archie Bunker's Place* in 1979–1980, and Stapleton agreed to appear as Edith in a few episodes (there was also a two-part Thanksgiving episode in the fall of 1979 that featured a reprise of all four main leads). The final episode of *AITF*, "Too Good Edith," focused on Edith's phlebitis and carried with it intimations of death (see the analysis of this episode in chapter 6). It was initially unclear how Stapleton's character would make an exit, but after extensive discussions it was decided that Edith would die offscreen in her sleep between the first and second seasons of *Archie Bunker's Place*, and that the first two episodes of the show's new season would focus on Archie's bereavement.

Stapleton looked toward her departure unsentimentally. "You know, I really don't feel anything at all," she told the TV critic Tom Shales in 1980, after Edith's departure was announced. "It's like talking about something that really doesn't die. Edith still exists in the imagination. And in reruns." Shales seemed to be only half-joking when he wrote "Jean Stapleton has decided to put her own interests above the best interest of the nation. She refuses to make any more appearances on television as the seemingly immortal Mrs. Bunker. And so the producers of *Archie Bunker's Place* sequel to the classic *All in the Family* have put out a contract on the beloved old dingbat. They will stifle her for once and for all."[19]

Actually, Lear himself was having trouble letting Edith go. "He could not say yes to allow Edith to die," Stapleton recalled many years later. "Norman, you realize she's only fiction," Stapleton told him. Lear's reply: "To me she isn't." Lear arranged for CBS to make a $500,000 donation to the National

Organization of Women to establish the Edith Bunker Memorial Fund for the Equal Rights Amendment."[20] Alas, the ERA, like Edith herself, would also perish in the early 1980s.

By that point, of course, Edith Bunker had become something of an institution. Indeed, her chair was placed alongside Archie's at the Smithsonian's National Museum of American History. Because, in effect, everybody knew Edith. But history is a process of remembering and forgetting, and as the decades passed fewer and fewer Americans would have any memory of the show at all, much less Edith—or what she stood for. But we would all do well to keep her in mind. She made the world a bigger place.

8

Left In

The Liberal Arts
of Michael Stivic

If Edith was the heart of *All in the Family*, her son-in-law Mike was the show's conscience. The best educated of the four principals—the only character with a college degree, which is not necessarily to say he was the smartest— Mike was also the one who wrestled most actively to know and do what he felt was right. Archie's instinct was always for self-interest; Edith, while she could be confused and slow to grasp the shape of a situation, had an ethical compass that pointed true north. Gloria, who fell somewhere between her parents, was also a person who tended to react intuitively, even viscerally, to situations, though she certainly had ideological convictions (principally feminist ones). But from the very beginning, years before he finished college, Mike tended to view his circumstances in a wider social context, striving to understand, and prioritize, the interests of those less fortunate than himself. He wanted to become a sociologist because he thought it was a way in which he could help people while achieving upward mobility for himself—doing well by doing good.

As such Mike was the quintessential late twentieth-century liberal and a fledgling member of the "New Class" described by the neoconservative intellectual Irving Kristol in an influential 1975 essay for the *Wall Street Journal*.[1] The term, which would become a fixture of right-wing discourse for the next half century, describes a cultural elite that used public institutions to gain power—cultural power, which they hoped would convert into political power—and attack that of the economic elite, all the while thinking of themselves as regular folk. This is pretty much what Mike was all about.

"The character wasn't all that far from me," Rob Reiner remembered four decades later.[2] Indeed, Reiner would wear his liberal politics on his sleeve for the next half century as an actor, writer, director, and producer. He was the most successful of the four principals in his post-*AITF* career, a celebrated director of classic films such as *This Is Spinal Tap* (1984), *When Harry Met Sally* (1989), and *A Few Good Men* (1992). He was also the most prominent of the four as a social activist at the forefront of issues such as gay marriage and early childhood education, and as a fund-raiser/cheerleader for Democratic presidential candidates Al Gore, Howard Dean, and Hillary Clinton. He had a fancier, more prominent life than Mike, whose aspirations focused on a tenured professorship, would likely ever have. But their hearts were in the same place.

Michael Lear

All this said, Reiner's Michael Stivic was really a stand-in for Norman Lear. Archie Bunker was based on his father, Herman Lear, who commonly referred to his son as a "meathead"—dead from the neck up, a line Archie would utter the first time he met Mike. Lear the younger often argued with Lear the senior, to no effect. As noted in chapter 2, Herman and Archie embodied the generational conflict of the old and new—which in many cases amounted to the suspicious and cynical against the hopeful and optimistic. "What is it with your generation, anyway?" Archie asked Mike in a 1978 episode. "You gave us ten years of misery with all the long hair and the dope and the guitars and spoiling the Vietnam War," he complained. He later described Mike as "a guy who goes to a John Wayne movie and roots for the Indians." Archie's description of Mike and his generation is substantially correct; their disagreements were less about the facts than what they meant and where their sympathies lay.

Mike's role in *All in the Family* was particularly crucial for providing the show's writers with a means to insert periodic mini-lectures that seemed entirely in character—on what other TV show would one witness an explication of Germaine Greer's feminist classic *The Female Eunuch* the way Mike offers in the 1973 episode "Battle of the Month"?—as well as a vehicle for articulating what Lear and his collaborators considered the responsible, practical, and moral outlook of the show, leavened by humor. This is something that the most insightful commentator on *All in the Family*, David Marc, pointed out in 1989:

> Archie, though the center of the viewer's attention, is by no means the persona of *All in the Family*. Instead, Lear's omniscient narrative sensibility serves that function. Unseen, but never unfelt, the Lear zeitgeist continuously serves to point out Archie's errors and thus, by indirection, its own vision of the brighter day. Mike and Gloria (Sally Struthers), though riddled with minor faults, are the heroes of *All in the Family*. Their "liberal" views are consistently presented as centrist and reasonable, while Archie's "conservative" views contain obvious and glaring flaws of logic and/or character. Edith's heart of gold is precious, but her subservience to a rigid, constraining role-destiny makes her something less than a model for social evolution.[3]

Rob Reiner explained how the logic Marc describes played out in practical terms over the eight seasons of the show: "We never let [Archie] get away with just saying something." *All in the Family* may have allowed any manner of bigotry to be expressed, but was scrupulous in having someone—usually Mike—on hand to refute it. "Mike was the voice of reason," said *AITF* writer Larry Rhine decades later.[4] As Marc observes, the show's ideological outlook may have been unseen, but it certainly was not unheard—frequently expressed by a live audience that regularly weighed in with laughter and applause to indicate its support any time Archie was put in his place by Mike or other characters.

Mike's importance in playing this role was in part a function of his status as something of an outsider among the Bunkers, a figure from the wider world who expands and reconfigures family dynamics, the way the partners of grown children do. The quintessential baby boomer, Michael Casmir Stivic was born in Chicago circa 1946 and orphaned after his parents died in a car accident. Mike was raised by his uncle Casmir, an ex-Marine lieutenant who went on to become a florist (a neat fusion of traditional gender occupations, and perhaps an indication of how Mike's liberal sensibilities may have been fostered). As his name suggests, Mike's background is Polish, and thus virtually by definition Catholic, though only the former identity means much to him—and that's at least partly because Archie is so relentless at needling him about it (in the decades after the Second World War, Poles were stereotyped as dumb and, like Italians, were ridiculed for military defeats early in the conflict). By twenty-first-century standards, the Gloria Bunker–Michael Stivic matrimonial merger is wholly unremarkable: a marriage of two white people. But while it would be an overstatement to call it a mixed (ethnic/religious) marriage by the 1970s, the memory of a time when such blending was notable was still alive, and there for Archie to pick up as a cudgel.

All in the Family opens in medias res, when Mike is twenty-four years old, a new husband, and a full-time college student. It's not clear what school he attends; since he lives with the Bunkers at 704 Hauser Street, he could presumably be commuting anywhere in the city, though Queens College, part of the City University of New York system, would be a plausible guess, given that it's located in Kew Gardens, not far from the Bunker home in Astoria. Mike is a little old to be in college, especially as a freshman, which we know because the episode about his graduation airs in the spring of 1974. Demographic trends were on their way to establishing eighteen-to-twenty-two-year-olds as the standard issue for full-time college students (part-time students were and are another story), though there were still plenty of exceptions in the 1970s. In some respects, Mike is a throwback in that he's a married man whose wife is supporting him—Gloria works in a department store to provide them with an income—a pattern that had been common in the years after the Second World War when men attended college on the GI bill while their wives worked, presumably temporarily, to help pay the bills until men got degrees that would literally pay off. But Mike is also very much a person of his time in the sense that many young men started or finished college late, given the shadow of the Vietnam War, where matriculated students could get draft deferments. He also attended college in a relatively strong national economy where a bachelor's degree was not necessarily essential to getting a remunerative full-time job.

It's only in later episodes that we get glimpses as to how this whole scenario was established. In the 1977 episode "Mike and Gloria Meet," we see mutual friends of the two (Priscilla Lopez and Christopher Guest, who would go on to have a long career as an actor, director, and Reiner collabo-

rator) plan a double date to take place at the Bunker home on a night Archie
and Edith are away. Her tight curls and nervous anticipation mark Gloria
as an innocent; Mike's bushy beard, tie-dye shirt, denim jacket, and peace
sign pin make him the very personification of the hippie. When his buddy
informs him that he's fixed Mike up with a girl, Mike demurs—he has plans
to picket Nixon's inaugural at the Waldorf Astoria (which means this is taking place in January 1969). When his friend says Mike is just being bitter,
he eagerly agrees. "I am damned disappointed in a country that would elect
Richard Nixon and not Eldridge Cleaver," he says—a remark that suggests
how comically out of touch Mike is for believing a leader of the Black Panthers could ever be elected president. What follows is the quintessence of
the awkward first date, made all the more so because Mike and Gloria's
respective friends quickly disappear, leaving them to grope for things to say.
It's only when they agree that they've made a mistake that they begin to
bond. It turns out that they both love ballroom dancing, which Archie
taught Gloria. "He sounds like a great guy," Mike observes, a hilariously
ironic prediction given what we've seen in the previous eight seasons. "You'd
love him," Gloria responds, which is even funnier.

It was many years earlier, in the 1971 episode "Mike Meets Archie," that
we see how the relationship between the two great adversaries was established. The episode begins with Mike and Gloria's first anniversary, which
means they would have been married in 1970, the year after they met. They're
celebrating with Chinese food—Archie referring to the Chinese as "chinks"
and Mike expressing his distaste with the slur and proceeding to a disquisition on ethnic differences between Asian populations—when the conversation turns to the day they met, at which point the episode goes into a flashback. It's clear before Mike ever walks in the door that Archie doesn't
regard any boy as good enough for his little girl. But the boy who does show
up—wearing the same tie-dye shirt he dons in the "Mike and Gloria Meet"
episode—is simply appalling to Archie, his disgust written all over his face.
Mike, oblivious to the dynamics of the Bunker household (he makes the
mistake of sitting in Archie's chair), tries to engage his girlfriend's father, who
buries his head in the *Daily News*.

Mike asks what he's reading about, and learns of the arrest of a couple
hundred Vietnam War protesters, a development Archie heartily endorses.
Mike tries gentle devil's advocacy, only to be stunned to learn that Archie is
indeed an America-love-it-or-leave-it kind of guy. When Mike tries to further remonstrate, Archie begins reciting the lyrics from Irving Berlin's 1918

song "God Bless America" (an anthem that led Woody Guthrie to respond in 1940 with his Marxist-tinged "This Land Is Your Land").[5] As Mike's rejoinders grow more insistent, Archie begins to belt out the song at full volume, prompting Edith and Gloria to come into the living room to find out what's going on. Mike gets up and leaves; Edith looks on in horror; Gloria breaks into tears. It's the first of what will be just another normal day at the Bunker residence as the proverbial curtain drops on act I and we cut to a commercial. The clip would become a staple of the *All in the Family* canon.

Conflicting Partners

No aspect of the show would be more central, and more commonly repeated, than the sparring between Archie and Mike. Mike would have more than his fair share of zingers, but as noted in chapter 6, Archie fired off a steady stream of putdowns, beginning with one that was established in the "Mike Meets Archie" episode: "meathead." ("I get called that literally every day of my life," Reiner reported almost a half century later, perhaps more amused than upset given that he's had a distinguished life after Mike.)[6]

Though clearly a more informed and socially skilled man, Mike had two vulnerabilities in his contests with Archie. The first was his economic dependency: at the end of the day Mike was living under Archie's roof and eating at Archie's table, weapons Archie effectively employed to shut Mike up. The other was Mike's emotional vulnerability: Reiner's acting made it clear that Archie really had the power to hurt Mike's feelings. Over and over again, Mike would feel compelled to take the bait and defend himself, a tendency that abated as the series progressed and his hide got tougher—and as he and Gloria struck out on their own. Archie was in many ways besieged by the culture that surrounded him in the 1970s, but he was relatively secure in his manhood, a trump card he was able to play with Mike, among others, for years.

One could fairly wonder how anyone could live with Archie for any length of time given the emotional discord, even chaos, that characterized life at 704 Hauser Street (though of course we know that people put up with all kinds of abusive situations that may seem incomprehensible to others—or, in retrospect, even to themselves). One could argue that *All in the Family* was just a TV show and shouldn't be mistaken for real life. That's true, though in some sense the show's claim to fame rested on its unprecedented sense of realism in its honest portrayal of family dynamics. But in watching the show one can also infer that the relationship between Archie and Mike was not simply or only one endless conflict. Though it's rarely a focus of a given episode, we learn of the two men going to ball games or going fishing together (there's a comic routine in which Mike and Archie argue over whether Mike should put a shoe on one foot before he's put a sock on the other). And not all their conflicts are a matter of ideological struggle; one recurring motif in the show is the two getting stuck trying to get through a doorway at the same time—a metaphorical statement about their relationship, to be sure, but one that's more slapstick than it is philosophical debate.

In at least one respect, Mike and Archie have something in common: they both have trouble coming to terms with feminism. This is something most viewers take for granted with Archie, but it's a little more surprising when it comes to Mike, who Reiner has characterized as "a bit of a chauvinist even though he was liberal-minded."[7] The evidence of this chauvinism—more than a bit, actually—is clear early in the first season of the show with the 1971 episode "Women's Lib," in which Gloria discusses her burgeoning gender identity with Edith, only to bump up against the sexism of her father, leading her to ask Mike to weigh in. But Mike says it's none of his business. "Repressed blacks are your business," Gloria observes. "Discrimination against Puerto Ricans and Jews and Poles and every other minority are your business. What about discrimination against women?" (The supposition seems to be that minority = female. And that women = white.)

"Gloria, it's not the same thing," Mike replies.

"How can you say that, Michael?"

"I don't believe in a woman opening up her mouth around the house, so shut up, would ya?"

"Like hell I will!"

Gloria storms off upstairs, and Mike follows in an effort to reason with her (by his lights). "I believe in total equality between men and women," he tells her in their bedroom. "But that equality can only come about when the female partner is willing to confess her total inequality." Gloria, infuriated, storms off and leaves the house to stay with a friend, leaving him awkwardly behind with his in-laws. When she returns to get her things, Edith nudges him to make an effort to repair the damage, but he demurs. "Oh, men!" she responds in a rare complaint. Mike tries to make common cause with Archie, asserting that men should be the kings of their castles. But Archie notes that his son-in-law has no castle. Ultimately Mike will reach out to mend the relationship, after a fashion. "We are totally equal—" he says as they kiss and make up—"in this room. In here you're my equal. Out there you're my wife." That apparently is good enough for Gloria, at least for the time being.

Mike's unabashed sexism here seems a bit out of character—or, at any rate, the character he would become. In a way, it seems to say less about him than about the state of feminist discourse in American society at large in the early 1970s, a time when statements and behavior that would later be widely regarded as unacceptable were regarded as routine. One thinks, for example, of the celebrated 1973 "Battle of the Sexes" between tennis stars Billie Jean King and Bobby Riggs, in which Riggs mocked feminists with lines like "Women belong in the bedroom and the kitchen, in that order." (The buildup to their celebrated tennis match was vividly captured in the 2017 movie *Battle of the Sexes*.) But while Mike's sexism was rarely as frank and convoluted as it was in the "Women's Lib" episode, it was certainly no anomaly. Another early episode focused on his reluctance to undergo surgery with a female doctor, unaware that the doctor who ultimately performs the procedure is a woman as well. In less dramatic fashion, his chauvinism was evident in a habit that would later be called "mansplaining" as well as his tendency to make decisions without consulting Gloria, as when, in the 1974 episode "Gloria's Shock," he announces that the couple will not be having children, or the 1976 episode "New Year's Wedding," when he invites a buddy—played by Billy Crystal—and his fiancée to be married in their living room. There's also his penchant for lapsing into condescension, which prompted another of Gloria's departures in the 1976 episode "Mike and Gloria Split." In the later years of the show their marriage would be one of growing tension, and its offscreen end would become the premise of a 1982 spin-off series featuring Gloria as a single mother.

Liberally Misguided

The most sustained critique of Mike's character—and perhaps the most sustained critique of the liberal imagination *All in the Family* ever undertook—was in the 1973 episode "Games Bunkers Play." The game in question was Group Therapy, a real-life board game with a strong psychotherapeutic overlay that was popular in the early 1970s. Mike is the enthusiastic cheerleader for the game, which will take place at the Bunkers with himself, Gloria,

Edith, the Lorenzos, and Lionel (Archie beats a hasty retreat to Kelsey's Bar). The basic idea is that a person picks a card requiring some degree of personal disclosure, and advances around the board depending on whether other characters decide the statement is "with it" or a "cop out." Things start out lighthearted enough with Frank Lorenzo, but when Lionel draws a card that literally requires him to push back against someone in the room, he chooses Mike and expresses his discomfort about what he regards as a patronizing subtext in their conversations. "You're always bending over backward for me, Mike," Lionel says. "I can't even get into a good argument with you because you're so quick to agree with me."

"Lionel, we're supposed to be friends," Mike replies, surprised and hurt.

"Yeah, that's why I'm telling you this." He goes on, "Just once I'd like you to talk with me as if I was Lionel Jefferson and not a representative of the whole black race."

"What do you *want* me to talk with you about, the weather?"

"Yeah. Sometimes. Black people have weather sometimes too, you know."

Mike, incredulous, decides this must be a joke. "You really had me faked out there! What an act! But I don't believe it." He holds up his card indicating that Lionel's remarks are a cop-out. But everyone else votes in favor of with-it.

Things go downhill from there. Gloria gets a card that tells her to say something to the person with whom she's closest. She's about to say that Edith dresses too conservatively when Mike interrupts, amazed that she doesn't consider *him* the person with whom she's closest. By now, Mike's initial manic bonhomie has deflated into a sullen grievance.

Then it's his turn. Mike's card tells him to explain to those in the room what makes him mature (some guffawing at this). "I'm open-minded. I'm tolerant of the other guy's opinions," he says.[8]

Gloria laughs. Mike, irritated, wants to know why. "Just thinking about you and daddy," she replies.

Mike is angered by what he regards as a false equivalence. "The man is a walking monument to intolerance!" (Every sentence now ends with the cadence of an exclamation point.)

Lionel, for his part, is also skeptical about Mike's claims, prompting him to retort, "I'm not the bigot in this house! He is!"

"Yeah, but he doesn't know any better."

Gloria delivers a particularly devastating criticism: "You sound just like daddy."

Mike tries to rise above it all. "I'm tolerant enough to know you're all dead wrong."

But Mike's ordeal is not over. Irene draws a card telling her to sit on the lap of the person who's making her most uncomfortable, and of course that's Mike. But it's Edith who (reluctantly) saddles Mike with what he considers the last straw when she's told to say something she's been meaning to say for a long time. "Mike, I don't like the way you've been acting so stuck-up lately. I think it's mean to call Archie names and make fun of him the way you do." Mike replies by pointing out Archie's tendency to say ignorant things, leading Edith to deliver the coup de grâce: "If you was really smarter than Archie, you'd be smart enough not to let him see that you're smarter than him." (This of course is precisely what Lionel does with Archie.) At this point the audience breaks into applause. Mike, furious, upends the board and playing pieces and storms upstairs. Gloria manages to coax him back downstairs, but it's not long into an apology when it's clear that Mike is still wallowing in self-pity and passive aggression. ("So you picked on me a little.") When Edith begins to tell a story about a man who saved another man's life, Mike tries to cut her off. The others insist that she proceed, whereupon Edith gets to the moral of her story, which is that sometimes those who owe a great debt to others (read: Mike) can be resentful of them. Her son-in-law, furious again over what he considers an unfair criticism, charges off into the kitchen. Gloria is about to intervene, but Edith says no, let me do it.

Mike's character has taken a beating in this episode, and, actually, one could argue that some piling on did take place. But Edith's character changes course by reaching out to him. "I told you why you yell at Archie," she tells him. Don't ya wanna know why Archie yells at you?"

"I know why," Mike replies, irritated and exhausted. "He hates me."

"Archie yells at you because he's jealous of you."

Mike waves this off, but she demands his attention. "You will listen to me," she commands. "Archie's jealous of you going to college. You got your whole life ahead of you. Archie had to quit school to support his family. He's never going to be nothin' more than he is right now. But you, you got a chance to be anything you want to be. That's why Archie is jealous of you. He sees in you all the things he could never be. So the next time he yells at you, try to be more understanding." There's audible applause as Edith leaves Mike to consider this, making clear to him that everyone in the living room will be there for him when he returns.

Mike realizes she's right. And so when Archie enters the house through the kitchen door, annoyed that the whole crowd is still in the living room, Mike ignores his bad mood. "I wanna tell you something," he says to Archie. "I understand." He embraces an uncomprehending Archie as the episode ends.

All the characters of *All in the Family* experience emotional growth. Mike's is perhaps the least obvious, in part because he starts from the highest baseline level. Certainly he and Archie have years of arguing to go. But Mike remains the sensible one in the years that follow as he finishes college, gets a master's degree, and gains momentum in establishing an academic career. His IQ is matched by his EQ, as when he returns the favor Edith did him in "Games Bunkers Play" with meaningful support when she has a spiritual crisis (see chapter 7). Even when he wavers in his ideological convictions, as when he correctly fears he will lose out in competing for a job against a black friend, he ultimately accepts his defeat in good cheer and takes the colleague and his wife out for dinner. Initially panicked by Gloria's two pregnancies (one a miscarriage and the other their son Joey), he grows into the role of father and provider. He also accommodates Gloria's growing assertiveness, whether in supporting her protest against getting fired from her job over her pregnancy (see chapter 9) or acceding to her demand that he get a vasectomy, given his strong feelings about limiting family size. After *All in the Family* had run its course, he and Gloria make a reprise appearance on *Archie Bunker's Place*, where we're told that Mike has lost his teaching job because he participated in a naked protest in California. The kicker, which we learn at the closing moment in the Bunker kitchen, is that he was following Gloria's lead. Whatever problems may mark their marriage, Mike does seem at the very least to be adapting to changing times with at least some degree of grace.

He also, in a gradual development that marks a real cadence in the series, ultimately makes his peace with Archie. At the end of the 1974–1975 season, Mike, who has a paying fellowship as part of his graduate studies, earns (barely) enough for he and Gloria to establish their own household. After some difficulties in finding a place they can afford, they rent the Jefferson homestead (George Jefferson makes the price irresistibly attractive to the Stivics, knowing it will irritate Archie to have "the meathead" nearby). This gives Mike new power in his dealings with Archie, as does the birth of his son the following season. The final step in his transition occurs at the end of the 1977–1978 season, when Mike lands a teaching position in Santa

Barbara. When Archie and Edith visit the Stivics out there in the final season of the show, Archie forsakes calling Mike a meathead, a real statement in the changing relations between them.

But the real turning point occurs in the eighth-season finale, "The Stivics Go West," when the two finally have to part. "You've been like a father to me," Mike tells him with his cab to the airport waiting.

"Well, you've been just like a son," Archie replies. "Never do a thing I told you to."

Mike's embrace of Archie is unreserved—"I know you always thought I hated you, but I love you," he says—while Archie's is tentative but real. After the cab drives away, we see Archie looking through the curtains of 704 Hauser, his face dappled by the streetlight. "There was no acting with the goodbye scene," Reiner later remembered. He poured his feeling about leaving the show, and O'Connor, into what remains one of the emotional highlights of the series.[9]

In the final analysis, *All in the Family* is really more of a show about Archie and Edith than it is about Gloria or Mike. Archie in particular took up most of the psychic energy of the show's creators, and the friction between his benighted worldview and his essential humanity sparked the energy that drove the show forward. But *AITF* never could have worked without the character—in the broadest sense of that term—of Michael Stivic. He was, amid all the tumult of 200 episodes, a reality check, whether or not he happened to be on our television screens.

9

"Little Girl" to Mother

The Working-Class Feminism
of Gloria Bunker Stivic

No character in *All in the Family* changed more than Gloria, the youngest member of the quartet that formed the sitcom's core. And yet Gloria tended to get overshadowed by the other three. She was often caught in the endless battles between Archie and Mike, while her words and behavior tended to be less striking (if more intelligent) than those of her mother, Edith. Thus, Gloria was a reflection of her times, in that young women of a half century ago tended to be overlooked more often than they are now, when topics like sexual harassment—a term first coined in 1975, amid the show's run—and equal pay were active, if unresolved, subjects of popular discourse.[1] The series went on the air a year before congressional passage of Title IX, an education law that provided government protection for equal treatment of men and women in public education.[2] That law was part of a larger wave of social change for women that occurred in the 1970s, one captured, in both its accomplishments and its limits, by *AITF* over the course of its run in that decade.

All in the Family reflected its times in another way as well: it was a male-dominated production. Norman Lear and his partner Bud Yorkin were men, as were all of the directors (mostly John Rich and Paul Bogart, with H. Wesley Kenney helming Season 5 in 1974–1975). Men dominated writing duties as well, but there were at least thirteen women who received writing credits for shows, among them Irma Kalish (who wrote the 1973 episode "Edith's Christmas Story," which dealt with breast cancer), Helen Levitt (whose credits stretched from *The Donna Reed Show* in the 1950s through *That Girl* in the 1960s to *The Bionic Woman* in the 1970s), and Susan Harris (who would go on to become a television impresario as the creator of successful sitcoms that included *Soap*, *Benson*, and *The Golden Girls*). This was about 12 percent of the total.[3] The writers of the final episode of the series, Patt Shea and Harriett Weiss, would be deeply involved in *Archie Bunker's Place* and *Gloria*, as indeed would many female writers for *All in the Family* in its spin-offs, suggesting at least some effort on Lear's part to recognize and promote women. All four casting directors for *All in the Family*—notably Marion Dougherty, who handled the pilot and had a distinguished career in film, as well as Jane Murray, credited with 135 episodes—were also women. So was Brigit Jensen (later Jensen-Drake), listed as associate producer for ninety-five episodes. This was more than tokenism.

But it was hardly equality. And nowhere was this more apparent than when it came to dealing with Gloria. Actually, this was something those behind the camera realized early on. "It's been easy to underwrite her, to let her serve as a feeder of lines," John Rich observed at the time. "We received letters from a women's lib group asking 'What does she do? What's her job, her education? Is she just around all the time?'" Rich said he and Lear discussed the matter, and Rich concluded that "we should write stories that give her another function than being another ear on the set."[4] That happened, but Gloria nevertheless remained a relatively recessive figure. As Sally Struthers herself noted of the character in 1973, "She's not as much a nitwit as she is a nonentity." As late as the sixth season of the show, when Gloria gives birth to her son Joey, screenwriter Larry Rhine remembered Struthers saying, "I'm having the baby and everyone else is doing the talking."[5]

Struthers was an up-and-coming actor when she joined the cast in 1970. Born, like Reiner, in 1947, Struthers grew up in Portland, Oregon, the granddaughter of Norwegian immigrants.[6] She joined a theater company in Pasadena, California, and did commercials before she first made a mark as a comic actor with a small role in the 1970 Jack Nicholson vehicle *Five Easy*

Pieces. She appeared in the short-lived 1970 TV series *The Tim Conway Comedy Hour*—actually, it was getting let go from that show that gave her the opportunity to read for *All in the Family*. Lear, who had seen her performing a tap dance routine on the *Smothers Brothers* show, described her as "a little pool of light," a remark that conveys admiration as well as diminution (though in fact her five-foot, one-inch frame was over a foot shorter than Reiner's). Lear described Struthers's audition as Gloria for the 1970 pilot in the same terms he did O'Connor's and Stapleton's: a sense of instant recognition of her rightness for the part. Unlike those two, however, she had much more competition, reputedly beating out 200 other prospects. Struthers also lacked the previous professional and personal ties to Lear that Stapleton and Reiner had. But her chemistry with Reiner (whom she briefly dated before he married Penny Marshall) clinched the part.[7] "Of the four principals, I knew Sally Struthers least well," Lear reported in his memoir. "I envisioned her as a Kewpie doll on the outside with an inner strength that would be enhanced over the seasons." Lear said he considered her the head of the Stivic family by the time the series finished its run in 1979.

As noted in chapter 2, two other actors had played Gloria in the first two pilots. Kelly Jean Peters had an earthy appeal and a bit of an edge to her; her successor, Candy Azzara, was a more traditional and earnest character (both would go on to have steady film and television careers). As with Reiner's performance of Mike, Struthers's Gloria was a fusion of her predecessors, with a strong physicality that co-existed alongside something that resembled innocence. "She had a wonderful little girl touch to the character," Rhine recalled.[8] But Struthers also exhibited a strong sense of craft. "What I liked about working with Sally is that she would try anything," Reiner later recalled.[9] Like Reiner, she had an ability to improvise and was a gifted mimic who worked imitations of Mae West and Lily Tomlin into her performances.

Gloria's backstory was the sketchiest of the four principals. She was born eleven months after Archie and Edith got married, which probably means 1949, a year or so after Mike. She grew up at 704 Hauser Street, though there are relatively few references to her childhood. As noted in chapter 7, we're told that after Gloria's birth, Edith's doctor informed her it would not be safe for her to get pregnant again, and so Gloria was raised as an only child. We're also told in the pilot that she was diagnosed as anemic and therefore was treated protectively by her parents. One of her childhood friends was Sidney Schapiro, the son of the Bunker family physician, with whom Gloria played doctor as a kid and who grew up to become one. (Played by George Wyner, he appears in a pair of episodes, including the final one. The elder Schapiro, played by Gene Blakely, delivers Gloria's son Joey in Season 6.) Even as a child, it seems, Gloria had a healthy interest in sex, and indeed, Gloria's unapologetic sexuality is one of the most striking, and progressive, aspects of her character—and a way in which she differs from her parents, something viewers at the time were likely to chalk up to the generation gap that separated uptight elders from more culturally emancipated youth.

Daddy's Woman

That may be, though outcomes like these are typically not reducible to single causes—and, in the final analysis, can be quite mysterious. Gloria's relationship with her parents is actually one of the more intriguing aspects of the show. In a number of ways, Gloria is her father's child. She has his mercurial temperament, which includes a penchant for blowing raspberries at people who say things she doesn't like (usually Archie). For the length of the show, he refers to Gloria as "little girl," and given her growing feminist consciousness, it's interesting that she doesn't resist this designation. However, the dynamics of the two characters vividly demonstrate the difference between temperament and ideology: while Gloria may share any number of traits with Archie, she resolutely rejects his political views, regularly arguing with him alongside Mike as well as on her own.

The bond between father and daughter is established early on. Gloria learns she's pregnant in the 1971 episode "Gloria Has a Bellyful," a development that has her (and Edith) overjoyed. "I hope I have triplets!" she exclaims. Mike reacts with panic—as he will over the course of three real or possible pregnancies, only one of which will result in the birth of a child. At this point in the series he's a college student without a job or a home to raise a family. (Archie, for his part, is less than thrilled to hear Edith volunteer for night feedings, for babysitting, and to clear beer out of the refrigerator to make room for an infant's needs, comically glaring at Mike as if to say, "Nice work, deadbeat dad!"). Mike decides to get a job, rent an apartment, and continue his studies through night school, something Gloria insists on as a basis for a more secure economic future for the family. But not long after this plan is set in motion she has a miscarriage. Archie, who was not at home at the moment of crisis, returns shortly after a doctor has attended to her upstairs and assures the family that she's fine and will still be able to bear children. By this point Archie has come around to the prospect of becoming a grandfather, and comes through the front door with an enormous toy panda. He's confused and angry to learn Gloria has lost the baby—for a moment he believes Mike talked her into an abortion—but as he absorbs what happens his grief starts to sink in. "Ah, gee," he says, his face registering a sense of sorrow that's striking because it's so rare.

Archie heads upstairs to see Gloria, who's in bed. "I didn't do a very good job, did I," she laments. He gets mad on her behalf: "Who said that, some dopey doctor?" But Archie, it's clear, is at a loss for words. "You want to say something?" Gloria asks him. "No, nothing," he responds, his inarticulateness palpable. (In this early episode, as in a number of early episodes, there's a piano soundtrack, which is distracting.) Gloria, understanding both his motives and his difficulties, finally steps in for him. "You love me," she says. Archie nods: it's hard for him to say the words. "I love you, too, Daddy," she says. The episode ends with the two of them holding hands, their connection no less powerful for being unspoken.

In some respects, Gloria's relationship with her mother is more fraught. The affection between them is evident, and Gloria appreciates Edith's goodness in ways Archie far too often overlooks, something she repeatedly points out to him. (Like O'Connor and Reiner, Struthers and Stapleton were close, referring to each other as mother and daughter; she also considered O'Connor a surrogate father.)[10] But Edith is also a problem for Gloria, because it's clear to her, as it is to the audience for the show, that she's a problematic role model in her unswerving subservience to Archie. At times this leads Gloria to be dismissive, even mean, as when she calls Edith "a doormat," "a zero," and "a nothing" in the 1973 episode "The Battle of the Month" (see chapter 7). But as noted, Edith can be articulate in defending herself when necessary, and that includes parrying Gloria, something her daughter recognizes, if at times belatedly. It's precisely this complexity that sustains the loving tension between the two women over the course of the show. Gloria's challenge, one shared by many women who go on to be wives and mothers, involves balancing the lessons and values of her mother while charting her course in a changing world.

Multiple Assaults

The frictions between mother and daughter come into sharpest relief when comparing the experiences of each in dealing with sexual violence. Gloria's crisis occurs first, in the 1973 episode "Gloria the Victim" (a title that would never fly today; "survivor" is considered the more acceptable term). The attack takes place at a construction site where Gloria had been subjected to catcalls when walking by, and had avoided as a result. But the episode is set on a Saturday morning, and she had been hoping to take a shortcut by crossing the site when she was suddenly seized. She managed to escape and has returned home in a stricken daze as Mike and Archie conduct one of their usual arguments. "It's bad enough it's a jungle in the streets," she says irritably. "Do I have to come home to one?" Mike recognizes something is wrong but she won't talk to him.

Gloria proceeds to the kitchen, where she finds a cheerful Edith, who is slow to recognize Gloria's distress. As she gropes to broach the subject of her assault, Edith reacts to a request that they talk by chirping, "This reminds me of when you was a little girl. We used to talk a lot in the kitchen. Remember?" But as what happened to Gloria dawns on Edith, she swerves in a different direction: distressed denial. Edith begins talking about the color of her neighbor Mabel Hefner's new couch as Gloria breaks down, but Edith—as she so often does—finds the wellsprings of her empathy and embraces Gloria.

It's Edith who goes back to the living room to prepare Archie and Mike to be attentive to what Gloria has to say. Gloria describes what happened: she was grabbed suddenly, had a sock stuck in her mouth, and felt her clothes being torn off. Gloria passed out in sheer terror, and her assailant, apparently frightened, fled. She proceeded to a friend's house where she took a shower and borrowed some clothes. Mike comforts her and elicits the information that the attack did not pass the threshold into rape. "Thank God for that," a grave Archie says.

Archie wants to take action by reporting what happened to the police, though his reasoning is typically coarse and offensive. When Edith tries to dissuade him as he picks up the phone, telling Archie that Gloria is not ready to take such a step, he replies, "Why is she afraid to say anything about it? I mean, as long as the guy didn't get her, she's got nothing to be ashamed of." Archie notes "the guy might still be lurking around the neighborhood like Jack the Raper" (*sic*), observing to Edith that "he could attack *you*—those guys don't care who they grab." (Both of these lines elicit laughter at his tone deafness.) When Archie reaches the local precinct on the phone he reports not rape—"if it was rape I wouldn't say nothing about it"—but rather "assault with batteries."

Scenes like this push what might be termed the Lear principle—an insistence on finding, or even inserting, comedy in the most serious of situations—to its very limits. In addition to depicting Archie's cluelessness as a joke, it also means a silly subplot involving twelve-inch hot dogs that Edith plans to serve for dinner that night, which she stored at the Jeffersons' place because her freezer was full. With a distraught Gloria upstairs, Lionel rings the doorbell to explain to Archie that Wilma, the Jeffersons' dog, ate the defrosting hot dogs and that he's Louise Jefferson's emissary in offering TV dinners as compensation.

Amid such distractions, Gloria is racked by fear and embarrassment when she learns Archie is calling the police. Mike encourages her to report the incident. "Why are you putting me through this?" she asks, anguished. Edith seconds Mike's suggestion, prompting Gloria's anguished reply, "Not you, too, Ma." When the detective, played by the great character actor Charles Durning, arrives at 704 Hauser to take Gloria's statement, Mike expresses relief that now maybe justice can be done. Not so fast, the detective says: "Apprehending a suspect is one thing; convicting him is something else." He notes that in the previous year (1972), there were 40,000 rape-related arrests in the United States, but a conviction rate of less than 10 percent. He then goes on to give Gloria a grueling preview of what's likely to happen when she takes the stand: a defense attorney noting she walked by after her husband warned her to stay away from the site, wondering why she walked down the same side of the street as the site, asking her what clothes she was wearing, and so on. Mike wonders if the detective is taking a little too much pleasure in his devil's advocacy. The ensuing conversation references a previous episode in which Gloria posed nude for a painter friend of her and Mike's, which the detective casts in a new light, suggesting how a story like this could be easily used against her as an example of her libertinism. (Amid this tension, Henry Jefferson comes by to inform Archie that Louise still feels bad about the hot dogs and is sending him to the market to get some, prompting the detective to ask that Henry get him some too.)

Gloria, understandably feeling as though she's being assaulted all over again, retreats to the kitchen. Edith, now fully emotionally engaged with Gloria, tells a tragicomic story about being lured under the boardwalk at

Rockaway Beach as an adolescent, where the promise of a milk shake led her to be grabbed and pushed by a sexual predator.

"Just like me," Gloria observes, eager to bond with her mother. Like Gloria, Edith got away; Gloria asks how. "My father taught me two things," Edith explains. "One was never to order a hamburger in a drugstore. And the other was something about knees." (Laughter and applause.)

"Gloria, I never told no one about this before, because in my time we was too scared to talk open," Edith says. "Over the years I wondered how many other girls that man got under the boardwalk. And how many didn't get away."

Gloria absorbs this parable and returns to the living room resolved to make a statement. But the detective has continued warning Archie and Mike how likely it is that "a cute dame like her" will be psychologically mauled if she testifies. Mike counsels against it, but Gloria says she wants to proceed. The detective says "good," which angers Mike: everything he's said indicates it's a bad idea. To the contrary, the police officer responds; "As a police officer I say make the complaint and follow through with it all the way." Archie, now against the idea, pushes Mike to persuade her to withdraw the decision: "Ask her about her duty to herself. Ask her about her duty to the family. Ask her if she wants to be in the papers." Mike tells the detective no: "I know what's best for my wife." The detective leaves, expressing hope that "the colored guy" will actually get the twelve-inch hot dogs. Archie reassures him: "Don't worry about that. He's one of the good ones."

Gloria is uneasy with their decision. "Michael, are you sure we're doing the right thing?" she asks. "No, I'm not sure we're doing the right thing, Gloria. I don't know what the right thing is. All I know is I'm trying to do the right thing for you." When Gloria protests she needs to speak out on behalf of future assault victims, he breaks in to say, "All I care about is you"—a statement that, he reluctantly acknowledges, puts him in agreement with his father-in-law.

Archie, for his part, has no doubts. He paraphrases Richard Nixon's second inaugural address of two months earlier: "You're on your own. Don't expect nuthin' from nobody, especially the government."[11] The audience reacts uproariously to Archie's bowdlerized, but nevertheless accurate, distillation of the spirit of Nixon's message. "Take care of your own. That's the rule. That's what we did here today. We took care of our own." As he speaks the camera leaves Archie and gradually tightens on Gloria. Her face is riven by distress and despair and she holds back her tears. The camera fades to commercial break.

All in all, "Gloria the Victim" is a remarkably complex and ambiguous episode. Gloria's decision—one pushed on her by the men in her life—is pragmatic and defensible, though clearly not the one the creators of the episode embrace, as it is voiced by Archie, by the least credible character in the cast. Yet there's a recognition that it would be unfair to insist that someone who has sustained as deep an injury as Gloria has should willingly subject herself to more. The blame here—unwittingly revealed in the voice of authority of the police officer, and justified by the president of the United States—is on a patriarchal order that casts shadows on women's lives that are barely acknowledged, never mind addressed.

And yet, in true Lear fashion, this isn't the last word. As mandated by network executives (an injunction he would later throw off), there's a final coda scene in the little teleplay, credited to Irma Kalish with her husband Austin as well as *AITF* regular Don Nicholl. The family is finally sitting down for the hot dog dinner, which is marred for Archie because Henry Jefferson ended up buying six-inch hot dogs, not twelve. Mike reasonably suggests that Archie put two in a roll, but Archie is having none of it. "Six-inch hot dogs taste shorter," he says. A jarringly trivial conclusion, perhaps. But also one that insists—as so much of *All in the Family* does—that the quotidian co-exist alongside the existential, the squalid alongside the transcendent.

The series returned to the subject of sexual assault four years later in the two-part episode "Edith's 50th Birthday" (see chapter 7). This time it's Edith who's attacked, which turns out to be a more protracted ordeal—and one that's portrayed, within the boundaries of network television standards, onscreen. Now Edith is the one who doesn't want to come forward when a suspect has been apprehended for her to identify—she refuses to leave the house for weeks, obsessively washing and ironing clothes. And now it's Gloria who wants her mother to be proactive. Unlike Edith, however, Gloria is more insistent, perhaps because of her own emotional involvement in the matter. She finally loses her temper. "I'm ashamed of you," she says, her words landing like blows. "The mother I knew always helped other people. You know something? You are selfish! You're not my mother anymore."

At that point, Edith slaps Gloria in the face (a move reminiscent of the way she slapped Archie after she learned he lapsed back into his habit of betting on horses in the 1973 episode "Archie the Gambler"). But it appears that Gloria has reached her morally and emotionally. "C'mon Archie," she says to a hapless husband who has been at a loss about how to help his wife. The two head for the police station in what clearly marks a resolution to the crisis. "You can put all that away, Gloria," she says of her housework. "I ain't gonna do any more ironing." The comic coda to the episode comes after Edith and Archie have left, when Gloria touches her smacked face and begins to cry like a child, comforted by Mike.

The Marital Is Political

Archie and Edith loom large in Gloria's psyche over the course of nine years of *All in the Family*. But the pivotal relationship of her adult life is with Mike. The Stivic marriage, like the Bunker marriage, is a complex one, and one whose contrapuntal contrasts give the series much of its texture. The most obvious difference is that Gloria and Mike are much more comfortable with their sexuality, its expression a constant source of irritation to Archie ("Your whole generation does nothing but think with its glands," he complains when he learns of his daughter's pregnancy in "Gloria Has a Bellyful"). As with Archie groping to express his emotions after Gloria's miscarriage, Edith is painfully awkward when she tries to discharge what she regards as her obligations in discussing sex with Gloria on her wedding day (once again, Gloria comes to a parent's rescue by making clear what she doesn't need to hear). But over the course of the series the two couples will discuss any number of sexual matters with each other, including the impotence of each of the men. And as with Archie and Edith, Mike and Gloria will each have ardent suitors—Bernadette Peters (in an early role) for Mike; a mentally disabled delivery boy for Gloria, who will ultimately have an extramarital affair after she and Mike move to California.

When *All in the Family* opens in January 1971, Gloria is a newlywed. She first crossed paths with Mike on a blind double date in January 1969, a moment rendered in a flashback during the 1977 episode "Mike and Gloria Meet" (see chapter 8). Her wedding, which took place in 1970, was also rendered in a flashback during a pair of 1972 episodes focusing on the desire of Mike's guardian, Uncle Casmir, to have a Catholic ceremony while Archie insists on a Protestant one (yet one more example of Gloria getting pushed into the background). The *All in the Family* historian Donna McCrohan describes Gloria in these episodes as a stand-in for "Shirley Temple on the Good Ship Lollipop."[12] There's still a sense of girlishness, suggested by her tight curls, in the first season of the show, though her hairstyle changes fairly quickly to suggest that of a more mature woman.

Indeed, Gloria shows a rising assertiveness early in the show's run. The eleventh episode of the first season, "Women's Lib," aired in March 1971, a time when feminism was achieving prominence in public consciousness. (Gloria Steinem's *Ms.* magazine would be launched later that year.) As noted in the discussion of this episode from Mike's perspective in chapter 8, Gloria articulates a powerful critique against Mike's at best incoherent, and at worst hypocritical, sexism. But her victory at the end of the episode is partial, as Mike is willing to explicitly grant Gloria equality only in private, not public, settings.

Still, this is hardly the last word on the subject. A good example is the 1973 episode "Henry's Farewell." When Archie demands that Edith get him some toast, Gloria asks, "Do you have to treat her like a slave?" To which Archie responds, "I treat her like a housewife." "Case closed," Gloria ripostes. The comparison between racial and gender oppression continues when Henry Jefferson and Archie discuss the prospects for a black president of the United States (not good, Archie says—God has to make a black pope first). "How about a woman president?" Gloria asks. Archie and Henry agree on this much: it's a bad idea. "Gloria's right," Mike weighs in. He's about to make his own disquisition when Gloria cuts him off: "I'm talking, Michael." Henry responds to Gloria by saying "I don't know a ghetto for women," prompting Gloria's comeback: "What do you call a kitchen?" At this point Louise Jefferson notes that Shirley Chisolm, the African American woman who ran for president in 1972, said she encountered more discrimination as a woman than she did because she was black. Gloria builds on the point: "Mr. Jefferson, you've come a long way, baby, but from now on it's we women who have to overcome, right?" She turns to Louise and Edith. "Do you know what I think?" Edith asks. When Gloria, curious, asks what, she replies, "I think we oughta eat." Gloria throws up her hands in disgust. But she, at least, is not giving up the fight in articulating a classic liberal white feminist position.

Gloria's feminism also surfaces in less pointed ways. One of the signature routines of *All in the Family* is Archie's return home from work, which often sets the scene for an episode by revealing his state of mind. But Gloria frequently provides a counterpoint to these moments because she's a working-woman who also regularly returns home from her job at the fictive Kressler's department store, where she labors as a retail clerk. She often brings news of the outside world, and she regularly registers fatigue on her face. As such she's a crucial figure in anchoring *All in the Family* in a working-class milieu, even as Mike pursues a dream of upward mobility for himself and his family.

There are times when Mike is less of a sexist hindrance than an active feminist ally. In the opening scene of the 1975 episode "Mike Faces Life," he's explaining the couple's financial pressures to Edith when Gloria comes home from work and discovers a pink slip in her paycheck. A colleague tells Gloria, who will give birth to her son Joey later that season, that Gloria was fired over her pregnancy. (Asked by Mike why one of their bosses divulged such sensitive information, the colleague slyly responds that he talks in his sleep, the meaning of which dawns on Mike, and the audience, gradually.) Outraged by this illegal sex discrimination, Mike and Gloria descend on the office of an executive at Kressler's to demand an explanation. Exasperated and intimidated, he speaks off the record: "Your wife was fired because she is pregnant. Kressler's has an image of fashion, style, beauty. That image isn't going to be helped by a girl who very soon is going to look like Alfred Hitchcock in drag." Infuriated, Gloria notes a male colleague with a pot belly as prominent as that of any pregnant woman, only to be told he fashions skiwear for the "portly."

The Stivics aren't ready to quit. The next scene shows them rushing home and setting up a portable television so that they and Edith can watch a local newscast. The camera cuts to the television screen, where we see pregnant women picketing in front of Kressler's store. The voiceover notes that police came to the scene—and that one of the officers, herself pregnant, joined the picketers. The reporter notes Gloria got her job back. Edith, amazed, asks Mike how they did it. He explains that the protest was his idea but that Gloria was the one to call her obstetrician and ask him to send his pregnant patients. "And so," says the news anchor on the television set, "along with black power, brown power, and red power, we now add preggo power." The scenario is lighthearted, but the message is clear: activism works. (The results will be a little less effective, though no less amusing, four years later when the two participate in a nude protest over a nuclear power plant in California that results in Mike losing his job.)

However important to her, Gloria's return to Kressler's is temporary. Once Joey is born—an event that coincides with growing earning power on Mike's part—she makes the transition from daughter to mother. That transition is also one for the series as a whole. It occurs halfway through its sixth season, clearly a gambit to reinvigorate the narrative of a series in middle age. As befits a major plot development, it's a two-part episode that ends in the maternity ward and unfolds on a lighthearted note. Seconds after the baby is born Mike suggests they have another, leading Gloria to reply, "Not now, Michael, I have a headache." Edith even brokers an embrace between him and Archie in the waiting room. For the next two seasons, baby Joey becomes another character in the mix until the Stivics leave for California. (The infant is played by twins Jason and Justin Draeger.) Joey became something of a landmark figure in the history of television broadcasting, because he's the first male character to be depicted with full frontal nudity—the scene where an incompetent Archie changes his diaper during a poker game is classic. In 1976, the Ideal Toy Company issued a fourteen-inch "Joey" that was billed as the first anatomically correct male doll.[13]

One of the more curious aspects of *All in the Family*, however, is that it does relatively little in the way of engaging what motherhood might actually mean for Gloria. To be sure, we see plenty of her and the baby, doing all the appropriate things one would expect. But all this is largely in the background. One searches in vain for an episode in the seasons that follow that shows her grappling with issues like postpartum depression, child care woes, or any number of other challenges young mothers face. In the year following the birth of the baby episodes, there are only two in which Gloria figures prominently. One focuses on her lack of sexual desire in the months following Joey's birth; the other on what turns out to be a false belief that she's pregnant. In both cases, the storylines are at least as much about Mike as they are about her—his frustration about sex (a matter on which Archie is surprisingly reassuring) and his anxiety about getting a vasectomy.

Class Dismissed?

One might say that expecting an exploration of Gloria's gender identity would be an unrealistic demand to make of a sitcom—except that *All in the Family* was so good at exploring so many other subjects, including subjects important to women, for so many years. One can only speculate as to the source of this omission: Struthers's availability (she was reportedly restless and eager to leave the show in its later years), for example, or the need to juggle episodes around other characters. One might think the relative inexperience of the scriptwriters with such issues (writing for a television show is not exactly a family-friendly proposition) would be an explanation, but as Lear said, "I can't think of a single writer on my shows that wasn't married or had children. They all seemed to have families. The pool we drew from was the national culture."[14] Whatever the reason, it seems like a lost opportunity.

In the final years of the series, the principal theme of Gloria's storyline is the gradual, but unmistakable, rise in marital tensions with Mike. This is hardly surprising, given that his completion of an undergraduate and then graduate degrees gives him new economic and personal leverage at a time when Gloria is more immersed than ever in the domestic sphere. It's clear that Mike isn't a bad guy; it's equally clear that he's not always attentive to his wife and the things she cares about most. In the final season of *All in the Family*, Archie and Edith take a Christmas trip to visit the Stivics in southern California, where we learn the Stivics are trying to pretend everything is fine despite the fact that they're headed for a divorce. We also learn that Gloria has been having an affair with one of Mike's colleagues—a bit unexpected, in that one might think Mike would be the one with more opportunities to stray, but again not hard to believe given the challenges that Gloria faces.

Some of which, it should be said, are cultural: Gloria is swimming against the tide of history. Her character is a stay-at-home mom at a time when more and more women were leaving the home for paid labor, whether out of necessity or by choice. As indeed will Gloria herself. In *Gloria*, a spin-off that ran for a single season in 1982–1983, we see her after Mike has left her for another woman to live on a commune. Gloria takes Joey, now about seven years old, and comes back to rural New York to be closer to her father and work for a veterinarian (played by a close friend of O'Connor's, the acclaimed Burgess Meredith). It's an uphill battle for Gloria, as well as for the series, in which Lear had no involvement. O'Connor, initially a producer of the series that ran in tandem with *Archie Bunker's Place*, withdrew his support over unhappiness about the way it was unfolding.[15]

It's instructive to compare Gloria's fate with that of her fictive contemporary, Mary Richards, the protagonist of *The Mary Tyler Moore Show*, which ran for years as part of the same killer stable of CBS sitcoms in the 1970s. Mary is about the same age as Gloria when she leaves small-town Minnesota in the aftermath of a broken engagement and goes to the big city of Minneapolis. Like Gloria, Mary lacks a college education. Unlike Gloria, she also lacks a romantic partner—which, at least superficially, would appear to place her in a weaker economic position. But over the course of the next seven years, we see Mary rise from a secretarial job to that of a producer at a local television station, gaining authority both personally and professionally. She also experiences upward economic mobility, as indicated by her move to a larger and more stylish apartment later in the series. Mary never does settle down with a man or have a child—active decisions on the part of the producers, who sought to make a feminist statement about a person who does indeed make it after all. It seems safe to say that most girls who tuned in week after week to watch *All in the Family* and *The Mary Tyler Moore Show* would prefer to end up like Mary, not Gloria.

In fact, of course, most women ended up more like Gloria than Mary. (Or like Rhoda, Mary's best friend, a New York Jew who was closer in spirit to Gloria despite Gloria sharing a WASP background with Mary.) The point here is not to detract from the importance of Mary—she was indeed a worthy aspirational figure whose own struggles were depicted with a bracing dose of realism—or to privilege the gender politics of one over the other. Rather, it's to return our focus to the foundational element of *All in the Family*: its class dynamics, dynamics that are rooted in culture at least as much as they are in money. Gloria Bunker Stivic was a working-class feminist. It was an uphill battle. It still is. More than anyone else in the show, she fought a good fight. And one that's ongoing.

10

Family Resemblance

The Rise and Fall of the Lear Television Empire

First, *All in the Family* was an idea. Then it became a pilot, followed by a full-fledged TV show. From there, it became a hit and a cultural phenomenon. Ultimately, it laid the foundation for a broadcasting empire that dominated 1970s television and created a legacy that lives in collective memory to this day.

When we last visited the subject of *AITF*'s place on the television map in chapter 3, it was to note that by 1972 the show had survived early doubts about its appeal and criticism of its content to become a bona fide success in a fiercely competitive network television landscape. For the next five years, it would routinely rule the airwaves as the most popular show—not just sitcom but show—on TV. It also achieved the unprecedented feat of winning four places on the Top 25 programs with the largest Nielsen ratings of all time, a statistic all the more impressive given that it was not for a special event like the Super Bowl.[1] But *AITF*'s success was more than a matter of mere ratings. So it's worth looking at some of the other metrics of its impact.

One, of course, was money. Remember that in the economic model of television broadcasting, the chief financial product was not the program but the people who watched it, who were sold as viewers to advertisers. The more people—or, perhaps more accurately, the more of the right *kind* of people, in a time when demographics were looming ever larger in American commerce—the more money a network could charge. In the 1975 *Guinness Book of World Records, All in the Family* was listed as commanding the highest advertising rate ever—$128,000 per minute—for any TV show.[2] This figure, too, has been eclipsed (indeed, it seems almost quaint given the inflation rate for the past forty years; Super Bowl ads are now measured in the millions) but is nevertheless a useful barometer of the show's currency at the time.

There were others. As noted, Archie Bunker became a form of political shorthand for Richard Nixon's political coalition (and the basis of more than a few political buttons, most of them ironic). But the show also became a touchstone in popular culture, a development with commercial implications. Sound recordings of the show's theme song and an *All in the Family* cast album were hits.[3] *All in the Family* also became something of a cottage industry in publishing. There was *Edith Bunker's "All in the Family" Cookbook*, whose cover featured an uncharacteristically gleeful Archie about to get his dinner from Edith. ("Best cookbook ever," notes one happy owner in a 2016 review on Amazon.com. "Have had mine for 43 years, pages falling out and unfortunately missing. Thankfully was able to get a replacement.")[4] There was also *The Wit and Wisdom of Archie Bunker*, a 184-page, 95-cent paperback consisting of Bunker musings divided into chapters including "Archie on Sex," "Archie on Women's Lib," and "Through Archie's Pinko-Colored Glasses."[5] Among the more ponderous literary entries came one from Presbyterian minister Spencer Marsh, who weighed in with *God, Man, and Archie Bunker*, published by the high-prestige house Harper & Row in 1975, when the show was at its height. "Archie's 'God' is a counterfeit, and he must die so that Archie and all those who are in so many ways like him can begin to know the God of revelation," Marsh opined. "When that 'God' dies, we who have wrongfully created him in our own image can be recreated by him in his image."[6]

The show's financial clout was also converted into other kinds. One of the most important was influence over the content of the show. Network executives are a skittish bunch and are disinclined to approve subject matter or language that may lead advertisers to demur from buying advertising. But the power dynamic shifts significantly when they're trying to keep a hit maker happy. "You couldn't have a battle with Norman, because he had all the ammunition," Fred Silverman, the CBS (later ABC) programmer who helped put the show on the air, later remembered. "And the network was not about to lose *All in the Family.*" Perry Lafferty, the vice president of programming, agreed. "They didn't talk Norman Lear out of doing much, I'll tell you that," he said. "He was older, he had more experience, and he was very tough. And he just held the line. It was like 'You don't want to do it this way? Let's not do it all.' It wasn't about whole shows, it was more about lines, and fights about maybe a scene or something . . . but the minute it got numbers, that was over!" Lear, who had a good relationship with the CBS director of program practices, William Tankersley, said he hated the expression "getting away with" to describe his attempts to stretch television conventions. "We were dead serious about what we wanted to do. And I think they caught on to that—that we were not playing games."[7]

Lear's leverage was internal as well as external. "He'd put in stuff, or make *you* put in stuff," Bob Schiller, a pillar of the writing staff, remembered. "But he owned the store, so there was not much we could say. So, that was that. But he certainly was an innovator, and had guts, and changed the face of television."[8] Lear's day-to-day presence receded somewhat as the show went on, but he continued to take a proprietary interest in it all the way through its nine-season run.

All in the Family was also powerful in what might be termed the politics of scheduling. In the days before streaming, network television shows lived or died by when they were broadcast—and what was broadcast around them. As we've seen, *AITF* was initially inserted into a relatively unprepossessing piece of programming real estate at 9:30 P.M. on Tuesday nights, following a string of very traditional comedies. But as its vast potential became clear, the show became a network showcase. By the time of the 1974–1975 season, it had become the anchor of the most legendary programming lineup in television history: *All in the Family* at 8:00 P.M., *The Jeffersons* (to be discussed shortly) at 8:30, *The Mary Tyler Moore Show* at 9:00, *The Bob Newhart Show* at 9:30, and *The Carol Burnett Show* at 10:00. That sequence, the television equivalent of the 1927 New York Yankees, didn't last long; the four sitcoms, each now considered a classic, would soon be redistributed to bolster weaker lineups in the network's schedule. "That night—that Saturday night we built at CBS—was the last night time that Saturday night was ever important. Anywhere," CBS executive Alan Wagner later remembered. "Nobody watches TV on Saturday nights anymore. Now it's the lowest audience numbers of any night of the week, but in those days, it was appointment viewing." Wagner called *All in the Family* "the linchpin" of its success.[9]

Lear's clout was also important in leading the counterattack against government regulation of network programming. In the early 1970s, a growing chorus of critics on the left as well as the right complained that there was too much inappropriate content—the left tended to complain about bigotry and violence, the right about sex and profanity—on the airwaves. The Federal Communications Commission (FCC) reported a rise in viewer complaints from about 1,200 in 1972 to 33,000 in 1973. In the face of such pressures, the agency, acting in concert with the National Association of Broadcasters and with the acquiescence of the networks, implemented Family Viewing Hour, a new rule barring "adult-themed" content on the air from 7:00 to 9:00 P.M. This pushed *All in the Family* out of its 8:00 P.M. timeslot and into 9:00 P.M. on Mondays, when it competed with ABC's new powerhouse programing, *Monday Night Football*. Lear teamed up with Alan Alda of *M*A*S*H*, Mary Tyler Moore, and O'Connor to sue the federal government on First Amendment grounds. A federal district judge in Los Angeles ruled in their favor in November 1977, allowing *AITF* to resume its place on Saturday night along with the Mary Tyler Moore and Bob Newhart shows. The decision was later overturned on technical grounds, but by that point there was new leadership at the FCC, which was moving in the direction of deregulation, reflecting the shifting political currents of the late Carter years, culminating in the abolishment of the Fairness Doctrine, whereby television stations were required to present multiple points of view on matters of public importance, in 1987.[10]

Beyond the impact of the show's individual episodes and collective imprint, the most important measure of *All in the Family*'s influence was its role in spawning a string of other shows that collectively became what might be termed the Lear sitcom empire. Some of these shows were spin-offs—and spin-offs of spin-offs. Others were separate but reflected Lear's liberal sensibility. Some were more successful than others. But taken together they represent a remarkable cultural achievement.

. . . And Then There's *Maude*

The beachhead for the *Maude* empire was *Sanford and Son*, which arrived in January 1972. Since the sitcom was a Tandem Production, Lear officially had a role, but the show was really a Bud Yorkin vehicle. It ran on NBC after CBS failed to seize it when offered the opportunity. Though the sitcom was entirely separate from *All in the Family*, the two shared a set of key traits. Like *AITF*, *Sanford and Son* was based on a British original, *Steptoe and Son*, which ran on the BBC from 1962 to 1965 and again from 1970 to 1974. The British series focused on a Cockney junkyard owner and his lazy son; as with *AITF*, the scenario was transposed into an American key, in this case to a black father-and-son team in the Los Angeles neighborhood of Watts. Like Archie, Fred Sanford—played by Redd Foxx, a veteran comedian whose work stretched back to the days of vaudeville, when he was friendly with Malcolm X—was a working-class figure with misguided prejudices, such as his animus against Puerto Ricans. But there was also something of a meta-textual dimension to the humor; as David Marc noted, "Instead of watermelon jokes, Lear offered jokes about watermelon jokes."[11] Like *AITF*, *Sanford and Son* was a midseason replacement when it launched in 1972; it would last for five more seasons.

The second sitcom to follow in *All in the Family*'s wake, and the first to be a direct spin-off of the show, was *Maude*. The character in question was Maude Findlay, one of a gallery of Edith's cousins who drove *All in the Family* plots over the course of its run. (There was cousin Amelia, for example, who persuaded Edith to attend their high school reunion, and cousin Liz, whose lesbianism was something Edith learned after her death. There was also cousin Floyd, who brought his daughter Stephanie into the Bunkers' lives in the final season.) Maude, played by the veteran stage actress Bea Arthur, made her first appearance halfway through the second season of *AITF* in December 1971. The "Cousin Maude's Visit" episode begins with three of the four Bunkers struggling with the flu—and Edith struggling to tend to them. Gloria pushes Edith to send for her beloved relative, but Archie will have none of it—the two have been at loggerheads for twenty-five years, ever since he appalled her with his juvenile antics to impress Edith at an ice cream parlor. Ultimately his objections are overridden, and Maude sweeps in—and past Archie. She's a juggernaut of activity, and amid her brisk efficiency makes clear why: "Dear, sweet Edith," she tells Archie. "I'd kill for that girl." (Her glare makes clear that she'd be happy to kill Archie.) "Gee, Maude, you already buried two husbands," Archie replies. "Ain't that enough killing for you?" Twice widowed, Maude would ultimately marry four times.

Archie and Maude are also political opponents, and an argument they have in this episode gives us an ideological backstory into her own series.

Maude has occupied Archie's chair and refuses to vacate it. Archie, know-ing how to get her goat, delivers a line he correctly believes will ultimately lead her to leap to her feet: "This country was ruined by Franklin Delano Roosevelt."

Maude's response: "You're fat."

"His whole family was for Roosevelt," Edith observes.

"That was for two terms and that was it!" Archie says. "We didn't know the guy was going to hold on to the job like the pope!"

"To save the country!" Maude exclaims. "The people adored him. He was a saint. That man had charisma." Maude clearly has the better of the ensu-ing argument; when Archie says, "FDR sold us out at Gibraltar," Maude points out that he means Yalta ("there too," he replies). But the ruse allows him to seize back his throne. "Archie, you can have your chair," Maude says. "Only don't move around too much. You'll crush your brains."

"Before it aired, I knew I was going to get a call very quickly to build a show around her," Lear later remembered. "There was nothing like her around. And, indeed, before I went to bed that night I got a call from Fred Silverman. Immediately: 'You've got to do a show with that woman, right away.'" Ironically, Lear was skeptical. "He didn't want to do it," Sil-verman remembered. "He just—I don't know, he had to be talked into everything."[12]

It was widely understood among insiders that Maude was actually based on Lear's second wife, Frances, to whom he was married from 1956 to 1985 and who founded *Lear's*, a magazine for women of a certain age after their divorce. "Maude *was* Frances," Lear's partner, Bud Yorkin, asserted. "There were similarities," Lear conceded, though in his memoir he said that of all the characters he's created, Maude is most like himself ("Oh, my Maude!" he exclaims at the end of the book). Susan Harris, who wrote for the new sitcom and went on to launch a few herself, viewed the character as a turn-ing point in the history of television: "No woman spoke the way Maude did."[13] Harris described Maude as a radical chic liberal, one whose opinions were inversions of Archie's, though sometimes rooted in presuppositions not all that different from his. So it was, for example, that she would say things like, "Everybody knows Jewish boys make the best husbands. It's a known fact. Look it up."

Once the decision was made to base a show on Maude, it came together quickly. The Season 2 finale of *AITF*, simply titled "Maude," broadcast in March 1972, was devoted to setting up the scenario for the sitcom to debut that fall. Archie and Edith travel to the suburban town of Tuckahoe—while the opening credits of *All in the Family* start in Manhattan and end in row-house Queens, those of *Maude* start in Manhattan and end up in leafy Westchester—where we meet the core characters: Maude, her current hus-band Walter, and her adult daughter by a previous husband, Carol, a divor-cee. (Carol is played by Marcia Rodd; she would be replaced in the series by Adrienne Barbeau.) *Maude* ran for six seasons; its theme song, "And Then There's Maude," sung by soul music luminary Donny Hathaway, was for a time as familiar as "Those Were the Days." *All in the Family, Sanford and Son, Maude*: Tandem had scored three hits in a row. *Time* magazine esti-mated that for 1972 alone, Yorkin and Lear's profits from the trio exceeded $5 million, a huge sum for the time.[14]

Like *All in the Family*, *Maude* engaged any number of socially charged subjects. But it would go significantly further—and generate more signifi-cant controversy—with one issue in particular: abortion. In the two-part 1972 episode "Maude's Dilemma," written by Harris, the forty-seven-year-old Maude is appalled to learn that she is pregnant. Her daughter is even more appalled and argues forcefully that Maude should terminate the pregnancy—something still illegal in many states at the time, though not in Maude's native New York. Walter carefully avoids taking a position, stating he will take his cue from his wife. For much of the two episodes, it appears that Maude is going to go ahead and have the baby. But in a bedside conversa-tion with Walter, it becomes clear she's principally doing this for the childless Walter, who, conversely, supports her having the baby only because he mis-takenly believes it's what Maude wants. The episode ends quietly with a deci-sion and an embrace—a mild resolution to a highly charged social issue.

Just how highly charged became apparent when Lear and company pro-ceeded with their plans to broadcast the episodes. Local affiliates refused to run it. (Only two in Illinois barred the first broadcast, though a total of thirty-nine did when it was rerun.) Advertisers refused to buy time for it. Protesters lay down in front of CBS chairman William Paley's car as he was driving into the network's garage. Hundreds of protesters picketed local TV stations in the Midwest; the network received 17,000 letters denouncing the show.[15] It's important to note here that the U.S. Supreme Court issued its *Roe v. Wade* decision guaranteeing the right to an abortion in January 1973, a signal event in the emergence of the New Right. The decision was announced between the premiere and the rerun of the episode, which may explain the hardening stance that solidified between the two airings.

While *Maude* was avowedly political, the show never lost sight of its mission to entertain even when it was stretching boundaries. For example, in the Season 3 episode "Walter's Heart Attack," Maude feels compelled to be nice to Walter amid a health crisis, even though she wrongly believes he's having an affair. When it's clear he's going to recover, she tells him how glad she is and then calls him "a son of a bitch"—a first in television profanity, but one even the CBS director of standards believed was the most logical and appropriate thing for the character to say in that situation.[16]

Black to the Future (with Class)

Maude also propelled a spin-off of its own. One key character in the series was that of the Findlay's wise, mild-mannered African American maid, Florida, played by Esther Rolle. At one point early in its run, the writers introduced her husband, a firefighter played by John Amos, soon to rocket to fame as the lead character of Kunta Kinte in the blockbuster ABC miniseries *Roots*. (The show's currency was great enough to be referenced in *All in the Family*.) Lear and his collaborators—who included Mike Evans, who played Lionel on *AITF*—thought the couple could form the basis for a show of their own and created *Good Times*, which ran from 1974 to 1979. In doing so, they recast Florida's backstory, situating her and her husband in a Chicago public housing project widely believed to be the notorious Cabrini-Green. The couple's oldest son, J.J., played by Jimmie Walker, had an expression—"Dy-no-mite!"—that became the signature line of the series. *Good Times* was the first network television show to depict a complete African American family. It also continued a pattern of Tandem Productions focused on the nuts and bolts of working-class life, to which *Maude* was an exception.

There was, however, a perception among some observers that *Sanford and Son* and *Good Times* peddled in demeaning stereotypes, criticism that was more prominent and durable than when similar complaints had been aired against *All in the Family*. A black writer in the *New York Times* said of *Sanford and Son* in 1973 that "there is nothing here that has traditionally motivated black humor—no redemptive suffering, no strength, no tragedy behind the humor. There is only the kind of selfishness and immaturity and bigotry that characterize contemporary American humor."[17] Jimmie Walker was widely criticized by evoking the damaging racial stereotype of the coon character in American minstrelsy.[18] Walker was also a lightning rod for criticism among his peers on the show as well, although Lear reported that largely black audiences at the tapings of the show were enthusiastic.[19] Whatever the merits of these criticisms—there are at least some—one senses an intra-racial class disagreement between African Americans over how they should be depicted in ways that can be witnessed by the outside world. It's a debate that stretches back to the conflicted career of Bert Williams at the turn of the twentieth century and continues through the work of comedians such as Dave Chappelle at the turn of the twenty-first.

Lear faced some of the challenges to his creative decisions directly. In his memoir he describes an unsolicited visit to his offices by three members of the Black Panthers (whose leader, Eldridge Cleaver, was once referred to by Archie as "Elder Cleavage") who asserted they had "come to see the garbage men." Lear reported they were upset in particular by *Good Times*, describing it as "nothing but a white man's version of a black family. . . . J.J. is a fucking putdown. . . . Every time you see a black man on the tube he is dirt poor, wears shit clothes, can't afford nothing. . . . That's bullshit, we got black men in America doing better than most whites." Hours later, Lear said, he and a colleague agreed to launch what proved to be arguably the most successful of all the *All in the Family* spin-offs, *The Jeffersons*.[20]

One suspects that the creation of *The Jeffersons*, whose family name is clearly meant to constitute ironic homage to a Founding Father, was a little more complicated than Lear made it sound. But however it came about, the show remains a landmark in television history not simply as a portrayal of black life but more specifically *affluent* black life, adding an important class dimension to popular discourse at a time when millions of white Americans were only beginning to achieve any sense of nuance in their understanding of African Americans. Of course, a television sitcom is a fairly primitive place to start. But for many it *was* a start in a cultural literacy project that is ongoing.

Actually, that start had been undertaken to a significant degree by *All in the Family*, where the Jeffersons were important characters in many episodes. Lionel Jefferson, of course, is there at the moment of creation, appearing onscreen as a college student in the pilot even before Archie or Edith do, offering viewers a character who can be instantly recognized as genial, sophisticated, and comfortable in his own skin. Lionel has apparently become friendly with the Bunkers because they are customers of his family's dry-cleaning business. But their relationship is put on a new footing in the eighth episode of Season 1, "Lionel Moves into the Neighborhood," when his parents buy a house at 708 Hauser Street, right next to the Bunkers—traffic between the two houses via their back doors will soon become commonplace. Archie, initially unaware that the black family in question is Lionel's, is annoyed at his neighbor, Jim Bowman, for not selling his house to a white family. (Bowman is played by Vincent Gardenia, who will also play a swinger seeking to participate in the sex partner switch with the Bunkers two years later before settling into the recurring role of Frank Lorenzo in 1974.) An avowed racist himself who sold the house to a black family only because he couldn't find a white buyer, Bowman suggests Archie and his neighbors pool their resources to buy out the new owners, a familiar racist tactic dramatized in the classic 1959 Lorraine Hansberry play *A Raisin in the Sun*. Archie describes the prospect of a black neighborhood as "our world is crumbling down—the coons are coming," leading Gloria to respond "I think it's wonderful." He approaches Lionel to be his mediator in making a buyout offer to the black family in question, which Lionel politely but firmly refuses to do, explaining that he's a member of the black family in question. By the end of the episode, Archie has accepted defeat and is giving Lionel his usually questionable advice to be on guard against the Italian butcher, the Armenian gas station manager, and the black sanitation workers. Thus is Lionel welcomed into the neighborhood by Archie's lights.

One key character we meet in this episode is Lionel's mother, Louise Jefferson, played by Isabel Sanford. Predictably, Archie mistakes her for a maid, but she and Edith rapidly become the fast friends they will remain for the next four seasons. Louise has Edith's kindly disposition but is considerably more worldly than Edith and more tactful than Archie. Her husband, George, played by Sherman Helmsley, remained offscreen for two years because of Helmsley's other acting commitments.[21] We instead are given George's brother Henry (Mel Stewart), who lives with his brother, nephew, and sister-in-law. The Bunkers mistake Henry for Louise's husband in the Season 1 finale, "The First and Last Supper," in which Archie reluctantly gives up tickets to the Mets game to have dinner with the Jeffersons, only to learn that George, whose prejudice against white people mirrors Archie's prejudice against black people, skipped the dinner to attend the very same Mets game, sending Henry to the Bunkers in his stead.

George Jefferson—a bantam-like figure of great energy, even ferocity—finally makes his memorable entrance in the 1973 episode "Henry's Farewell," whose plot turns on Henry's pending move to start a dry-cleaning business in upstate Dutchess County. Edith wants to throw a farewell party for him, which Archie refuses to do on racial grounds. When he learns that George has *also* refused to hold an interracial party, Archie changes course in an act of one-upmanship. What follows is a string of pointed topical dialogue between him and Henry (some of which is discussed in chapter 9). Toward the end of the evening, Henry proposes an ironic toast: "I want to thank you, Bunker, for letting me know, and letting me see, that some white folks are better than other white folks." A clueless Archie responds, "Well, I wish the whole world could hear that." Mike then suggests that Archie toast Henry, but we suddenly hear George shouting from outside that he wants to be the one to toast Henry. What follows is a kind of interracial form of the Dozens conducted by two men separated by a closed door. When Archie asks if George would actually like to enter, George responds, "I wouldn't come in there even if you got on your hands and knees and sang [the Al Jolson minstrel song] 'Mammy.'"

"If I was your brother I'd leave home too," Archie replies.

"If you were my brother I'd slit my throat."

"If I was your brother I'd give you the knife."

Archie opens the door and claims that George has entered, which George denies, leading to an argument about whether stoops count as interiors. "So, finally, the great Jefferson, who always reclined to cross my freshold," Archie says. But George is now focused on his brother. "Henry, when I was a kid I was always asking Ma for a brother. You know how poor we were. So all we could afford is you."

Louise, mortified, explains to the Bunkers that George is joking.

"The trouble with being a brother," George continues on a more serious note, "is that sometimes you can't say the things you really feel. Like how good it is to have somebody to rap to, somebody to kind of pick you up when you're so low that you have to reach to touch bottom. Well you know I'm not much of a talker, but there's one thing that needs to be said: I love you, brother."

Henry jokingly accuses George of theft—for stealing his words. The two men embrace. All acknowledge a lovely moment. "Just sorry it had to take place in a honky household," George says as he heads out the door.

Over the course of the first four seasons, the lives of the Bunkers and Jeffersons intertwine in convergent and divergent ways. So, for example, there's the pair of 1973 episodes titled "We're Having a Heatwave," broadcast about a month before Henry's departure, in which he and Archie team up to try to prevent a Puerto Rican family from moving into the residence next door. It is ultimately acquired, for unrelated reasons, by Irene and Frank Lorenzo, an Irish-Italian couple who add two additional layers of ethnic flavor to the roster of characters on the show.

One of the more amusing and ironic case studies in the Bunker-Jefferson relationship is the 1974 episode "Lionel's Engagement." At the start of the episode, Louise diplomatically explains to Edith that she, Mike, and Gloria are welcome to attend her son's engagement party, but that it's best that Archie not attend. So she's taken aback when Archie arrives on the scene as this conversation concludes and invites himself. "Mrs. J., you know how I feel about Lionel," he says. "I mean, I like him very much. I mean I practically watched the kid grow up." This is an exaggeration—as Edith points out, Archie has only known Lionel for four years. Archie waves that off. "I took him under my wing," he says delusionally. "Being colored, he naturally was a little green." Archie's paternalism is literally laughable, but there's little question about the sincerity of his affection for Lionel, however limited his angle of vision.

We soon learn that Louise's gentle suggestion that Archie not attend the party was actually an attempt to finesse what was a demand by George that he not be invited. When Louise reports while making dinner that Archie invited himself, George responds, "No way, Louise!" What follows is an argument that depicts what will become an ongoing dynamic in the Jefferson marriage: George's impetuousness, tempered by Louise's flexibility—to a point. Losing her patience, Louise, who makes clear that her affection for Edith is the lodestar guiding her actions, demands that George desist in complaining about Archie. "Are you telling me to shut up?" he asks angrily. "Do you see anyone else in this room?" she answers. When George says Archie will attend the engagement party "over my dead body," Louise tersely replies by saying "that's one way."

The great joke of this episode, and one that will carry over into the ensuing series, is that Lionel's fiancée, Jennie Willis, is the daughter of an interracial couple, something Lionel has put off telling his father until the party. George is appalled—and Jennie's black mother is appalled that George is appalled—that Jennie's father is white. When Mr. Willis gently tries to privately remonstrate with his wife, an observing George tells Louise, "That's what happens when you mix black and white. Ten more seconds he's gonna call her a nigger."

"Listen to that," Archie observes. "I ain't used that word in three years." This is an inside joke; the show had been on the air for only three years at that point, so Archie had never used the term—and, notwithstanding a self-described ignorant childhood reference in the "Shoebootie" anecdote discussed in chapter 6, never would—which was also uttered by Sammy Davis Jr. in the 1973 episode "Sammy's Visit." In retrospect, it's amazing that the taboo term ever got past network censors at all, though it's perhaps unsurprising that black characters were the ones to use it most directly and forcefully. When, in 2019, ABC broadcast a live episode of *The Jeffersons* as originally written but with a new cast, the epithet was uttered by Jamie Foxx's George Jefferson, but bleeped out by broadcast censors. (Foxx, by the way, born Eric Bishop, adopted his stage name in honor of *Sanford and Son* star Redd Foxx.)

In "Lionel's Engagement," Mr. Willis breaks the rising racial tension between the families by asking Louise to dance. When George starts to object, she says, "He asked me first." George and Archie repair to the bar, where they have a memorable exchange. "Bunker, what is this world coming to?" a bemused George asks. "Beats me, Jefferson," Archie replies. "All I got to say is"—raising his glass—"here's to yesterday."

The Jeffersons, like *Maude*, made its debut as a midseason replacement in 1975, and also like *The Jeffersons*, *Maude* was launched during an episode of *All in the Family*. (One difference, though, was timing: the *AITF* episode "The Jeffersons Move Up" was aired a mere week, not six months, before the series debuted.) The episode begins with a tearful goodbye between Edith and Louise ("Did I ever tell you that I love you?" Edith asks; "Every minute we spent together," Louise replies) before the action shifts to the Upper East Side of Manhattan and the family's new digs. The Willises, coincidentally, live upstairs in the same building though new actors, Roxie Roker and Franklin Cover, portray them. In the years that followed, the series, helmed by *AITF* veterans Don Nicholl, Michael Ross, and Bernie West, which was grounded in the Jefferson's apartment building and explored what became a familiar range of Learesque social issues, went on to become one of the most beloved and durable in television history, lasting eleven seasons and over 250 episodes (about 50 more than *AITF*). It had particular resonance for African Americans. As the black entrepreneur Russell Simmons noted in 2016, "*The Jeffersons* represented the American Dream for black people."[22]

King Lear

By the middle of 1975, the Tandem broadcast empire was at its peak. In the Nielsen ratings for the 1974–1975 season, *All in the Family* came in at number one, *Sanford and Son* at number two, *The Jeffersons* at four, *Good Times* at seven, and *Maude* at nine—domination reminiscent of the Beatles on the Billboard pop charts in 1964.[23] *All in the Family* reruns also entered into the daytime sweepstakes, competing with soap operas such as *Another World* and *The Edge of Night*. Lear wasn't entirely happy about the daytime broadcasts, because they involved more advertising time, requiring trims of *AITF* episodes. He tried to persuade CBS to forgo the additional revenue, but capitulated—and made a lot of money as a result. (One suggestion of Lear's wealth: his divorce settlement from Frances Lear in the mid-1980s was valued at over $100 million).[24]

Lear's success in the mid-1970s was prominent enough to attract the attention of one of the premier high-culture brokers of the era, the *New Yorker*. In a somewhat stilted omnibus review of Lear sitcoms, the critic Michael Arlen noted that roughly 125 million viewers watched one each week, which added up to about 5 billion a year. "Perhaps what is most fascinating about Mr. Lear's oeuvre is the dimensions of its success, for he seems to be one of those ordinary but uncommon figures who come along every so often in our mass-entertainment culture to achieve—more or less single-handed and with the appearance of naturalness—what tens of thousands of business geniuses and consumer theoreticians spend half the energies of the Republic vainly striving after, namely, a 'feel' for what the public wants before it knows it wants it, and the ability to deliver it."[25] (Not that Lear shows are very funny, or exhibit a genius recognized beyond the precincts of the *New Yorker*, mind you. Most of what he peddles, Arlen says, is anger couched in laughs.)

It is, however, in the nature of pop stardom of the kind that Lear was enjoying in the mid-1970s that a run of rapid-fire hits would eventually come to an end. This didn't happen right away. The year 1975 also marked the debut of one of Lear's most durable hits: *One Day at a Time*. The show featured Bonnie Franklin as a single white divorcée—a television first—raising two adolescent daughters (Mackenzie Phillips and Valerie Bertinelli) in Indianapolis. A fusion of working-class concerns and second-wave feminism, it lasted nine seasons alongside *The Jeffersons*, well into the Reagan era.

It was also in 1975 that Lear and Yorkin parted company. Like the later Lennon and McCartney, the two had largely focused on their own projects but shared the credit and the profits. After this point, however, Lear shifted his emphasis away from Tandem Productions to a new enterprise he dubbed T.A.T.—an abbreviation of the Yiddish phrase "tuchas affen tish," or "ass on the table."

But the Lear balloon was beginning to deflate. One of T.A.T.'s first projects—this one for ABC, which meant that Lear now had shows on all three networks—was *Hot l Baltimore*, a series based on a successful off-Broadway play about the denizens of a sleazy Maryland hotel (the "e" was missing from its sign). The series, which was developed by *Maude* producer Rod Parker, featured two prostitutes as its main characters. It lasted only one season, perhaps because its sexual innuendo was regarded as sensationalistic.

Lear pushed television frontiers in a different direction by developing not simply a new show but a new *kind* of show with *Mary Hartman, Mary Hartman*, a satiric soap opera that he launched in 1976. (The title was a kind of homage to the classic early 1950s sitcom *The Goldbergs*, in which the family matriarch Goldberg called out to her neighbor through her window, "Yoo-hoo, Mrs. Bloom! Mrs. Bloom!")[26] Like traditional soaps, *Mary Hartman, Mary Hartman*, colloquially known as *MH2*, aired five times a week, but in an unprecedented move was scheduled for late nights. Set in the fictive town of Fernwood, Ohio, the opening scenario set the tone for what followed: it began with the mass murder of a five-member family, along with two goats and eight chickens, down the street from the eponymous Mary Hartman (Louise Lasser). But Mary is less impressed by the crime than the label of a household product she's using in a home where the television is always on. Oh and by the way, the neighborhood flasher turns out to be her grandfather. In subsequent episodes, characters will die via drowning in chicken soup, electrocution in a bathtub, and impalement by a Christmas tree (the actor depicting this last mishap, Martin Mull, would go on to have a distinguished comic career in movies, television, and comedy clubs).

Lear had persuaded CBS to bankroll the first few episodes of *MH2*, but the network quickly pulled out. When neither of the other two major networks expressed an interest, Lear made the bold decision to syndicate the show himself, selling the series to 128 individual stations around the country and demonstrating—on the eve of cable television's rise to prominence—that there were alternatives to network broadcasting for producers of new programming. This approach also allowed the show's creators to stretch standards at a time when other shows, notably *Saturday Night Live*, which premiered in 1975, were just beginning to test such waters in new ways.

In terms of its overall success, *MH2* was a mixed bag. It lasted for only a year and a half. *Fernwood 2 Night*, a summer spin-off show about a late-night local TV talk show that starred Mull and a sidekick played by Fred Willard, ran for a mere three months in 1977 (it was rebooted as *America 2 Night* in 1978). But all these shows developed cult followings and remained beloved for decades after cancellation (*America 2 Night* ran on Nick at Nite in the early 1990s). And they showed that Lear's spirit of restless experimentation extended beyond content, paving the way for generations of successors to find new audiences.[27]

But other Lear shows simply flopped. Indeed, in the second half of the 1970s there was a growing cascade of failures. These included the 1976 T.A.T. production *All's Fair*, starring Richard Crenna as a conservative congressman and Bernadette Peters as his photographer girlfriend. It was canceled after one season. *The Dumplings*, about an overweight couple who own a New York deli, lasted for ten episodes in 1977. *The Nancy Walker Show*, a vehicle for the veteran star of stage and screen whose strong cast included William Daniels and James Cromwell (who played the minor character of Stretch Cunningham in *AITF*), made it through thirteen episodes in 1976–1977. *Apple Pie, All That Glitters, Mr. Dugan*: such shows were little more than blips that came and went in 1977 and 1978. Some were conceptually daring—*All That Glitters* was an avowedly feminist show with women occupying key production positions, and *Mr. Dugan* was about a black congressman, though members of the real Congressional Black Caucus expressed concerns about his characterization—but failed to find audiences.[28]

It's important to keep in mind that this string of failed sitcoms did not mean that Lear was considered damaged goods. Even as these shows foundered, others, like *The Jeffersons* and *One Day at a Time*, hummed along. *All in the Family* gave way to *Archie Bunker's Place*, which enjoyed good ratings well into the early 1980s. *Diff'rent Strokes*, about a wealthy family that adopts its deceased housekeeper's sons, was a bona fide hit that ran for eight seasons between 1978 and 1986. But it was the only Tandem Production show in which neither Lear nor Yorkin was a producer. Lear's magic touch was fading. In 1984 he launched *A.K.A. Pablo*, television's first all-Latino prime-time series, featuring Paul Rodriguez as an aspiring stand-up comic in L.A. It lasted six weeks. By this point, Lear was losing energy for, and interest in, the television business and appointed Alan Horn, a talented executive who would ultimately become the head of Walt Disney, to run his empire.

Fall Season

Lear's decline, if that's the right term to describe someone whose body of work was so large and so durable, can be attributed to a number of factors. It seems safe to surmise that to at least some degree he was a victim of his own success. Supervising the creation of so many shows over the course of a single decade simply had to distract him. One can also discern a dilution of his talent into a gimmick of throwing odd political bedfellows against each other to see what happens. On the other hand, the quality of collaborators, especially writers and actors, that Lear attracted was always first-rate. Indeed, some of the most memorable episodes of *AITF* were produced in its final seasons, when he was no longer a day-to-day fixture on the set.

The network television environment in which Lear operated and prospered was also changing. He lost a key ally when Fred Silverman left CBS in 1975 to take over as president of ABC, inaugurating a string of successes that would become legendary in the annals of television—with shows that competed directly with Lear's. The controversy surrounding Family Viewing Hour suggested that audiences were less receptive to content that challenged their ideological predilections, while network executives focused protecting their bottom lines from potentially problematic content. By the early 1980s, the big three saw themselves less as stewards of the public good than businesses answering to shareholder value. Such intensifying economic imperatives were also reflected in the networks' shrinking patience in giving shows time to find an audience. One can plausibly wonder if *All in the Family*, which was not an immediate hit, could have succeeded had it gone on the air later than it did. It's commonplace to lament the narrow-mindedness of the networks in such programming decisions, which in many cases was real enough. But corporate pressures in an age of megamergers (typified with ABC's swallowing by the much smaller Capital Cities collection of stations in 1985) and the new challenges of cable made their concerns anything but imaginary as the 1970s gave way to the 1980s.[29]

But the biggest challenge Lear faced was more broadly cultural. As has been made clear over multiple chapters in this book, he rode a wave of change in social mores as the 1960s gave way to the 1970s. As the 1970s gave way to the 1980s, however, that tide receded—or, at any rate, shifted.

Actually, the 1960s underwent a reappraisal in the 1980s.[30] While the liberationist ethos of the Age of Aquarius had a durable appeal among the public at large, there were also gathering cultural currents in the 1980s that questioned, even rejected, the oppositional quality of the 1960s, embracing the sense of cohesion and stability associated with the 1950s, which experienced something of a revival. As we've seen, nostalgia was certainly an important part of television long before *All in the Family* came along, but it took on new contours, often in the form of fond memories of earlier, gentler challenges to the status quo. This tendency was apparent even early in the 1970s with nostalgia acts like Sha Na Na—featured in a TV series in the late 1970s—and with the success of the 1972 Broadway musical *Grease*, which became a smash hit movie in 1978. (The star of *Grease*, John Travolta, was featured in the ABC show *Welcome Back, Kotter*, a sitcom about a high school that ran from 1975 to 1979 with strong sentimental accents in its depiction of rebellious, but harmless, adolescents.) Nowhere was this nostalgia more obvious than in sitcoms, where two of the most successful of the decade were *Happy Days* (1974–1984) and its spin-off *Laverne & Shirley* (1976–1983), developed by impresario Garry Marshall, a man who was comparably successful to Lear but with little of his interest in engaging social or political questions—which was at least in part why he was so successful. Those shows, by the way, were supervised by none other than Fred Silverman, who assembled a 1978 Tuesday night lineup (one that included *Taxi* and *Three's Company*) that rivaled the CBS Saturday night lineup of 1974–1975 in terms of ratings, if not quality.

The new conservatism was a matter of not only avoiding political issues but engaging them head-on. This was apparent in one of the biggest sitcoms of the 1980s, *Family Ties* (1982–1989), in which Michael J. Fox—star of the time-traveling *Back to the Future* trio of films (1985–1990)—played a young conservative at odds with his post-hippie parents. The creators of the show originally intended the parents to be the stars, but Fox, and the politics of his character, stole the show.

Even television shows that were meant to showcase social progress had deeply traditional accents. *The Cosby Show* (1984–1992) was widely hailed as a landmark sitcom for the quality of its writing and acting. It featured an affluent African American family in a cast headed by the well-established comedian Bill Cosby. This was not a novelty; indeed, *The Jeffersons* had led the way. Even in the Reagan era, the patriarchal families of 1950s sitcoms such as *The Adventures of Ozzie and Harriet* (1952–1966) were far too retrograde for the post–women's movement of the 1980s. But with a black man in the lead it was once again possible to smuggle in the message that sometimes, anyway, father may really know best. The legacy of the show was severely corroded, however, in the 2010s amid allegations against Cosby that resulted in his conviction on three counts of sexual assault in 2018.[31]

Other shows that marketed themselves as socially liberal could have strong, even reactionary, countercurrents. A new wave of T&A ("tits and ass") television shows, among them the sitcom *Three's Company* (1977–1984) and the crime drama *Charlie's Angels* (1976–1981), used presumably feminist premises—unmarried cohabitation, women as daring private investigators—to showcase highly sexualized stars such as Suzanne Somers and the iconic Farrah Fawcett. As the feminist writer Barbara Ehrenreich argued in her important 1983 study *The Hearts of Men*, the benefits of sexual liberation tended to favor men more than women, and such shows were at least as much about capturing the male gaze as they were about empowering women.[32]

Actually, feminism took on distinctive accents in the 1980s. The hallmark of the movement in the 1960s and 1970s was a drive for equality, especially in terms of issues like equal pay for equal work. That quest continued, but there was also a more conservative version that tended to define the concept as a matter of succeeding on male terms. One could glimpse it, for example, in the fashion fad of the power suit: trousers, oversized blouse, and a (typically double-breasted) suit jacket with padded shoulders, an ensemble that suggested empowerment through mimicking male couture. Yet this message was also often coupled with more traditional notions of femininity. The two were memorably fused in a perfume ad from the era that featured an attractive woman in a power suit (among other outfits) singing, "I can bring home the bacon / fry it up in the pan / and never let you forget you're a man."[33] Domesticity remained instinctive, even for female breadwinners unafraid to assert their sex drives.

By the mid-1980s, then, the world of *All in the Family* and its ilk could seem surprisingly far away. Indeed, by the early 1990s it had become the stuff of nostalgia, memorialized in a twentieth anniversary special in 1991. It was around that time that rebroadcasts of the show became a fixture of the cable network Nickelodeon's "Nick at Nite" lineup. Like a pop star who has amassed a lucrative catalog, Lear could rest on his laurels and receive the plaudits of a generation of successors—as indeed he did. In some ways he had no choice, as it was no longer easy to get his shows financed and launched. His focus shifted back to films, where it had been before *AITF* came along. In 1982 Lear, Yorkin, and Jerry Perenchio teamed up to purchase AVCO Embassy Pictures, a production company into which he folded Tandem and T.A.T. (Yorkin sold his share in the enterprise to the other two). The company financed Rob Reiner's directorial debut *This Is Spinal Tap* in 1984 before AVCO's sale to Coca-Cola, at vast profit, the following year. Lear received an executive producer credit on Reiner's *The Princess Bride* (1987), widely considered a classic, as well as the hit movie *Fried Green Tomatoes* in 1991.

Citizen Lear (and Papa Lear)

Much of Lear's focus in the 1980s and 1990s, however, was civic. Concerned about the rise of the evangelical right, which he regarded as a threat to religious liberty, Lear became a tongue-in-cheek minister in the (mail order) Universal Life Church, which allowed him to officiate at four weddings, one of which was for *South Park* creator Trey Parker. More significantly, Lear spearheaded the founding of People for the American Way, a liberal political action organization, in 1981. In the decades that followed, PFAW became a prominent counterweight to organizations such as the Reverend Jerry Falwell's Moral Majority, engaging in fund-raising and political action for a variety of Democratic candidates. Characteristically, Lear nevertheless enjoyed good relations with the genial Ronald Reagan before, during, and after his presidency. In 1980, Reagan consented to Lear sending a reporter and camera crew to cover his first campaign for president. He presented an edited ninety-minute video interview drawn from the experience to Reagan's widow Nancy in 2002.[34]

Perhaps Lear's most notable civic undertaking was his purchase of a rare original copy of the Declaration of Independence in 2000. The following year, he took it on a fifty-state, one-hundred-city tour designed to inspire Americans "to participate in civic activism, to exercise their rights, and to vote." The Philadelphia stop of the tour included a reading of the Declaration at Independence Hall by a string of Hollywood luminaries that included Michael Douglas, Whoopi Goldberg, and Benicio Del Toro.[35] Lear's effort was reminiscent of the Freedom Train tour of 1947 in which the National

Archives sent a collection of important documents around the country (but refused to stop in segregated cities) and a similar effort to commemorate the nation's bicentennial in 1975–1976.

The closing decades of the century were busy ones in Lear's personal life as well. Following his divorce of Frances Lear (itself following a four-year marriage to his first wife, Charlotte), Lear wed for a third time in 1987 when he married Lyn Davis, who was twenty-five years his junior. He has a total of six children from his three marriages; the youngest three, with Lyn, were born in the closing decades of the century. Lear was again a father at a time when men are more commonly grandfathers—or even great-grandfathers.

He continued to try his hand with television. In 1991 Lear unveiled *Sunday Dinner*, a series about an older widower (Robert Loggia) engaged to a much younger environmentalist (Teri Hatcher), much to the outrage of his children. The series lasted for six episodes. Lear returned three years later with *704 Hauser*, in which he resurrected a key character from *All in the Family*—the Bunker homestead—and populated it with a black family, the Cumberbatches, who flipped the Bunker-Stivic script by having the parents (Lear favorite John Amos and Lynie Godfrey) bemused by their high-powered conservative son (T. E. Russell). Somewhat improbably, the now-grown Joey Stivic (Casey Siemaszko) comes by to see his grandparents' old place in the pilot episode, and finds himself snacking with the bickering Cumberbatch clan. This show, too, lasted for only six episodes.

In the second decade of the twenty-first century, the nonagenarian Lear experienced something of a professional quickening. "Suddenly I'm extremely wise, and everyone is asking me for advice," he noted puckishly as a ninety-four-year-old.[36] The high-profile publication of his 2014 memoir, *Even This I Get to Experience*, brought him a new round of attention, followed two years later by an installment of the PBS American Masters documentary series titled *Norman Lear: Just Another Version of You*, which featured heartfelt tributes from across the entertainment industry. Lear generated national headlines in 2017 when he was selected to appear in the Kennedy Center Honors ceremony, but announced he would not participate in any activities involving President Donald Trump. "I will not go to this man's White House," he said. "I will not go to *my* White House as long as this man is president." The president and first lady subsequently declined to participate in festivities marking the event.[37]

Lear's renewed cultural currency appears to have translated to some new clout in Hollywood. He struck gold for the first time in forty years in 2017 with a Netflix reboot of *One Day at a Time*, this iteration featuring a Cuban family led by the stage and screen legend Rita Moreno. It finished a second season in 2018 and was renewed for a third in 2019.[38] In its wake, *Entertainment Weekly* reported that Lear inked a deal with Sony Pictures for reboots of *All in the Family*, *The Jeffersons*, *Maude*, and *Good Times*, though Lear quickly disavowed his desire to see them resurrected.[39] One thing that did happen, however, is a live rebroadcast of the "Henry's Farewell" episode, a pet project of talk show host Jimmy Kimmel that aired on ABC in the spring of 2019. The production featured Woody Harrelson as Archie and Marisa Tomei as Edith; Lear himself, ninety-six-years young, was on hand to deliver crisp patter. (A *Jeffersons* episode was part of the same show, as was a documentary that followed the two.)

It seems unlikely all these series would succeed if rebooted. It also appears likely that at least one of them would catch on in some form at some time. At this point in the history of popular culture, hit TV shows are a little like beloved novels or plays that get picked up, revised, or reimagined by subsequent generations. We live in a postmodern society in which *King Lear*, *Little Women*, *Star Wars*, and *Harry Potter* jostle with newer works of imagination that cross multiple media platforms. Archie Bunker was quintessentially a man of his (fading) time. But he lives on in collective memory—and, perhaps more importantly, in digital storage—waiting to be brought back to life by those who may find him relevant in ways we can scarcely imagine. The Bunker files are closed. But the possibility, maybe even the necessity, that they may be reopened lives on.

Conclusion

Just Like Us

In March 2018, as work on this book was getting under way, the ABC television network broadcast the first episode of its *Roseanne* reboot. The show, a big success during its first run in the 1980s and 1990s, was part of a wave of sitcom reboots in the 2010s that included *Will and Grace*, *Murphy Brown*, and Norman Lear's own *One Day at a Time*. This *Roseanne* got off to a very successful start; the initial broadcast of the episode generated 18 million viewers, a figure that jumped to almost 22 million when delayed screenings were factored in. As we've seen, such numbers would be considered anemic in the broadcast era of *All in the Family*, but this was the most viewers for a comedy show since 2014. The future for the show looked bright; ABC renewed *Roseanne* for a second season three days later.[1]

Yet almost from the start, the reboot was a troubled proposition. There were persistent rumors of problems on the set, many involving the show's star and lodestar, Roseanne Barr. Barr was a vocal supporter of President Donald Trump, who returned the favor by calling her to congratulate her in the aftermath of the premiere and invoked her at a campaign rally in Ohio the next day. "Look at Roseanne! Look at her ratings," he said. "They were unbelievable! Over 18 million people! And it was about us."[2] Trump's notion of "us"—the white working class that formed the core of his political base—was as clear as who "us" wasn't: people of color, elite liberals, and the like. To be sure, there were people who defied easy categorization, but American society in the Trump years was as polarized as it had been for at least a century, a development Trump himself was happy to foster.

Barr herself didn't help matters any. She had been a lightning rod for criticism long before the *Roseanne* reboot, as when, for example, she grabbed her crotch during a mangled performance of "The Star-Spangled Banner" at a San Diego Padres baseball game in 1990.[3] Her vocal support of Trump had alienated her from many potential viewers long before the show aired, and she generated outrage for describing the former U.S. ambassador to the United Nations Susan Rice, who is African American, as an ape. Amid falling ratings—by early May, viewership was about half of what it had been at the premiere—Barr committed the fatal mistake of attacking Valerie Jarrett, the former presidential adviser to President Barack Obama, by tweeting, "if the muslim brotherhood & planet of the apes had a baby = vj." Within hours of the appalling tweet, the show was canceled.[4]

Color Television

Roseanne Barr the person always generated more heat than Roseanne Connor, the character she played in her sitcom. Indeed, there was often a complexity to the latter that made the show a bona fide heir to *All in the Family* in its nuanced portrayal of the white working class. The second episode of the reboot, for example, shows Roseanne protecting her grandson against homophobic bullies when he decides to wear a purple blouse and skirt to school. But this Roseanne could also spark Trumpian controversy. Of particular note was the conclusion of the third episode, which aired on April 3. She and her husband Dan have fallen asleep while watching the game show *Wheel of Fortune*, and are awakened hours later during late-night programming. "We missed all the shows about black and Asian families," Dan laments.

"They're just like us," Roseanne replies. "There, now you're all caught up."

This joke seems to have rankled a lot of people. As a number of observers noted, Dan seemed to be referring to two other hit sitcoms, *black-ish* and *Fresh off the Boat*—which, probably not coincidentally, also aired on ABC. "Here's why the Roseanne joke about 'missing all the shows about Black and Asian families' matters," Kelvin Yu, an Asian American writer and director, wrote in a front-page opinion piece in the Arts section of the *New York*

Times. "At the very least, it's reductive and belittling, as if to say those shows are nothing more than 'Black' and 'Asian' in their existence." Over at the *New Yorker*, the Pulitzer Prize–winning television critic Emily Nussbaum was also disturbed. In a piece titled "White-ish," she asserted that "Roseanne's joke makes no sense. The ABC Tuesday night 'black and Asian' family sitcoms aren't 'they're just like us!' stories: to the contrary, they're downright gonzo in their cultural specificity spiked with in-jokes."[5]

What's a little surprising about such criticism of Roseanne's joke is how they seem to miss the point—and fail to acknowledge its double-edged quality. Yu asserts that she's saying "these shows are nothing more than 'Black' and 'Asian,'" when in fact she's saying precisely the opposite: that such people *share* common experiences with the Connors, among others.[6] For a long period of American history, this truth was something a great many Americans refused to recognize. Indeed, it's something that *All in the Family* went out of its way to affirm, a cultural project that was undertaken with trepidation and resistance but something it to a great degree helped convert to the status of common sense by the end of the twentieth century.

This of course is not the whole story, and one in any case can't judge a joke solely on the basis of its (verbal) language. Far from a considered judgment or sentimental bromide, a dismissive air seems to suffuse "just like us": these people *think* they're different. They think that their "cultural specificity," in Nussbaum's words, is the most important thing about them, but it isn't really. In this context, Roseanne's remark is a sharp, pointed rebuttal to the prevailing logic of identity politics in the early twenty-first century, a logic that reflects elite opinion of what it wants the world to be (a cosmopolitan bazaar of diversity) rather than what it really is (the same class-bound culture whose true colors never change). In this regard, Yu is right: the remark *is* belittling, and as such can reasonably be regarded as objectionable. But it can also reasonably be regarded as a usefully provocative political critique aimed at a culture of particularity.

Unfortunately, as matters currently stand, you can't make up your own mind about this. The joke—along with the rest of the *Roseanne* reboot—has been scrubbed from the internet. It was not enough to cancel the show; ABC removed any trace of it. This was of course its legal right; as a nongovernmental entity it enjoys freedom of speech, which includes the freedom *not* to speak. But there are also more substantial reasons beyond a mere right that can plausibly be advanced to justify the decision—one made, perhaps not incidentally, by ABC president Channing Dungey, the first African

American female head of a major television network. The first is that Roseanne in particular, and *Roseanne* by association, was causing pain to people who have historically been subject to ill-advised humor that has been thoughtless at best, and malicious at worst. The other related reason is that social media content of the kind Barr posted foments hatred, and that allowing her show to continue was tantamount to condoning, if not endorsing, sentiments that might amplify if allowed to continue. Certainly there's plenty of evidence of a dangerous mob mentality on the internet, as Kelvin Yu discovered to his dismay when he posted his own comments challenging the "just like us" joke and was confronted by vitriol that no person should have to face for expressing an opinion.

Democratic Faith

The animating spirit of this book—a spirit deeply informed by the formative experience of watching *All in the Family* as a child—nevertheless regards the decision to erase the series as a mistake.[7] When Norman Lear said in 2016 that his credo, expressed in a proverbial bumper sticker, can be summed up as "just another version of you," he knew he was making a contestable assertion. The moment he does so in the documentary of the same name was part of a segment depicting an argument he had in the mid-1970s with the actors of *Good Times*, Esther Rolle and John Amos. They were concerned about the depiction of black characters on the show. "There were lines that were dropped on you that were meant for you to say because you were black," Rolle recalled in a 1990 interview, which she felt honor-bound to contest. Lear disagreed, responding in footage of a script conference from the 1970s, by saying, "You guys [the black actors] know the language, the behavior, but we share the same feelings." This was "just like us"—but us in a key of empathy and a search for common ground. Was Lear right? Maybe so: "Norman Lear was part of the healing in what he gave us," the black entrepreneur Russell Simmons says at another point in the documentary. Maybe not: Rolle and Amos are pretty compelling to see and hear in making their own case. "I insist that you can have comedy without buffoonery," Rolle says, understandably concerned about the dangers of caricature. But the documentary reflected the spirit of Lear's vision, so palpable in *All in the Family*: give us the argument, not the resolution. As *AITF* showed us, sometimes such arguments are a good deal less than civil—or, for that matter, logical. But its animating faith—and to be clear, a great many principles that guide our behavior really *are* a matter of faith that we should understand and treat as such—is that more candor is better than less. This faith is at heart a democratic faith, and one that is now under active question on the left no less than on the right, where the notion that individuals can and should be trusted to make up their own minds is now regarded as naïve at best and pernicious at worst. In an age of big data, where powerful forces of media manipulation lurk, there are reasons to think this way. But there are also reasons—reasons rooted in our history, a history where, in the words of the flawed president Bill Clinton, "There is nothing wrong with America that cannot be fixed by what is right with America."[8] We should strive to keep the faith.

It has been a long time since *All in the Family* was a household commonplace. Generations of children born since 1980 have grown up without ever seeing the show—very possibly without ever hearing of it. To at least some extent, the affection it still commands for those born in the middle of the American Century is a matter of nostalgia—not simply a general hankering for a lost childhood but also for a nation whose population was a good deal whiter and a good deal more tolerant of sexism and racism as we understand those concepts in the early twenty-first century (understandings that will soon be revised, as the implacable rule of time commands). It's hard to imagine the show getting made now: "There's much more political correctness now than there was when we were on a playing field where we hadn't played before," Lear notes.[9] And in many ways that's a good thing. But we would do well to remember, and perhaps to recover, its generous common spirit, one that helped stitch our country together. The show inspired the love and loyalty from which history is made, and from which it is born anew.

Acknowledgments

Yesterday's Man

Those Were the Days began in front of a living room television set, circa 1970. It was completed in front of a laptop computer at a local Starbucks, circa 2020. In between those two moments of fluid duration, I have produced over a dozen works in the chosen medium that has defined my life: the printed book. Thus, this is a work of history as well as a historical artifact. It's a book about a man whose world is increasingly receding into the past by an author who is having a similar experience. To quote a lyric from the 1980 song "Girls Talk" by Elvis Costello—a once-rising star who took his stage name from a falling one—"you may not be an old-fashioned girl / but you're gonna get dated." That includes you, dear reader.

In closing before opening, a few words of thanks:

First to my agent, Roger Williams, of the Roger Williams Agency, who steered me through some choppy waters. Also to my editor Lisa Banning, who acquired the book and steered it into print with efficiency and good will. Production editors Daryl Brower of Rutgers and Mary Ribesky of Westchester Publishing Services pushed the project through the pipeline. Liz Schueler copyedited the manuscript with skill and tact. Thanks also to Rutgers Director of Sales and Marketing Jeremy Grainger and Publicity Manager Courtney Brach for their enthusiasm. For the past two decades I have had the good fortune to teach at the Ethical Culture Fieldston School in

New York, which has provided material, emotional, and intellectual under-pinnings for my life. In particular, I'd like to thank my History Department colleagues, especially Andy Meyers (now of Whittle School and Studios), and William Norman of the Performing Arts Department. Head of School Jessica Bagby was notably supportive in multiple ways, in particular with procuring illustrations for the book. Fieldston student Anna McNulty (Fieldston class of 2019, Stanford Class of 2023) provided valuable research assistance en route to what will no doubt be a distinguished career. And Wally Levis, to whom this volume is dedicated, has been a cherished fellow traveler.

I finish this book amid an emptying nest. My children, Jay, Gray, Ry, and Nancy, have been welcome company on my journey; I look forward to the prospect of savoring theirs. My wife, Lyde, remains by my side. I'm not entirely sure why. But I'm grateful she does.

—Jim Cullen
Hastings-on-Hudson, New York
Summer 2019

Notes

Introduction

1 Rosenthal made these comments in the PBS American Masters documentary *Norman Lear: Just Another Version of You,* first broadcast in 2016.

2 Horace Newcomb, *TV: The Most Popular Art* (New York: Anchor, 1974), 39–41.

3 Poehler makes this comment early on in *Just Another Version of You.*

4 See Peter Biskind, *Easy Riders, Raging Bulls: How the Sex-Drugs-and-Rock 'N' Roll Generation Saved Hollywood* (New York: Simon & Schuster, 1998). On the strengths of the old order, see Thomas Schatz, *The Genius of the System: Hollywood Filmmaking in the Studio Era* (1988; repr., Minneapolis: University of Minnesota Press, 2010).

5 For one account of this trajectory, see David Nasaw, *Going Out: The Rise and Fall of Public Amusements* (New York: Basic, 1993).

6 The term "peak TV" was coined by FX network president John Landgraf, circa 2015. He and others have been using it ever since. See Megan Garber, David Sims, Lenika Cruz, and Sophie Gilbert, "Have We Reached Peak TV?," *The Atlantic,* August 12, 2015, accessed August 25, 2018, https://www.theatlantic.com /entertainment/archive/2015/08/have-we-reached-peak-tv/401009/.

7 See Chris Anderson, *The Long Tail: Why the Future of Business Is Selling Less of More* (2006; repr., New York: Hachette, 2008).

8 Chuck Tryon, *On-Demand Culture: Digital Delivery and the Future of Movies* (New Brunswick, N.J.: Rutgers University Press, 2013), 2.

9 Barry Schwartz, *The Paradox of Choice: Why More Is Less* (2004; repr., New York: Ecco, 2016).

Chapter 1 Situation Comedy, Situation Tragedy: The Transitional World of *All in the Family*

1 "Blast Hurts 27 During Vietnam Riot," *New York Times,* January 12, 1971, accessed June 10, 2019, https://www.nytimes.com/1971/01/12/archives/blast-hurts-27-gis

-during-vietnam-riot.html; "Food Stamps Bill Signed by President, *New York Times,* January 12, 1971, accessed June 10, 2019, https://www.nytimes.com/1971/01/12/archives/food-stamps-bill-signed-by-president.html; "Blanda Is Selected Male Star of the Year," *New York Times,* January 12, 1971, accessed June 10, 2019, https://www.nytimes.com/1971/01/12/archives/food-stamps-bill-signed-by-president.html.

2 Joshua B. Freeman, *American Empire: The Rise of a Global Power / The Democratic Revolution at Home* (New York: Penguin, 2012), 297.

3 James Patterson, *Restless Giant: The United States from Watergate to Bush v. Gore* (New York: Oxford University Press), 8–9.

4 Freeman, *American Empire,* 302.

5 "Vietnam War Time Table," *United States History,* accessed June 10, 2019, http://www.u-s-history.com/pages/h1959.html (March 21, 2018).

6 Alan Wolfe, *America's Impasse: The Rise and Fall of the Politics of Growth* (Boston: South End Press, 1981), 38.

7 Freeman, *American Empire,* 297.

8 Patterson, *Restless Giant,* 7–8.

9 Freeman, *American Empire,* 304–305.

10 Martin Shefter, introduction to *Political Crisis / Fiscal Crisis: The Collapse and Revival of New York City* (1985; repr., New York: Columbia University Press, 1992). See also Andreas Killen, *1973 Nervous Breakdown: Watergate, Warhol, and the Birth of Post-Sixties America* (New York: Bloomsbury, 2007), 194–196, 204–207.

11 Freeman, *American Empire,* 350–351.

Chapter 2 The Revolution, Televised: Origins of the *Family*

1 Much of the narrative on the origins of broadcasting that follows derives from Jim Cullen, *A Short History of the Modern Media* (Malden, Mass.: Wiley-Blackwell, 2014). See especially chapter 5.

2 David Grimsted, *Melodrama Unveiled: American Theater and Culture, 1800–1850* (1968; repr., Berkeley: University of California Press, 1987), 182–183.

3 Donna McCrohan, *Archie & Edith, Mike & Gloria: The Tumultuous History of All in the Family* (New York: Workman, 1988), 40.

4 Cullen, *Modern Media,* 176–180.

5 Figure cited in Janet Staiger, *Blockbuster TV: Must-See Sitcoms in the Network Era* (New York: New York University Press, 2000), 77.

6 For more on the reconceptualization and fragmentation of advertising, see Lizabeth Cohen, *A Consumer's Republic: The Politics of Mass Consumption in Postwar America* (New York: Vintage, 2003), especially chap. 7, "Segmenting the Mass"; Tim Wu, *The Attention Merchants: The Epic Battle to Get Inside Our Heads* (New York: Vintage, 2017), especially chap. 13, "Coda to an Attentional Revolution." Richard Adler notes this concern with increasing audience specialization in the context of CBS and *All in the Family* in particular in his introduction to his edited anthology *All in the Family: A Critical Appraisal* (New York: Praeger, 1979), xvii–xviii.

7 The line is actually that of Lear's friend and playwright/screenwriter Herb Gardner; Lear cites it as an apt description of his own family life in his memoir *Even This I Get to Experience* (New York: Penguin Press, 2014), 21.

8 Lear, 21, 221. In the 1940s, an appliance company founded by Herman Lear was dissolved by a court because of financial irregularities (108).

9 Lear makes this confession at the end of *Norman Lear: Just Another Version of You*, a 2016 PBS documentary. He explains that he had a childhood friend whose grandfather did this. "I adopted it," he says with some emotion. "Or, more honestly, I stole it."

10 Lear makes these remarks during *Another Version of You*.

11 Lear, *Even This I Get to Experience*, 27.

12 Lear, 56.

13 Lear, 64.

14 Actually, the best thing about the movie is the Coplandesque score by newcomer Randy Newman, who would go on to have a brilliant, under-the-radar career as a recording artist and arranger.

15 Todd Gitlin, *Inside Prime Time* (New York: Pantheon, 1985), 212; Lear, *Even This I Get to Experience*, 67, 267.

16 Lear, 196.

17 McCrohan, *Archie & Edith*, 11.

18 Bud Yorkin, Archive of American Television interview, 2015, accessed May 5, 2018, https://www.youtube.com/watch?v=b17aM3K6fio.

19 Allan Neuwirth, *They'll Never Put That on the Air: An Oral History of Taboo-Breaking TV Comedy* (New York: Allworth Press, 2006), 125.

20 Neuwirth, 126.

21 Lear, *Even This I Get to Experience*, 221. Yorkin has told his side of the story in different venues; his belief that the show would not make it to the American airwaves is cited in the 2016 PBS documentary *Norman Lear: Another Side of You*.

22 McCrohan, *Archie & Edith*, 41.

23 Lear, *Even This I Get to Experience*, 223.

24 Lear, 223.

25 Richard Severo, "Carroll O'Connor, Embodiment of Social Tumult as Archie Bunker, Dies at 76," *New York Times*, June 22, 2011, accessed May 1, 2018, https://www.nytimes.com/2001/06/22/arts/carroll-o-connor-embodiment-of-social-tumult-as-archie-bunker-dies-at-76.html.

26 Lear, *Even This I Get to Experience*, 223–224.

27 Lear, 222; David Marc, *Comic Visions: Television Comedy and American Culture* (Boston: Unwin/Hyman, 1989), 182.

28 Jean Stapleton, Archive of American Television interview, 2015, accessed May 5, 2018, https://www.youtube.com/watch?v=ye274MRHON8. Adler, in *Critical Appraisal*, reports it was actually shot in January 1969 (xx). It's not clear how many times the pilot was rehearsed or taped.

29 Executive Leonard Goldberg, quoted in Neuwirth, *They'll Never Put That on the Air*, 131.

30 Lear, *Even This I Get to Experience*, 224–225. Adler, in *Critical Appraisal*, reports the second episode as being taped in March (xx). The sources of these dates seem to be the memories of the principals; in any event, the general time parameters are clear enough.

31 Gitlin, *Inside Prime Time*, 206, 213.

32 Gitlin, 213; "Turn-On George Schlatter Tells the True Story," February 4, 2010, accessed May 5, 2018, https://www.youtube.com/watch?v=Gbz3irCcMEo.

33 Lear, *Even This I Get to Experience*, 231.

34 Silverman recollections in Neuwirth, *They'll Never Put That on the Air*, 134.

35 Marc, *Comic Visions*, 176.

36 Gitlin, *Inside Prime Time*, 235.

37 Severo, "Carroll O'Connor"; Carroll O'Connor, *I Think I'm Outta Here: A Memoir of All My Families* (1998, repr., New York: Pocket Books, 1999), 173.

38 Lear, *Even This I Get to Experience*, 235.

39 Rob Reiner, Archive of American Television interview, 2015, accessed May 6, 2018, https://www.youtube.com/watch?v=ImoNQvvNroA. Lear described Struthers as a "little pool of light" in the *Birth of All in the Family* documentary included in the DVD complete series for the show published by Shout! Productions in 2012.

40 Lear, *Even This I Get to Experience*, 235.

41 The *TV Guide* graphic and text are reproduced in McCrohan, *Archie & Edith*, 32.

42 Lear, *Even This I Get to Experience*, 238.

43 Gitlin, *Inside Prime Time*, 212–213; Staiger, *Blockbuster TV*, 81–83.

44 Fred Ferretti, "TV: Are Racism and Bigotry Funny?," *New York Times*, January 12, 1971, 71, accessed May 6, 2018, https://www.nytimes.com/1971/01/12/archives/tv -are-racism-and-bigotry-funny-cbs-family-series-may-shock-some.html.

45 Lear, *Even This I Get to Experience*, 235.

Chapter 3 Fuzzy Reception: Meeting the Bunkers

1 In a flashback episode from the second season in which Mike meets Archie, however, the bearded Mike is wearing tie-dye and a necklace.

2 "'All in the Family': THR's 1971 Review," *Hollywood Reporter*, October 21, 2014, accessed June 10, 2019: https://www.hollywoodreporter.com/news/all-family-thrs -1971-review-736435.

3 Donna McCrohan, *Archie & Edith, Mike & Gloria: The Tumultuous History of All in the Family* (New York: Workman, 1988), 33–34.

4 Janet Staiger, *Blockbuster TV: Must-See Sitcoms of the Network Era* (New York: New York University Press, 2000), 93; George Gent, "*All in the Family* Takes First Place in the Nielsen Ratings," *New York Times*, May 25, 1971, accessed May 6, 2018, https://www.nytimes.com/1971/05/25/archives/all-in-the-family-takes-first-place -in-nielsen-ratings.html.

5 The Armory and Haynes reviews are reproduced in Richard P. Adler, ed., *All in the Family: A Critical Appraisal* (New York: Praeger, 1979), 84–85, 89–90; Jack Gould, "Can Bigotry Be Laughed Away? It's Worth a Try," *New York Times*, February 21, 1971, 15, accessed May 7, 2018, https://archive.nytimes.com/www.nytimes.com /specials/seinfeld/aif71.html; McCrohan, *Archie & Edith*, 35.

6 Stephanie Harrington, "The Message Sounds Like 'Hate Thy Neighbor,'" *New York Times*, January 24, 1971, accessed May 6, 2018, https://www.nytimes.com/1971/01 /24/archives/the-message-sounds-like-hate-thy-neighbor-hate-thy-neighbor.html.

7 *The Brady Bunch* (1969–1974) was a hit series that straddled the cultural changes of the era. The sitcom chronicled the lives of a widow with three daughters and a widower with three sons who marry, engaging the social changes typified by blended families while sidestepping the still-thorny issue of divorce.

8 Josh Ozersky, *Archie Bunker's America: TV in an Era of Change, 1968–1978* (Carbondale: Southern Illinois University, 2003), 69–70; Staiger, *Blockbuster TV*, 90. Young's piece is reproduced in Adler, *Critical Appraisal*, 85–87.

9 This exchange can be seen on the PBS American Masters Series *Norman Lear: Just Another Version of You*, which first aired in 2016.

10 Nixon quoted in Norman Lear, *Even This I Get to Experience* (New York: Penguin, 2014), 244. Nixon was probably reacting to the fourth episode of the series, which involves a friend of Mike and Gloria's that Archie incorrectly suspects is gay—only to learn an ex-football player he admires and with whom he discusses his suspicions turns out to be gay himself.

11 Unnamed *Life* reviewer quoted in McCrohan, 36; John Leonard, "Bigotry as a Dirty Joke," *Life*, March 1971, 11, accessed May 6, 2018, https://books.google.com /books?id=iVMEAAAAMBAJ&pg=PA10&lpg=PA10&dq=bigotry+as+a+dirty+j oke+john+leonard&source=bl&ots=y_vVMkPv3y&sig=nJNa7Ip _es6EiUdjxSvHCIgc5OE&hl=en&sa=X&ved=0ahUKEwioupObqPHaAhUkxVk KHbmWA6oQ6AEILDAC#v=onepage&q=bigotry%20as%20a%20dirty%20 joke%20john%20leonard&f=false.

12 Laura Z. Hobson, "As I Listened to Archie Say 'Hebe' . . . ," *New York Times*, September 12, 1971, accessed June 10, 2019, https://www.nytimes.com/1971/09/12 /archives/as-i-listened-to-archie-say-hebe-as-i-listened-to-archie-as-i.html.

13 The word did make it to the airwaves—overcoming what one has to imagine were serious concerns among network censors—in the famous "Sammy's Visit" episode of February 1972. Significantly, however, it was uttered by a black man, Sammy Davis Jr. Another black character, George Jefferson, says it in the 1974 episode "Lionel's Engagement," whereupon Archie notes that he himself hasn't used it in years. He recollects using the term as a child in the 1978 episode "Two's a Crowd," not realizing it was offensive (and getting beaten up by an African American boy after doing so).

14 Hobson "As I Listened."

15 Lear, *Even This I Get to Experience*, 246.

16 Norman Lear, "As I Read How Laura Saw Archie," *New York Times*, October 10, 1971, D17, accessed May 8, 2018, https://www.nytimes.com/1971/10/10/archives/as -i-read-how-laura-saw-archie-as-i-read-laura-.html.

17 Staiger, *Blockbuster TV*, 92; Adler, *Critical Appraisal*, xxix. The Adler anthology includes a set of such research reports. See Part VI (123–180).

18 Lear, *Even This I Get to Experience*, 245.

19 Peter N. Carroll, *It Seemed Like Nothing Happened: America in the 1970s* (1990 repr., New Brunswick, N.J.: Rutgers University Press, 1990), 62.

20 Carroll O'Connor, American Academy of Television interview, accessed July 11, 2018, https://interviews.televisionacademy.com/interviews/carroll -oconnor#interview-clips.

21 Lear, *Even This I Get to Experience*, 266–267.

22 Robert Lewis Shayon, "Love That Hate," *Saturday Review*, March 27, 1971, included in Adler, *Critical Appraisal*, 92–94.

23 Lear, *Even This I Get to Experience*, 246–247; Hobson, "As I Listened."

24 Lear, *Even This I Get to Experience*, 246; McCrohan, *Archie & Edith*, 36. Lear makes the point that the show still had new episodes while others were in reruns in a 2012 interview included in the complete series DVD set issued by Shout! Factory.

25 Gent, *"All in the Family* Takes First Place"; McCrohan, *Archie & Edith*, 36; Staiger, *Blockbuster TV*, 110.

26 Lear, *Even* This *I Get to Experience*, 247. The actual size of the theater audience—
sometimes 250, sometimes 300—seems to fluctuate, depending on who's remembering it when. The point in any case is that the intimacy of a small-scale theatrical
performance was the hallmark of an *AITF* taping.

Chapter 4 Producing Comedy: Making *All in the Family*

1 Norman Lear, *Even* This *I Get to Experience* (New York: Penguin Press, 2014), 147.
2 Richard P. Adler, ed., *All in the Family: A Critical Appraisal* (New York: Praeger,
1979), xxii; Donna McCrohan, *Archie & Edith, Mike and Gloria: The Tumultuous
History of All in the Family* (New York: Workman, 1987), 126. In the interview
included in the complete DVD set of *All in the Family* issued by Shout! Factory in
2012, Lear says he won the argument over the number of breaks. Rob Reiner
describes the development routine in chapter 4 of his interview for the Archive of
American Television, accessed July 20, 2018, https://interviews.televisionacademy
.com/interviews/rob-reiner#interview-clips.
3 McCrohan, Archie & Edith, 127; Dennis McLellan, "John Rich Dies at 86;
Director of Landmark Sitcoms," *Los Angeles Times*, January 30, 2012, accessed
June 11, 2018, https://www.latimes.com/local/obituaries/la-me-john-rich-20120130
-story.html.
4 Adler notes O'Connor's desire to end the live tapings on page xxii of *Critical
Appraisal*. (Viewers hear his voice at the end of each episode of the final season,
noting that they were shown to audiences, whose live response was recorded.)
Stapleton's, O'Connor's, and Reiner's remarks on the dynamic air of tapings can be
found in their interviews for the American Academy of Television, accessed June 11,
2018, https://interviews.televisionacademy.com/interviews.
5 Shales makes this point in the booklet accompanying the complete DVD set for *All
in the Family*, distributed by Shout! Factory (16).
6 McLellan, "John Rich Dies at 86."
7 Reiner, Archive of American Television interview.
8 Steve Winn, "O'Connor's 'Labor Day' May Be Heartfelt, but It's No Holiday," *San
Francisco Chronicle*, September 26, 1997, accessed June 12, 2018, https://www.sfgate
.com/performance/article/O-Connor-s-Labor-Day-May-Be-Heartfelt-But-It-s
-2804591.php.
9 Carroll O'Connor, *I Think I'm Outta Here: A Memoir of All My Families* (1998;
repr., New York: Pocket Books, 1999), 5. O'Connor discusses *AITF* from pages 191
to 201.
10 This was David Dukes, who played the notorious rapist in the 1977 two-part
episode "Edith's 50th Birthday." See McCrohan, *Archie & Edith*, 134.
11 O'Connor, American Academy of Television interview.
12 O'Connor, *I Think I'm Outta Here*, 194–195.
13 Lear describes this episode in *Even* This *I Get to Experience* (248–250). McCrohan
also notes it in *Archie & Edith* (129).
14 Isabel Sanford, Archive of American Television interview, chap. 4, ca. 2002,
accessed August 5, 2018, https://interviews.televisionacademy.com/interviews
/isabel-sanford#interview-clips.
15 "The Playboy Interview: Carroll O'Connor," *Playboy*, January 1973, 74, 205. In the
1970s, *Playboy* interviews were a high-profile measure of stature for media

celebrities. (Yes, people really did read *Playboy* for the articles.) McCrohan notes the contrast between Gleason and O'Connor on page 129 of *Archie & Edith*; Ball also played a bigger role, with husband Desi Arnaz, in launching *I Love Lucy* than O'Connor did with *All in the Family*. His 1978 complaint is included in a farewell profile, "Farewell to the Family," *People*, March 27, 1978, accessed August 26, 2018, https://people.com/archive/cover-story-farewell-to-the-family-vol-9-no-12/.

16 McCrohan, *Archie & Edith*, 230.

17 Lear, *Even This I Get to Experience*, 316; O'Connor, *I Think I'm Outta Here*, 195.

18 Lear, *Even This I Get to Experience*, 251.

19 Lear, 318.

20 McCrohan, *Archie & Edith*, 131–132.

21 O'Connor, *I Think I'm Outta Here*, 195.

22 Dennis McLellan, "Paul Bogart Dies at 92; Emmy-Winning TV Director," *Los Angeles Times*, April 18, 2012, accessed June 14, 2018, https://www.latimes.com /local/obituaries/la-xpm-2012-apr-18-la-me-paul-bogart-20120418-story.html.

Chapter 5 The Character of Home: Chez Bunker

1 Archie uses the phrase "Here in Astoria" while sitting in his house in the 1976 episode "Archie Finds a Friend." Astoria is cited as his address later that year in "Mr. Edith Bunker" and again in the 1977 episode "Archie's Chair," when Archie names his address as "704 Hauser Street out in Astoria, Queens." In the 1978 episode "Bogus Bills," he says he owns a bar in Astoria, which is a few blocks from his house.

2 Sam Roberts, the legendary *New York Times* reporter and expert in the city's history, noted that Lear wasn't much help when he sought clarification on the matter in 1993, shortly before the sitcom *704 Hauser*, set in the former Bunker home, made its debut. Roberts notes, however, that a spokesman for Lear specifically rejected Astoria as its location and named Corona as a likely prospect. See "The Cranky Spirit of Archie Bunker Haunts This House," *New York Times*, December 19, 1993, accessed June 3, 2018, https://www.nytimes.com/1993/12/19 /arts/the-cranky-spirit-of-archie-bunker-haunts-this-house.html.

3 On the Glendale home and its rise and fall as a pop culture shrine, see Vivian Lee, "Fewer Fans Visit 'All in the Family' TV Home," *New York Times*, June 2, 2013, accessed June 3, 2018, https://www.nytimes.com/1993/12/19/arts/the-cranky-spirit -of-archie-bunker-haunts-this-house.html.

4 "Hauser Family History," Ancestry.com, accessed June 10, 2019, https://www .ancestry.com/name-origin?surname=hauser.

5 It's a little unclear exactly where. Archie's father owned a house in Woodside, and he apparently attended Flushing High School. In *Archie's Bunker's Place*, Archie is depicted as a native of Long Island City. These neighborhoods are scattered across Queens, but they're Queens nonetheless.

6 The Bunkers are literally conversant with the musical. This becomes clear in the 1974 episode "Mike's Graduation," when Archie, hoping that he will finally be able to convert his daughter and son-in-law's bedroom into a study, comes downstairs in a cardigan sweater with a pipe in hand, comparing himself to Professor Henry Higgins. (Naturally, his hopes for the bedroom conversion prove unfounded: Mike takes a fellowship and will thus remain at 704 Hauser.)

7 Chana Joffe-Walt, "Mortgage-Burning Parties Almost Extinct," Morning Edition, National Public Radio, July 3, 2009, accessed July 1, 2018, https://www.npr.org /templates/story/story.php?storyId=106242731.

8 David Marc, *Comic Visions: Television Comedy and American Culture* (Boston: Unwin/Hyman, 1989), 181. In fact, it's not clear whether the Bunkers live in a detached single-family home. The actual house in Glendale on which their home is based is a duplex, which is to say a two-family house. The Lorenzos and Jeffersons are sometimes referred to as living next door, but it's not clear whether this is a literal or figurative designation for people who in any case are clearly neighbors.

9 Horace Newcomb, *TV: The Most Popular Art* (New York: Anchor, 1973), 219.

10 Jim Cullen, *The American Dream: A Short History of an Idea That Shaped a Nation* (New York: Oxford University Press, 2003), 150.

11 Marc, in *Comic Visions*, also makes this point (180).

12 Christopher Lasch, *Haven in a Heartless World: The Family Besieged* (New York: Basic Books, 1978). Lasch, whose next book would be the best-selling *Culture of Narcissism: American Life in an Age of Diminishing Expectations* (New York: W. W. Norton, 1979), chronicled the growing contempt for traditional values in a long career that hit its stride in the heyday of *AITF*.

Chapter 6 Not Bad for a Bigot: The Making of Archie Bunker

1 In the first iteration of the song, performed solo by O'Connor in the first pilot, there was an additional set of lyrics, whose frame of reference is the 1930s: "Had my twelve-tube radio / Loved the *Eddie Cantor Show* / Oh where did all that beauty go? / Those were the days!" It may also be worth noting that O'Connor is credited with co-writing (with Roger Kellaway) the tune (no lyrics) that ran during the closing credits of each episode.

2 Donna McCrohan is among those who discuss the etymology of Archie's name. See *Archie & Edith, Mike & Gloria: The Tumultuous History of All in the Family* (New York: Workman Publishing, 1988), 38–39.

3 McCrohan notes the contradictions in Archie's family background on page 213 of *Archie & Edith*.

4 Lear makes this remark in the 2016 PBS American Masters documentary *Norman Lear: Just Another Version of You* as the clip is being shown.

5 Jonathan Cobb and Richard Sennett, *The Hidden Injuries of Class* (1972; repr., New York: Norton, 1993).

6 W.E.B. Du Bois, *Black Reconstruction in America, 1860–1880* (1935; repr., New York: Free Press, 1995), 700–701.

7 This point is made by David Marc: "It's hard to imagine him as anything but a New Deal Democrat who has switched allegiances away from the party during its post-Lyndon Johnson drift to the McGovern left." *Comic Visions: Television Comedy and American Culture* (Boston: Unwin/Hyman, 1989), 181.

8 The Bunkers' Episcopalianism doesn't really make sense from a class standpoint. At best, they should be Methodists, a step or two down the Protestant ladder—respectable and striving.

9 Norman Lear, *Even This I Get to Experience* (New York: Penguin, 2014), 221.

10 Marc, *Comic Visions*, 181.

11 Lear, *Even This I Get to Experience*, 249.

12 Lear, 317.

13 Dan Avery, "The First Drag Queen on Network Television," Logo, June 30, 2016, accessed July 17, 2018, http://www.newnownext.com/tbt-the-first-drag-queen-on -network-television/06/2016/.

14 For a discussion of this and illustrations, see McCrohan, *Archie & Edith*, 190–191.

Chapter 7 A Really Great Housewife: The Character of Edith Baines Bunker

1 Claire Cain Miller, "The Costs of Motherhood Are Rising, and Catching Women Off Guard," *New York Times*, August 17, 2018, accessed August 19, 2018, https:// www.nytimes.com/2018/08/17/upshot/motherhood-rising-costs-surprise.html.

2 For more on the concept of social capital and its decline in American life, see Robert Putnam, *Bowling Alone: The Collapse and Revival of American Community* (2000; repr., New York: Simon & Schuster, 2001).

3 Norman Lear, *Even This I Get to Experience* (New York: Penguin, 2014), 197.

4 Tara Siegel Bernard, "When She Earns More: As Roles Shift, Old Ideas on Who Pays the Bills Persist," *New York Times*, July 6, 2018, accessed July 19, 2018, https:// www.nytimes.com/2018/07/06/your-money/marriage-men-women-finances.html. See also Claire Cain Miller, "When Wives Earn More Than Husbands, Neither Partner Wants to Admit It," *New York Times*, July 17, 2018, https://www.nytimes .com/2018/07/17/upshot/when-wives-earn-more-than-husbands-neither-like-to -admit-it.html?searchResultPosition=1.

5 *All in the Family* is chock full of such cultural references from its beginning. In one knowing intertextual aside, Edith responds to news that Mike might get a job in Minnesota by exclaiming, "Minnesota? Isn't that the place where Mary Tyler Moore keeps losing her hat?" Edith is referring to the opening title sequence of *The Mary Tyler Moore Show*—at one point part of the same killer Saturday night lineup as *All in the Family* on CBS.

6 Sander Vanocur, "Foxxy ABC Is Gathering Stars," *Washington Post*, April 9, 1976, 29; Donna McCrohan, *Archie & Edith, Mike & Gloria: The Tumultuous History of All in the Family* (New York: Workman Publishing, 1987), 64.

7 McCrohan, 64.

8 The butcher, played by the fine character actor Theodore Bikel, returns the following season in "A Girl Like Edith," in which the joke is that his new fiancée is an Edith look-alike—and the even bigger joke is that the look-alike, a notably cold German, is played by Stapleton (credited as Giovanna Pucci).

9 Lear, *Even This I Get to Experience*, 221–222. Stapleton's similar account can be heard in her interview with the Archive of American Television, accessed July 15, 2018, https://interviews.televisionacademy.com/interviews/jean-stapleton.

10 Lear, *Even This I Get to Experience*, 222.

11 Bruce Weber, "Jean Stapleton, Who Played Archie Bunker's Better Angel, Dies at 90," *New York Times*, June 1, 2013, accessed July 15, 2018, https://www.nytimes.com /2013/06/02/arts/television/jean-stapleton-who-played-archies-better-angel-dies -at-90.html.

12 Stapleton talks extensively about landing the role and her vision of Edith in the Archive of American Television interview. See especially the chapter 2 segment of the video.

13 Edith's sexual innocence in this exchange is foreshadowed at the start of the episode when, entering their hotel room, Edith wonders why the clerk asked if Archie wanted the room by the hour, and her puzzlement over the advertised adult film (*Goldilocks and the Three Bares*).

14 See the comments of Barry Harman, who got a story credit for the episode, in Allan Neuwirth, *They'll Never Put That on the Air* (New York: Allworth Press, 2006), 152–153. Lear's comment follows.

15 McCrohan, *Archie & Edith*, 73.

16 Emily Nussbaum, "In the Current Climate: TV's Reckoning with #MeToo," *New Yorker,* June 3, 2019), p. 60.

17 Lear, *Even This I Get to Experience*, 254.

18 Lear, 314–315; McCrohan, *Archie & Edith*, 161.

19 Tom Shales, "A Death in the Family: Dirge for the Dingbat," *Washington Post*, April 23, 1980, accessed July 18, 2018, https://www.washingtonpost.com/archive /lifestyle/1980/04/23/a-death-in-the-family-dirge-for-the-dingbat/7e06b1bf-c0f1 -494b-8c57-33738a4f2da0/?utm_term=.d1d00e9f41e4.

20 Stapleton, Archive of American Television interview; Lear, *Even This I Get to Experience*, 317.

Chapter 8 Left In: The Liberal Arts of Michael Stivic

1 Irving Kristol, "Business and 'The New Class,'" *Wall Street Journal*, May 10, 1975, ProQuest. Kristol elaborated on this idea elsewhere, notably in his book *Two Cheers for Capitalism* (New York: Basic Books, 1978). The concept of the New Class was borrowed from Marxism, loosely correlating with people who were also known as apparatchiks, or Communist Party functionaries.

2 Rob Reiner, Archive of American Television interview, chapter 3, accessed July 20, 2018, https://interviews.televisionacademy.com/interviews/rob-reiner#interview -clips.

3 David Marc, *Comic Visions: Television Comedy and American Culture* (Boston: Unwin/Hyman, 1989), 183.

4 Larry Rhine, Archive of American Television interview, ca. 2007, accessed July 21, 2018, https://interviews.televisionacademy.com/interviews/larry-rhine.

5 On "This Land Is Your Land" as a response to "God Bless America," see Joe Klein, *Woody Guthrie: A Life* (1980; repr., New York: Delta, 1999), 140–145. But "God Bless America" was also appropriated by the American left. See Sheryl Kaskowitz, "'God Bless America': One Hundred Years of an Immigrant's Anthem," *New York Times,* July 2, 2018, accessed July 22, 2018, https://www.nytimes.com/2018/07/02 /arts/music/irving-berlin-god-bless-america.html. Archie would have been most familiar with Kate Smith's version, which became a patriotic standard in the late 1930s and early 1940s. The song enjoyed a resurgence of popularity in the aftermath of 9/11, when it once again had a right-leaning valence. But Smith's version, which had been a fixture of Philadelphia Flyers and New York Yankee games, was banned by both organizations in 2019 after it was revealed Smith had recorded racist songs in the 1930s, a decision that also sparked charges of excessive political correctness. See "Kate Smith's 'God Bless America, Dropped By Two Major Sports Teams," National Public Radio, April 22, 2019, accessed June 11, 2019, https://www.npr.org/2019/04 /22/715918211/kate-smiths-god-bless-america-dropped-by-two-major-sports-teams.

6 Reiner, Archive of American Television interview.
7 Reiner, Archive of American Television interview.
8 There is a body of sociological evidence suggesting that liberals tend to overestimate their own tolerance and are less good at representing conservative opinion than conservatives are in rendering liberal opinion. For one such analysis, see Jonathan Haidt, *The Righteous Mind: Why Good People Are Divided by Politics and Religion* (New York: Vintage, 2013), 334.
9 Reiner, Archive of American Television interview.

Chapter 9 "Little Girl" to Mother: The Working-Class Feminism of Gloria Bunker Stivic

1 Rory Dicker, *A History of U.S. Feminisms* (New York: Seal Press, 2008), 70–71.
2 The text of the law reads, "No person in the United States shall, on the basis of sex, be excluded from participation in, be denied the benefits of, or be subjected to discrimination under any education program or activity receiving Federal financial assistance." See U.S. Department of Justice website, accessed June 11, 2019, https://www.justice.gov/crt/title-ix-education-amendments-1972.
3 This figure was determined by culling a list of writers for the show on the Internet Movie Database, accessed July 26, 2018, https://www.imdb.com/title/tt0066626/fullcredits.
4 Donna McCrohan, *Archie & Edith, Mike & Gloria: The Tumultuous History of All in the Family* (New York: Workman, 1987), 56–57.
5 Larry Rhine, Archive of American Television interview, chapter 5, accessed July 28, 2018, https://interviews.televisionacademy.com/interviews/larry-rhine#interview-clips.
6 Struthers mentioned her ancestry in congressional testimony in 2001, available at the U.S. Commission of Affordable Housing and Health Facility Needs for Seniors in the 21st Century, November 7, 2001, accessed June 11, 2019, http://govinfo.library.unt.edu/seniorscommission/pages/hearings/011107/struthers.html (August 1, 2018).
7 Lear makes this remark in the *All in the Family Is on the Air* documentary included in the 2012 DVD set of the series issued by Shout! Factory as well as in his memoir, *Even This I Get to Experience* (New York: Penguin, 2012), 233, where he also describes her casting. Struthers explains her firing from *The Tim Conway Show* in Alan H. Falluck, "Sally Struthers on '9 to 5,' Life, and Topless Scene with Jack Nicholson," *Newsday*, July 25, 2012, accessed July 28, 2016, https://www.newsday.com/search/sally-struthers-on-9-to-5-life-and-topless-scene-with-jack-nicholson-1.3858275. McCrohan renders the circumstances of Struthers's casting on page 19 of *Archie & Edith*. Lear's comments on Struthers appear in *Even This I Get to Experience* (253).
8 Rhine, Archive of American Television interview.
9 Rob Reiner, Archive of American Television interview, accessed July 28, 2018, https://interviews.televisionacademy.com/interviews/rob-reiner#interview-clips.
10 Struthers says this on what appears to be a local television news clip from the mid-1980s, when she appeared in a Broadway production of *The Odd Couple*. See "Sally Struthers: After *All in the Family*, She Could Not Get Work," You Tube, May 31, 2017, accessed June 11, 2019, https://www.google.com/search?q=sally+struthers+and+jean+stapleton&ei=EKZfW6qgFNC-ggeXyJTQBw&start=10&sa

=N&biw=709&bih=363. On her relationship with O'Connor, see "Farewell to the Family," *People*, March 27, 1978, accessed August 26, 2018, https://people.com /archive/cover-story-farewell-to-the-family-vol-9-no-12/.

11 A key excerpt of what Nixon actually said on January 20, 1973: "A person can be expected to act responsibly only if he has responsibility. This is human nature. So let us encourage individuals at home and nations abroad to do more for themselves, to decide more for themselves. Let us locate responsibility in more places. And let us measure what we will do for others by what they will do for themselves." Transcript available at The American Presidency Project, published by the University of California at Santa Barbara, accessed June 11, 2019, https://www .presidency.ucsb.edu/documents/oath-office-and-second-inaugural-address.

12 McCrohan, *Archie & Edith*, 232.

13 McCrohan, 59–60; See also Fandom.com's *All in the Family* wiki, accessed June 11, 2019, http://all-in-the-family-tv-show.wikia.com/wiki/Joey_Stivic.

14 Matt Zoler Seitz, "Norman Lear on Redefining the Modern Sitcom and the Best Family TV Show He Didn't Create," Vulture, January 17, 2018, accessed August 3, 2018, http://www.vulture.com/2018/01/norman-lear-family-shows-and-his-next -project.html.

15 Tom Shales, "Archie Bunker, Stifled," *Washington Post*, May 12, 1983, accessed July 31, 2018, https://www.washingtonpost.com/archive/lifestyle/1983/05/12 /archie-bunker-stifled/24c686e5-aa3d-400e-863c-ffdb8fe5cocd/?utm_term= .ca2b11616176.

Chapter 10 *Family* Resemblance: The Rise and Fall of the Lear Television Empire

1 See the introduction of *All in the Family: A Critical Appraisal*, ed. Richard P. Adler (New York: Praeger, 1979), xxxiv.

2 Adler, xxxiv.

3 Donna McCrohan, *Archie & Edith, Mike & Gloria: The Tumultuous History of All in the Family* (New York: Workman Publishing, 1988), 141. Both were released in 1971; in 1977, Sammy Davis Jr. sang a disco version. See the "Those Were the Days" entry at the Songfacts website, accessed June 11, 2019, https://www.songfacts.com /facts/archie-and-edith-bunker/those-were-the-days-theme-to-all-in-the-family.

4 The book was published by the Popular Library in 1971. See the entry (and review) on Amazon, accessed August 6, 2018, https://www.amazon.com/Edith-Bunkers -All-Family-Cookbook/dp/0445081953/ref=sr_1_1?s=books&ie=UTF8&qid=153 3563434&sr=1-1&keywords=Edith+Bunker%27s+all+in+the+family+cookbook.

5 *The Wit and Wisdom of Archie Bunker* (New York: Popular Library, 1971).

6 Spencer Marsh, *God, Man, and Archie Bunker* (New York: Harper & Row, 1975), 7.

7 See Silverman and Lafferty comments in Allan Neuwirth, *They'll Never Put That on the Air: An Oral History of Taboo-Breaking Comedy* (New York: Allworth Press, 2006), 144. On Lear and Tankersley's rapport—something they both affirmed— see pages 194–195. The Lear quote appears on page 144.

8 Schiller's comments appear in Neuwirth, *They'll Never Put That on the Air*, 147.

9 Wagner's comments appear in Neuwirth, *They'll Never Put That on the Air*, 153.

10 Norman Lear, *Even This I Get to Experience* (New York: Penguin, 2014), 282–287; McCrohan, *Archie & Edith*, 150–153; David W. Rintels, "Why We Fought the Family Viewing Hour," *New York Times*, November 21, 1976, accessed August 6,

2018, https://www.nytimes.com/1976/11/21/archives/why-we-fought-the-family-viewing-hour.html. For a good overview of the issues involved, see Erik Barnouw, *Tube of Plenty: The Evolution of American Television*, 2nd rev. ed. (New York: Oxford University Press, 1990), 474–481.

11 McCrohan, *Archie & Edith*, 138.

12 Lear and Silverman comments in Neuwirth, *They'll Never Put That on the Air*, 187–188.

13 Lear and Silverman comments in Neuwirth, 187–188; Lear, *Even This I Get to Experience*, 436. Harris quoted on page 188.

14 *Time* story quoted in McCrohan, *Archie & Edith*, 141.

15 Lear, *Even This I Get to Experience*, 265.

16 Neuwirth, *They'll Never Put That on the Air*, 194–195.

17 Eugenia Collier, "'Sanford and Son' Is White to the Core," *New York Times*, June 17, 1973, accessed August 8, 2018, https://www.nytimes.com/1973/06/17/archives/sanford-and-son-is-white-to-the-core-eugenia-collier-is-coeditor.html.

18 Walker addresses and responds to this criticism in his memoir *Dy-No-Mite! Good Times, Bad Times, Our Times* (New York: DaCapo Press, 2012), 99, 135.

19 Lear, *Even This I Get to Experience*, 274.

20 Lear, 276. In the 2016 documentary *Norman Lear: Another Version of You*, there is footage of Lear negotiating with the actors of *Good Times* over lines and situations in that show. John Amos and Esther Rolle, interviewed many years later, stand by their concerns. Lear, with a confidence that might be harder to sustain in a twenty-first-century climate, stands by his position, which is essentially that the show is engaging issues and questions that transcend racial lines.

21 Lear, *Even This I Get to Experience*, 275.

22 Simmons makes this remark in the *Norman Lear: Just Another Version of You* documentary.

23 Lear, *Even This I Get to Experience*, 279.

24 McCrohan, *Archie & Edith*, 144–145; Enid Nemy, "Frances Lear, a Mercurial Figure of the Media and Magazine Founder, Dead at 73," *New York Times*, October 1, 1996, accessed August 9, 2018, https://www.nytimes.com/1996/10/01/us/frances-lear-a-mercurial-figure-of-the-media-and-a-magazine-founder-dead-at-73.html.

25 Michael Arlen, "The Air: The Media Dreams of Norman Lear," *New Yorker*, March 10, 1975, 89–94.

26 Lear, *Even This I Get to Experience*, 293.

27 McCrohan, *Archie & Edith*, 145–147.

28 McCrohan, 154–156.

29 For details of the transaction, see David A. Vise, "Capital Cities Communications to Buy ABC for $3.5 Billion," *Washington Post*, March 19, 1985, accessed August 13, 2018, https://www.washingtonpost.com/archive/politics/1985/03/19/capital-cities-communications-to-buy-abc-for-35-billion/7e2d4fa9-144b-4704-8d2e-498bc5496057/?utm_term=.414fb87ba032.

30 Much of the material in the next five paragraphs draws on Jim Cullen, *Democratic Empire: The United States since 1945* (Malden, Mass.: Wiley-Blackwell, 2016), 223–224.

31 Eric Levenson and Aaron Cooper, "Bill Cosby Guilty on All Three Accounts in Indecent Assault Trial," CNN, April 26, 2018, accessed December 2, 2018, https://www.cnn.com/2018/04/26/us/bill-cosby-trial/index.html.

32 Barbara Ehrenreich, *The Hearts of Men: American Dreams and the Flight from Commitment* (1983; repr., New York: Anchor, 1987).

33 The ad, for the fragrance Enjoli, can be viewed on YouTube, accessed August 13, 2018, http://www.youtube.com/watch?v=jA4DR4vEgrs.

34 Lear, *Even This I Get to Experience*, 328–333, 308–312. The People for the American Way website remains active at www.pfaw.org (accessed August 14, 2018).

35 For an account of the trip, see the story on Norman Lear's website, accessed June 11, 2019, http://www.normanlear.com/citizenship/declaration-of-independence-road -trip.

36 *Just Another Version of You.*

37 Hank Stuever, "Norman Lear Put His Foot Down—and the White House Flinched," *Washington Post*, November 27, 2017, accessed August 14, 2018, https:// www.washingtonpost.com/entertainment/tv/norman-lear-put-his-foot-down— and-trumps-white-house-flinched/2017/11/26/1b08527a-c5b1-11e7-84bc -5e285c7f4512_story.html?utm_term=.b9736ab8813f.

38 Nellie Andreeva, "'One Day at a Time' Renewed for Season 3," *Deadline Holly- wood*, March 26, 2018, accessed December 2, 2018, https://deadline.com/2018/03 /one-day-at-a-time-renewed-season-3-netflix-1202353529/.

39 Nick Romano, "*All in the Family, The Jeffersons, Good Times, Maude* Are Up for Reboots," *Entertainment Weekly*, July 27, 2018, accessed August 14, 2018, https://ew .com/tv/2018/07/27/all-in-the-family-jeffersons-good-times-maude-reboots -norman-lear/. For one of many subsequently reported demurrals, see Dominic Patten, "No *All in the Family* or *Maude* Reboot Plans, Says Norman Lear—TCA," *Deadline Hollywood*, July 29, 2018, accessed December 2, 2018, https://deadline .com/2018/07/norman-lear-no-new-all-in-the-family-one-day-at-a-time-sony-deal -netflix-tca-1202436113/.

Conclusion

1 William P. Davis and Jacklyn Peiser, "'Roseanne' the Reboot: A Timeline," *New York Times*, May 29, 2018, accessed August 26, 2018, https://www.nytimes.com /2018/05/29/business/media/roseanne-reboot-timeline.html.

2 Davis and Peiser, "'Roseanne' the Reboot."

3 For a detailed account of the incident twenty-five years later, see Geoff Edgars, "Roseanne on the Day She Shrieked 'The Star-Spangled Banner,' Grabbed Her Crotch, and Got a Rebuke from President Bush," *Washington Post*, July 25, 2015, accessed August 26, 2018, https://www.washingtonpost.com/news/arts-and -entertainment/wp/2015/07/23/roseanne-on-the-day-she-shrieked-the-star -spangled-banner-grabbed-her-crotch-and-earned-a-rebuke-from-president-bush/ ?utm_term=.b2a43dd8a915.

4 Davis and Peiser, "'Roseanne' the Reboot"; Joe Otterson, "'Roseanne' Falls to *NCIS* in Ratings Tuesday," *Chicago Tribune*, May 2, 2018, accessed August 26, 2018, http://www.chicagotribune.com/entertainment/tv/ct-roseanne-down-ratings -viewers-20180502-story.html; John Koblin, "After Racist Tweet, 'Roseanne' Is Cancelled by ABC," *New York Times*, May 29, 2018, accessed June 11, 2019, https:// www.nytimes.com/2018/05/29/business/media/roseanne-barr-offensive-tweets.html.

5 Kelvin Yu, "'Roseanne': When a Punch Line Feels Like a Gut Punch," *New York Times*, April 13, 2018, accessed June 11, 2019 https://www.nytimes.com/2018/04/13

/arts/television/roseanne-bad-joke-controversy-kelvin-yu.html; Emily Nussbaum, "How One Joke on 'Roseanne' Explains the Show," *New Yorker*, April 23, 2018, accessed August 26, 2018, https://www.newyorker.com/magazine/2018/04/23/how-one-joke-on-roseanne-explains-the-show.

6 This is a point made by another Asian American writer, Ravi Chandra. See "Roseanne, Race, and 'They're Just Like Us,'" *Psychology Today*, April 23, 2018, accessed August 26, 2018, https://www.psychologytoday.com/us/blog/the-pacific-heart/201804/roseanne-race-and-they-re-just-us.

7 For an early iteration of this view, see Jim Cullen, "*All in the Family* Pushed the Envelope on Race and Gender. Has America Regressed Since Then?," *USA Today*, September 28, 2018, accessed December 2, 2018, https://www.usatoday.com/story/opinion/2018/09/28/all-family-shows-us-progress-50-years-columnists-opinion/1434863002/.

8 Text of Bill Clinton, first inaugural address available at American Presidency Project published by the University of California at Santa Barbara, accessed August 27, 2018, http://www.presidency.ucsb.edu/ws/index.php?pid=46366.

9 Lear makes this remark in the 2016 PBS American Masters documentary *Norman Lear: Just Another Version of You.*

Index

ABC network, 4, 6, 24, 29–32, 146, 148, 154, 156
abortion, 121, 138
Academy of American Television, 92
Adams, Lee, 63
Adler, Richard P., 50
Adventures of Ozzie and Harriet, The, 23, 150
affiliate station, 4
affirmative action, 70
African Americans, 11–12, 28–29, 139–145, 149–150, 155–156, 173n20. *See also* racial/ethnic issues
AIM. *See* American Indian Movement
AITF. See *All in the Family*
A.K.A. Pablo, 147
Alda, Alan, 135
Allen, Fred, 27, 49
Allen, Gracie, 27
All in the Family (*AITF*): advertising rates, 133; ancestors of, 2–3, 20–23, 29–31; bigotry/intolerance, 30, 63–84, 107, 135; Bunker home as set, 49–50, 56–62, 64, 152, 167nn1, 2, 168n8; cast (*see specific actors and characters*); characters and Lear's personal life, 72, 91, 106; class issues, 2, 131; coda scene, 102, 125, 126; comedy inserted in serious situations, 123; conservative form/progressive content, 48–52; cultural references, 89, 133, 153;

169n5; daring irreverence, 2–3; debut, 8–9, 18; Emmy Awards, 44–45, 90, 95; exploring American prejudices, 34; gender issues, 77–81, 127 (*see also* gender); heirs of, 2–3; high-profile recognition, 44–45; homosexual issues, 33, 40, 78, 95–96; indifference toward show, 38–40; living room setting, 20; longevity, 48; making of, 47–55; male-dominated production, 118; name of sitcom, 34; network advisory/censors, 34–35, 68; offensive language, 41, 66, 109, 135, 165n13; origins, 17–35; other settings, 49, 55; pilot episode, 29–32, 35, 163n28; popular/controversial show of all time, 9, 45, 132, 145; production schedule/procedures, 47–48, 49; props, 60; quality of scripts, 51; racial issues, 2, 41–44, 127 (*see also* racial/ethnic issues); reactions to show, 36–46; reboot, 153; sexual assault issues, 99, 117, 122–126; situation comedy formula, 3; spin-offs, 48, 55, 103, 112, 115, 118, 132–154 (*see also specific spin-off*); success of, 17–18, 132–154; theme song (*see* "Those Were the Days"); timing during social changes of the sixties, 4–5, 8–16, 28–29, 65, 138; timing of broadcast, 134; transition to *Archie Bunker's Place*, 103; use of multiple cameras, 49, 51, 55;

"generation gap," 11, 64–65, 106–110, 120
genocide, 11
genre. *See* formula
Gentleman's Agreement, 41
GI Bill, 64
Gilbert, Ray, 93
Gilford, Jack, 94
Gleason, Jackie, 22–23, 53–54, 166n15
Glendale section of Queens (New York), 56, 58, 168n8
Gloria, 112, 118, 130–131
"Glow Worm," 93
"God Bless America," 110, 170n5
Godfrey, Lynie, 152
God, Man, and Archie Bunker (Marsh), 133
Goldberg, Whoopi, 151
Goldbergs, The, 22, 146
Golden Girls, The, 90, 118
Goldensen, Leonard, 31
Good Times, 46, 139–140, 145, 153, 157, 173n20
Gore, Al, 106
Gould, Jack, 39
Grapes of Wrath, The, 62
Grease, 149
Great Depression, 15–16, 19, 23, 64, 66, 71, 87
Great Gatsby, The (Fitzgerald), 57–58
Green Acres, 24, 35
Greer, Germaine, 107
Griffiths, Martha, 12
gross domestic product, 9–10, 13
Group Therapy (game), 112–115
Guest, Christopher, 108–109
Guinness Book of World Records, 133
Guthrie, Woody, 110

ham radio, 18
Hansberry, Lorraine, 141
Happy Days, 149
Harrelson, Woody, 153
Harrington, Stephanie, 39
Harris Susan, 118, 137–138
Hatcher, Teri, 152
hate crime, 78–79, 100
Hathaway, Don, 138
Hauser Street, 56–57
Haynes, Pamela, 39

HBO, 6
Hearts of Men, The (Ehrenreich), 150
Hee Haw, 33, 35, 46
Heller, Meyer, 40
Helmsley, Sherman, 68, 141
Henrietta (queen), 57
Hobson, Laura Z., 41–42
Hollywood Reporter, 38
Homeland, 9
"homemaker." *See* housewife
homosexuality, 33, 40, 78, 95–96, 106, 165n10
Honeymooners, The, 2, 22–23, 39, 54
Hoover, Herbert, 64
Hope, Bob, 51
Horn, Alan, 147–148
Hot l Baltimore, 146
housewife, 60–61, 80, 86–88
Houston, Texas, 10
Hughes, Bernard, 97
Hulu, 6

Ideal Toy Company, 129
I Love Lucy, 2, 21–22, 23, 50, 51
immigrants, 14, 23, 58, 70
inflation, 13, 61, 70
Israel, 12
I Think I'm Outta Here (O'Connor), 52–53
"I Wish I Could Shimmy Like My Sister Kate," 93

Jackson, George, 12
Japan, 10
Jarrett, Valerie, 155
Jefferson, George (character), 68, 141–144
Jefferson, Lionel (character), 36–37, 75–76, 140–144
Jefferson, Louise (character), 93, 141–144
Jeffersons, The, 46, 48, 51, 53, 140–144, 145, 147, 149–150, 153
Jensen-Drake, Brigit, 118
Jewish Defense League, 76–77
Jewish religion, 26, 27, 42, 72
joblessness. *See* unemployment
Johnson, Lyndon, 12–13, 32, 71, 168n7
Josefsberg, Milt, 51
Joyce, James, 30
Julia, 25

World War II, 19, 23, 26, 64, 67, 69, 108
Wrubel, Allie, 93
Wyner, George, 120

yellow power movement, 12
Yorkin, Bud, 27, 29, 32, 45, 118, 136–138, 146,
   147, 151, 163n21

Yorty, Sam, 71
Young, Robert, 89
Young, Whitney, 39
Yu, Kelvin, 155–156,
   157

"Zip-a-Dee-Doo-Dah," 93

About the Author

JIM CULLEN, like Archie Bunker, is a native of Queens. He is the son of a New York City firefighter and a homemaker. He and his younger sister spent the first few years of their lives in Jackson Heights, adjacent to the Bunkers' Astoria. Jim later moved to Long Island, received a bachelor's degree in English from Tufts University and his master's and doctoral degrees in American studies from Brown University, and went on to teach at Harvard, Brown, and Sarah Lawrence College before settling into a longtime position as history teacher at the Ethical Culture Fieldston School in New York, attended by three of his four children. He is the author of numerous books, among them *The American Dream: A Short History of an Idea That Shaped a Nation*, *A Short History of the Modern Media*, and *Democratic Empire: The United States since 1945*. His essays and reviews have appeared in the *Washington Post*, *USA Today*, *Rolling Stone*, CNN.com, the *Journal of American History*, and other publications. Jim lives with his wife, the Sarah Lawrence historian Lyde Cullen Sizer, in Hastings-on-Hudson, New York.